RENEGOTIATING FAMILY RELATIONSHIPS: DIVORCE, CHILD CUSTODY, AND MEDIATION

RENEGOTIATING FAMILY RELATIONSHIPS
Divorce, Child Custody, and Mediation

ROBERT E. EMERY

THE GUILFORD PRESS
New York   London

©1994 The Guilford Press
A Division of Guilford Publications
72 Spring Street, New York, NY 10012

Printed in the United States of America

This book printed on acid-free paper.

Last digit is print number: 9 8 7 6 5 4 3 2 1

Library of Congress Cataloging-in-Publication Data

Emery, Robert E.
    Renegotiating family relationships : divorce, child custody, and
  mediation / Robert Emery
      p.   cm.
    Includes bibliographical references and index.
    ISBN 0-89862-214-X
    1. Divorce mediation—United States.   2. Custody of children-
  United States.   3. Divorced parents—Counseling of—United States.
  I. Title.

  HQ834.E48   1994
  306.89—dc20   94-12337
                                                        CIP

*To Kimberly, Maggie, Jacey,
and all of my family*

Preface

D ivorce, child custody, and mediation are important, controversial, and emotional topics. American families and families in most other industrialized societies have changed, but the evolution is not yet complete. This book touches upon many aspects of the evolution of the American family, including changing demographics, changing laws, and changing evidence from psychological research. The primary emphasis of this book, however, is on one specific consequence of family change: family conflict. Conflict is an inevitable consequence of change, particularly change in the face of uncertainty. Until our society negotiates a new set of prescriptive rules for families, conflicts between family members will continue as we all attempt to negotiate and renegotiate our rules and expectations for family relationships.

This book discusses my perspectives on how families renegotiate their relationships as a result of divorce and the conflicts that accompany divorce. Children are my overriding concern in the book; however, much of the discussion focuses on the parents rather than on the children. This is because both my research and practice strongly suggest that children's adjustment to divorce is greatly affected by their parents' conflict and cooperation. In one sense, partners who are also parents can never be completely divorced. They are joined by their bonds with their children and by concerns about their children's emotional health. Parents do not end their relationship when they divorce; but they must renegotiate it.

Mediation is a useful tool for helping parents to begin to renegotiate their relationship. Mediation is of value because it encourages parents to cooperate—a distinct contrast to the traditional method of adversary settlement. Mediation also is of value because underlying issues such as grief or hopes for reconciliation can be addressed during the process, at least briefly. Perhaps the greatest benefit of mediation, however, is that it helps parents to redefine new boundaries in their relationships. These boundaries are defined explicitly by the specific and detailed terms of a mediated agreement and implicitly through the process of negotiation that occurs in mediation.

In many respects, this book is the culmination of research on mediation that I began ten years ago and of the new clinical skills that I had to master in order to fulfill this task. Both research and practice are addressed in this volume, but the practitioner side of my professional personality contributes more to this volume than is typical in my writing.

I am grateful to the William T. Grant Foundation for funding the research that sparked my interest in mediation. The Grant Foundation also provided me with funding to participate in a consortium of divorce researchers. We have had exciting and stimulating meetings twice a year over the past seven years, and I would like to thank the members of that group as well. I am also extremely grateful to the James McKeen Cattell Fund and the Center for Advanced Studies at the University of Virginia for financial support for a one-year leave of absence during which most of this book was written.

There are numerous individuals who have been instrumental to me and my work. Joanne Jackson assisted with the original research and was my co-mediator during innumerable mediation sessions. Mavis Hetherington has been an influential and supportive colleague. Elizabeth Scott and John Monahan have taught me much about the law, as has my wife, Kimberly Emery. Many graduate students were extremely helpful and active in this research, particularly Susan Peterman, Melissa Wyer, Sheila Matthews, Danny Shaw, Jeff Haugaard, and, more recently, Katherine Kitzmann. Peter Dillon, another graduate student, helped extensively with the background research for Chapter 8. Linda Christian and Debbie Mundie also deserve thanks for their diligence in typing and retyping the manuscript. I have a special loving debt of gratitude to Kimberly Emery for letting me write early in the morning and to Maggie Emery for letting dad write in the afternoons after school.

Finally, I would like to thank the hundreds of parents with whom I have worked in mediation, particularly those who consented to participate in my research studies. I have learned much from all of them.

Contents

CHAPTER 1

Conflicting Perspectives
His and Her Divorce

Child custody disputes present problems from a variety of perspectives. Although most disputes are settled out of court, high divorce rates make custody contests one of the most frequent sources of litigation in the United States. Thus, custody disputes are expensive from the perspective of the public interest. The current standard for determining contested custody according the "best interests of the child" is a vague principle which, from the perspective of judges, often makes custody disputes extremely frustrating and difficult to decide. Custody cases are not attractive from the perspective of many trial lawyers either. These cases frequently are emotional, demanding, and financially and personally unrewarding. Legal expenses, fears about losing custody, and the divisiveness of a custody battle are a few of the many problems that custody disputes present from the perspective of each parent. Finally, from the perspective of children, a custody dispute epitomizes one of the worst things about divorce: getting caught in the middle between their parents.

Mediation is an alternative means of resolving custody disputes that holds the promise of alleviating some of these problems. Mediators encourage a cooperative approach, rather than viewing separated and divorced parents as adversaries whose interests must constantly be protected by legal advocates. The former partners meet together with an impartial mediator, who helps them to identify, discuss, and ultimately resolve the disputes that have arisen as a result of their divorce. Mediators often address some of the partners' emotional conflicts, thus the approach shares some features of family therapy as well as of legal negotiations. The goal of mediation is not to promote a marital reconciliation, however. Instead, the overriding goal of mediation is to help separated and divorced couples to negotiate a

1

written agreement that becomes a basis for their legal settlement, and the exploration of emotional issues is limited according to that goal.

Mediators urge parents to contain their painful emotions, communicate with each other, cooperate in rearing their children, and retain control over their children's lives by making their own decisions about custody and postdivorce childrearing. Custody mediation thus promises to reduce the frequency of litigation, relieve judges of the burden of determining custody, allow lawyers to concentrate their expertise on the financial aspects of divorce, and reduce the divisiveness of divorce for parents and especially for children. As discussed in Chapter 8, research indicates that custody mediation fulfills these lofty promises to varying degrees.

Mediators attempt to help parents to settle their custody disputes in a more simple, unemotional, and rational manner, to the benefit of all involved. Even though divorce has become common, it remains extremely difficult. For many people, divorce is not simple, unemotional, and rational. It is complex, emotionally charged, and irrational. The extreme upheaval that divorce often causes for real people and real families can get lost in the divorce statistics that are cited so frequently. There are better and worse ways to divorce, and there are better and worse ways to settle custody disputes, but there are no happy solutions. No approach, including mediation, is a panacea. The many dilemmas of divorce must be acknowledged, whatever one's role in or approach to resolving custody disputes.

Much of the complexity, emotionality, and irrationality of divorce is lost in empirical research, which by necessity must focus on more simple, quantifiable, and understandable aspects of the process. Research on divorce and child custody is essential for achieving an objective understanding of the issues, and for developing effective policies and interventions. However, clinical experience also is extremely valuable as a means of enriching an academic understanding of the divorce process, and especially for developing hypotheses about divorce and child custody that subsequently can be investigated empirically.

In order to enrich, enliven, and hopefully enlighten, clinical material is included at various points throughout this book together with a multidisciplinary consideration of academic analysis and empirical findings. Much of this first chapter is devoted to a consideration of case histories that illustrate common dilemmas in divorce and child custody disputes. These dilemmas convey some of the reasons why custody disputes are so problematic from the perspective of separated and divorced families, the legal system, and society. The emotional dilemmas also introduce topics that are addressed more academically in subsequent chapters.

CONFLICTING PERSPECTIVES ON MARRIAGE, PARENTING, AND DIVORCE

One goal of legal intervention in divorce and custody disputes is discovery, that is, uncovering the facts of a case. There are many impediments to uncovering the truth in custody disputes, however. One of the most important is that family members have conflicting perspectives on divorce and family life. There is much wisdom in the truism that "love is blind." Love makes people see what they want to see, believe what they hope is true. One dilemma in divorce is that the blinders of love are removed. When former partners answer the question, "What went wrong?," they often surprise themselves with complaints that they had only vaguely recognized in their marriage. When divorcing parents present the "facts" of their case to their attorneys, perspectives that already were in conflict can become even more polarized. Some of these conflicting perspectives on divorce are illustrated in the following two case histories.

The Case of Sheila

Sheila hoped that her separation would give her a new start at the age of 31. She had married right after finishing college, a decision that seemed impulsive and blind to her in retrospect. Her sweet college boyfriend soon became a distant and cold husband. They had been lovers and best friends, but once they got married, their relationship changed. They became housemates who had sex on occasion. Sheila's life grew increasingly empty, lonely, and meaningless. When she became pregnant at 23, she hoped that a baby would revitalize her marriage, but, much to her disappointment, her husband showed almost no interest in the infant. Sheila drew new energy from her little girl, but financial pressures and her husband's frustrations mounted when Sheila stopped working to stay home with her baby. At his insistence, she ended up returning to work long before she was ready.

Sheila resented giving up her daughter's infancy to day care, and she was doubly disappointed when her husband showed no interest in their second child, a boy. She was determined to spend a few years at home now that she had two children, but money and her "laziness" became the topics of constant fighting. Sheila stuck by her decision not to work for 2 years, but as much as she loved being a mother, her marriage was in shambles. When she returned to work, it was with a purpose in mind. She would build her income to the point where she and her two children could live on their own. She knew she had married the wrong man. She was frightened of divorce for herself and for her children, but the fighting and unhappiness were worse. Sheila was convinced that staying married "for the children's sake" was an excuse for making the safe, easy, and wrong decisions that she had made her whole life. She had no real husband, and her children had no real father.

It took Sheila several years to prepare for her move and to muster the courage to tell her husband that she was leaving him. When she finally confronted him, she was unsure of what to expect, but she knew it would be bad. He yelled, he screamed, he threatened. He refused to leave their home or to support Sheila or the children if she left. Sheila was prepared for this. She had already rented a furnished apartment, had money saved in a secret bank account, and had spoken with a lawyer who assured her that her husband would have to support the children, and perhaps her as well.

After she moved out of the house, the fighting stopped for a while, but the begging started. Her husband was sorry. He loved her. He loved the children. Life was worthless without them. He pleaded with her to come back. But Sheila had not made an impulsive decision this time. There was no going back.

And then it happened. Sheila and her husband had been separated for about 8 weeks. They had no legal agreement, but had settled into something of a pattern where the children would spend each Saturday night and Sunday morning with their father. But instead of getting the children back one Sunday afternoon, Sheila got a call from her husband. He said that he had filed for sole custody of the children. He might settle for joint custody, but he planned on keeping the children at least until the following Saturday no matter what. He would return them on that day, but only if Sheila signed a joint custody agreement that allowed the children to be swapped between them each week. If she refused to sign the agreement, he would not bring them back. When Sheila screamed into the phone to return her children immediately, he hung up on her.

The Case of John

Like Sheila, John had two young children who were the subject of a custody dispute. His circumstances were very different otherwise, however. John was very much a family man. He worked hard and his job was all right, but work was a means to an end for John. That end was his family. As soon as he left work, John headed for home, eager to see his wife and especially his children. John knew that his marriage was going through a rough period, but he also knew in his heart that everything would work out in the end. At least he thought he knew that.

John had gotten married and had children at a young age, but he knew that family life would make demands, and expected that there would be hard times. Certain things bothered him, of course. His wife had been sexy and kind of wild when they were dating, but sex became infrequent and dull early in the marriage. It just about disappeared after his first child was born. John believed that it was wrong for him to complain about sex, so he just kept quiet and kept trying. His sexual advances were rebuffed far more often than not, and that left John feeling rejected too. Still, he kept trying. Besides, there was more to life than sex. He enjoyed his family, and loved playing with his children, especially his little boy, who was beginning to share John's interest in sports.

John was much more worried about money than he was about his family life. His wife did some work, even after the children were born, but from John's point of view her working hurt as much as it helped. John felt that earning a good income was his responsibility. He had set a goal of having a nice house and a secure income by the age of 30, so the pressure would be off of everyone, especially him. Unfortunately, the economy worked against John. He was making ends meet, but he secretly felt like a failure. He sometimes saw his dreams as just that, dreams. He struggled to come up with new plans that would relieve the financial pressures, but nothing worked.

Nevertheless, John was far from giving up on his job, and he never considered giving up on his family. Then he got the shock of a lifetime. One day, out of the clear blue sky, his wife said that she was leaving him. John was shocked. Things had been rough at times, but nowhere near a divorce. He begged, he pleaded, he promised anything, but his words fell on deaf ears. Within a few days, his wife and children had moved out.

John was too stunned to do anything more than protest pathetically, but his objections had no effect. His wife had every move planned. Unlike him, she was not devastated. She seemed happy. She had a place to go, and money coming in from some mysterious source. John tried to pull himself together and figure out was happening. Then he came upon the explanation. His wife must be having an affair. He felt like an idiot. Of course, why else would she do something like this? She had planned it all too perfectly.

John's anger at being used energized him into action. Within a few weeks after the separation, he got himself a lawyer and a plan. His wife could go if that was what she wanted, but she was not going to take his children. He asked his lawyer to file for sole custody of the children, and upon hearing his lawyer's warning that "possession is nine-tenths of the law," he came up with another tactic on his own. He would not return the children after their next visit. At least he would keep them until he had a formal agreement that protected his relationship with his children. After all, he was their father, and his wife had walked out on him with no cause. He had rights, and so did his children.

As you may have guessed, John and Sheila were married to each other.

Sheila and John had shared much of their daily lives for 10 years, yet they experienced and remembered their time together very differently. Some of the differences in their stories may have been deliberate distortions on the part of one or both of them as they faced the separation and the custody dispute began. There is strong motivation to portray oneself as a saint and one's former spouse as a sinner because of the high stakes involved in custody disputes, and because extreme positions can be a strategic advantage.

However, many of the differences between Sheila and John surely were a result of legitimately different experiences, perceptions, and memories. His "family time" on Sunday afternoons may have been "football time" to her. His sexual initiations may have seemed like unrelenting and unfeeling demands to her. To him, they may have represented a stoic persistence to get close to his wife. He may have viewed his concern for his work as a part of his responsibility to his family. She may have seen him as being married to the job.

HIS AND HER DIVORCE

In her classic book, *The Future of Marriage*, sociologist Jesse Bernard (1972) wrote that couples have not one marriage, but two: "his" and "hers." Each member of the couple experiences their union so differently that functionally there are two marriages. Nowhere is this provocative idea more evident than during divorce. As with Sheila and John, many separated or divorced parents have widely conflicting perspectives on their own and each other's marriage and parenting.

Perhaps John was a cold and angry man who was as insensitive to his children as he had been to his wife. Or perhaps Sheila was a bored and self-centered woman who was unprepared for the realities of family life, and who was captivated by fantasies of an affair. It is tempting to conclude that the truth lies somewhere in between the two extremes, and it often does. But perhaps there is no "truth." Perhaps some of John's and Sheila's actions can be established as legal facts, but what a court determines to be the truth is unlikely to change John's or Sheila's perceptions of reality.

Even if they agreed about the facts of their relationship, John and Sheila would be likely to continue to disagree about the reasons for their problems. They would be likely to attribute different motivations to their own and each other's actions. Sheila might see her leaving as justified by John's long history of cold and calculated manipulation, manipulation poignantly exemplified by his refusal to return her children. In contrast, John might view his actions as justified by Sheila's selfish disregard of his relationship with his children both during their marriage and following the separation. In short, they both are likely to blame each other for past and present transgressions. They have conflicting memories about their past. They have conflicting views about their present motivations. Given this, it is not surprising that they would be in conflict about the terms of their separation and its future fairness for themselves and their children.

HIS AND HER ACCEPTANCE OF THE END OF THE MARRIAGE

In addition to "his" and "her" divorce, John and Sheila illustrate another common dilemma in custody disputes. Sheila and John differ in their acceptance of the end of their marriage. As with most divorces, they did not reach a mutual decision to end their relationship. Sheila had wanted to terminate the marriage for a long time. John still hopes that the marriage will continue. As with their conflicting views of the past, John and Sheila's very different desires for the future of their marriage greatly complicate their separation. Sheila's push for a divorce collides with John's hope for a reconciliation.

Disparities between partners in accepting the end of the marriage increase the likelihood of a custody dispute, and they greatly complicate attempts to resolve a dispute once it has arisen. John and Sheila differ not only in terms of what custody arrangement they want, they also differ on *whether* an arrangement is wanted.

John may resist any type of an agreement, or he may insist on one that is clearly unacceptable to Sheila. He may do so for the very simple reason that he does not want an agreement. For him, agreeing to a custody arrangement means accepting the separation, and John does not want to accept the end of his marriage. He certainly does not want to facilitate it by agreeing to some custody arrangement for which he is unprepared emotionally or practically. In fact, John is likely to become angry and uncooperative with professionals who try to hasten the process of reaching an agreement, whether those professionals are therapists, mediators, judges, or even his own attorney. From John's point of view, anyone who pushes for a settlement is on Sheila's side.

Unlike John, Sheila is much more ready to "do business." She has contemplated the end of her marriage for a very long time, and she has at least begun to consider what she wants and needs in a custody and separation agreement. She may see some of the obstacles that John raises for what they are: his refusal to accept the end of their marriage. But whether or not to end the marriage is not a question that Sheila wants to reopen. Even if she harbors some ambivalence, this is a feeling that Sheila is likely to want to conquer, not explore. It certainly is not a feeling that she wants to share with John. Sheila wants to get on with her life, but even after she has finally made her dramatic move, it feels as though John is in control. Sheila does not want to understand John's hurt and pain. She wants to get this over with, and the sooner, the better. Unlike John, Sheila therefore is likely to see those professionals who push for a resolution as being reasonable and helpful.

Thus, part of a couple's conflict over custody often reflects their opposing wishes for the future of their marriage. They fight over their children, and much of their dispute does legitimately concern the children. But when they fight about their children, they also often are fighting about whether or not to end their marriage.

Research on Fighting Divorce by Disputing Custody

My research on child custody mediation and litigation offers some support for this assertion. In over 60% of the families, 1 month after settling their custody dispute in mediation or in court, at least one partner indicated that they felt that they should have tried to stay together longer. Only in about one-quarter of all cases did both partners agree that they were glad that they finally made the break. In fact, in a handful of cases *both* partners indicated that they were only going ahead with the divorce because it was what their spouse wanted (see Figure 1.1).

Men were much less accepting of the end of their marriage than were women in this sample of parents who were disputing custody. Over 40% of the men reported that they were going ahead with the divorce only because their spouses wanted it, compared to less than 10% of the women. Similarly, over half of the men agreed that they found themselves wondering what their spouses were doing, whereas only about 15% of women did so.

This difference between men and women cannot be an indicator of gender differences either in who initiates divorce or in who is better able to cope with divorce, because other research finds a fairly even balance between the genders on these dimensions. Instead, the findings appear to reflect gender differences in what disputes are used

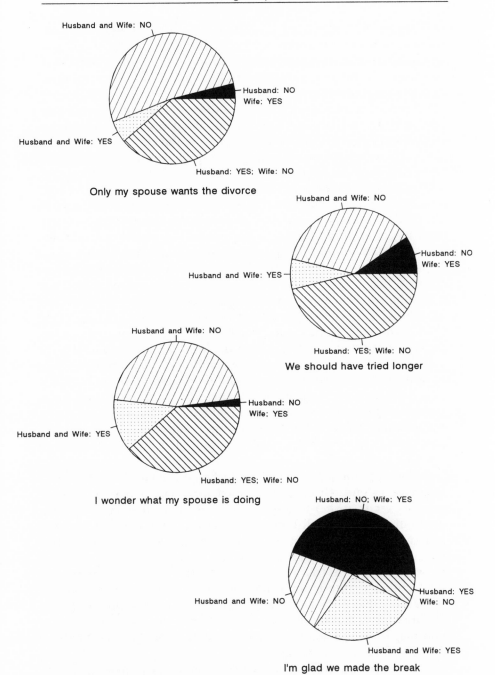

Figure 1.1. Couples' agreements and disagreements about the end of their marriage among parents disputing child custody.

as a means of indirectly contesting the end of a marriage. Men who do not want their marriage to end may be more likely to refuse to reach a custody agreement, while women who do not want their marriage to end may be more likely to refuse to reach financial agreements. Why may this be the case?

If one partner does not want to divorce, consciously or unconsciously they may become intransigent about reaching a separation agreement in order to delay or even prevent the end of the marriage. Of course, this tactic only works if the dispute is over an issue of great value to the partner who does want to end the relationship. Otherwise, the spouse who is more eager to proceed with the divorce would simply concede the point, thus allowing the process to move more quickly. Because men and women have greater or lesser investments in different aspects of their marriage according to traditional marital roles, this suggests that divorce disputes are likely to focus on different topics depending upon whether the husband or wife is more eager to divorce.

When a man does not want the marriage to end, disputing custody is likely to be a more effective means of blocking an agreement than disputing the financial terms of the divorce. Because of her greater investment in childrearing during a traditional marriage, a wife and mother is unlikely to make substantial concessions about custody even when she is eager to end the marriage. In contrast, she may be willing to compromise on finances because she views economic hardship as an inevitable consequence of her decision to leave the marriage. Thus, when custody disputes are examined, it is likely that more men than women will not want their marriage to end, as revealed in my study.

The opposite pattern may hold when a woman does not want a marriage to end. Given a traditional marriage, it may be a more effective tactic for her to dispute finances rather than custody when attempting to block a divorce settlement for emotional reasons. This is because her husband may be more likely to make childrearing than financial concessions. In a traditional marriage, the husband is likely to be invested in his role as breadwinner. He may feel like a hypocrite if he contests custody when he wants the marriage to end and he recognizes that his wife has assumed the primary responsibility for childrearing. Thus, more women who do not want their marriage to end may be found among partners who are disputing the financial terms of their divorce settlement.

Whatever the differences between men and women, it is clear that some partners object to a separation agreement, in part, because they object to the end of the marriage. By delaying the agreement, they delay the end of their marriage. The specific dynamics may vary according to gender and according to the individual marital relationship, but mediators must always consider the possibility that a dispute over custody also is a dispute over the future of the partners' relationship.

HIS AND HER GRIEF

Yet another dilemma in divorce and custody disputes that is illustrated by the case of Sheila and John is the couple's conflicting experience of grief. Many of the reactions that former spouses have to separation and divorce can be understood as a part of coping with loss. The problem of conflicting experiences and perspectives arises again in the experience of grief. Sheila and John experienced a very different type of loss when they separated. Metaphorically and emotionally, Sheila lost her marriage to a chronic, terminal illness. She knew for years that her marriage was dying, and this knowledge allowed her to prepare for its end both emotionally and practically. The actual separation undoubtedly was painful for her, but as with the death of a loved one following a long and trying illness, the pain was likely to be tinged with some guilty relief.

In contrast to Sheila, the metaphor for what has happened to John's marriage is a sudden, mysterious, and potentially deadly disease. John could comprehend that something terrible had happened. His marriage was in critical condition. Everyone around him acted somber and pessimistic. Still, he could cling to the hope of a miraculous recovery. Miracles sometimes happen, and as bad as the outlook may have been, no one could truthfully tell John that there was absolutely no hope for his marriage. And he could draw more hope from his contacts with Sheila, especially from her guilt-ridden attempts to be friendly to him. To John, these may have been signs of life in the marriage, because what was final to Sheila was far from final to John.

Even as he gradually recognized that his marriage was ending, John's grief would be likely to be much more erratic and intense than Sheila's. Sheila anticipated the end of her marriage, and she grieved for years before the separation. Sheila also made various practical preparations for her new, single life, and she looked forward to it with some optimism. Perhaps he was blind, but John's loss still was unanticipated. He did not have time to prepare for the separation, and the end of his marriage was not something that he wanted. He may have seemed controlling to Sheila, but he felt out of control. His intense and unpredictable grief put him on an emotional rollercoaster.

John and Sheila's differing experiences of grief can be yet another source of conflict. If he does not interpret her friendliness as a sign of hope, John may interpret Sheila's lack of distress as a glib reaction to the separation. Her absence of apparent grief may make him wonder if she ever loved him, or it may cause him to speculate that she is involved with another man. While John is hurt by Sheila's lack of strong reactions, Sheila is likely to be frustrated by John's devastation. She may wonder where his emotions were when they were together, or she may be angered by his self-pity and foot-dragging. In short, each may wonder why their partner does not feel the same way that they feel.

HIS AND HER CHILDREN

As with other emotional conflicts, a couple's disparity in the experience of grief can lead to fights about a variety of issues, including the children and custody. Because of their own, conflicting experiences of grief, Sheila and John are likely to have very different views on how their children are experiencing the separation. Sheila is likely to see the children as she sees herself: as accepting the separation and coping with it relatively well. John also is likely to see the children as he sees himself: as hating the separation and feeling devastated by it.

Each parent projects his or her own feelings onto the children. If no problems are apparent, John may argue that the children are hiding their feelings, protecting their mother, and defending against their terrible pain. Sheila may counter that the children's lack of reaction proves that they are doing fine. In fact, she may see them as happier than they were when they had been exposed to the daily tension, fighting, and unhappiness of the marriage. If the children do show obvious difficulties, this may demonstrate the need for a reconciliation to John, even if only for the sake of the children. To Sheila, the children's problems are proof of their need for stability and the paramount importance of having a clear and stable custody arrangement as soon as possible.

As with other emotional aspects of separation and divorce, a couple's conflicting experience and projection of grief means that custody disputes often involve conflicts about the children that reflect much more than the children. Some of the parents' conflicting interpretations of their children's feelings and needs certainly are due to legitimate differences of opinion. Even impartial mental health professionals have difficulty discerning how children feel and what they want following their parents' marital separation. Still, intentionally or unintentionally, parents in a custody dispute also are likely to project their own experiences onto their children, and thus adopt a somewhat self-serving and inaccurate view of their children's adjustment and needs.

THE CHILDREN'S PERSPECTIVE ON HIS AND HER DIVORCE

Perhaps the central dilemma in divorce and custody disputes is that children have a third perspective that often conflicts with the views of either parent. The children's needs are supposed to be paramount in custody disputes, yet it is distressing how frequently the children's perspectives on separation and divorce are forgotten in the parents' emotional turmoil. Too often, it seems, a concern for the "children's" needs masks an attempt to resist the end of the relationship, a search for signs of continued life in the marriage, a struggle to gain the upper hand in negotiations, or a punishment of the other parent with guilt, rejection, or isolation. Too often, parents expect the children to side with them against their father or mother, rather than recognizing that the children's perspectives may differ from their own.

Some children do side with one parent or the other following a separation or divorce. In other families, loyalties are so deeply divided that different children end up allying with a different parent. However, from the children's perspective, the biggest problem often is not choosing the right side but having to choose at all.

This is especially true in acrimonious divorces. As discussed in Chapter 9, empirical evidence consistently points to parental conflict as the factor that most consistently predicts maladjustment among children whose parents have separated or divorced (Amato & Keith, 1991b; Emery, 1982, 1988; Grych & Fincham, 1990). Clinical experience and recent research (Buchanan, Maccoby, & Dornbusch, 1991) indicate that a particular problem is when children feel caught in the middle of a custody dispute. Most children do not want to be forced to take sides with one parent against the other, and as fervently as they may wish for a reconciliation, children's foremost desire often is for their parents to stop all of their fighting.

SUMMARY AND OVERVIEW

Thus, there are three major conflicting perspectives within separated and divorced families: his, hers, and the children's. As is illustrated by the case of John and Sheila, it can be extremely difficult to determine which perspective is true, let alone which perspective is right. Perhaps Sheila was emotionally abused, and she needs a strong advocate who will help her to fend off her misplaced guilt and stand up to John at last. Perhaps John was used and manipulated, and he needs a strong advocate who will help him to put aside his grief and protect his rights as a father. Perhaps the children are being forgotten, and they need their own advocate who will insist that Shelia and John stop arguing about their lost rights and start assuming their continuing responsibilities as parents.

American Justice

A natural inclination when confronted with such conflicting possibilities is to dig further to uncover the truth. The American legal system and the American sense of justice are such that we believe that one true and right side will be found if only we dig deeply enough. We revel in righteous indignation. As suggested by the concept of "no fault" divorce laws, however, many divorces do not entail an ultimate right and an ultimate wrong. Perhaps there is no "truth" in many divorces and in many custody disputes. Perhaps much of each parent's concept of the truth reflects his and her conflicting perspectives on their marriage, on their parenting, and on their divorce.

We might discover that Sheila was having an affair, for example, but we also might discover that John had been verbally abusive. Does the verbal abuse justify the affair, or does Sheila's infidelity justify John's denigration? Do either of the facts bear directly on determining the best arrangement for the custody of their two children? From the children's perspective, does the conflict that is inherent in settling a custody dispute create more problems than it resolves? These are some of the substantive and procedural questions that confound legal intervention in divorce and custody disputes.

When one side clearly is the victim and the other is the perpetrator, legal advocacy, fact finding, and protection may be necessary irrespective of the divisiveness of a legal battle. The traditional benefits of the American legal system that ensure due process and protect the weaker party may be needed, especially in custody disputes that involve victimization in the form of a history of family violence or dramatically unequal power between two parents. Yet the same advocacy, fact finding, and protection that is so beneficial in some cases may only polarize conflicting perspectives on his and her divorce in others. Adversarial manuevering may turn differing experiences in understanding and in coping with a divorce into a family feud, a feud that ultimately is destructive to children, whose perspective on divorce is considered last in this chapter as it often is in custody disputes.

More than Legal Conflict

Whether one views custody disputes from a legal or psychological perspective, the difficulty of determining the accuracy of his, hers, and the children's perspective on divorce illustrates three essential observations. First, much of the interpersonal and legal conflict that occurs as a result of separation and divorce is caused by conflicts of perspective. Many disputes, including some formal, legal contests over child custody, involve conflicts over differing desires for the marriage's future, differing experiences of grief, and differing projections onto the children.

Second, different family members have conflicting perspectives on their family, relationships, and divorce, in part because of their different roles in the family and in the separation. Conflicting perspectives can be expected to be found between the partner who wanted the marriage to end and the partner who wants it to continue, between mothers and fathers, and between parents and children. As is discussed in Chapter 5, conflicting perspectives also can be expected to be found between different professionals who represent either one of the parents, the children, or the entire family in a custody dispute.

The third observation is that all of the adults involved in divorce and custody disputes would benefit from becoming more aware of the child's perspective. The perspective of one or the other parent is the one traditionally taken by family and friends and by the attorneys who represent each parent. One partner typically *is* seen to be the injured party. One party *is* expected to win custody. Divorce typically *is* viewed as the beginning of a family feud. From the perspective of children, however, past wrongs often are much less important than are current conflicts that continue to disrupt their daily lives. Perhaps we need to find a way to make divorce less divisive both legally and socially.

Overview

The observations made in this first chapter have been based primarily on clinical considerations. In subsequent chapters, the support for these assertions is examined based on further case histories, extensive empirical evidence, and the analysis of both legal and psychological concepts. In Chapter 2, my family systems view of divorce as the renegotiation of family relationships is introduced, and the issues of grief, identity conflict, and redefining boundaries are considered primarily from the perspective of former partners who remain parents. In Chapter 3, the same family systems model is extended to a discussion of the renegotiation of parent-child relationships and the triangular relationship between the child and both parents.

In Chapter 4, the complex and often vague guidelines that comprise the substance of divorce and child custody law are reviewed. A general overview of dispute resolution procedures is presented in Chapter 5, with a particular emphasis on the adversarial legal system, how it contrasts with mediation, and how the alternative approaches to dispute resolution mesh with mothers', fathers', and children's conflicting perspectives on divorce. Chapter 6 details a model for managing the process of mediation, especially in the first session, based on the dual and overlapping goals of renegotiating relationships and negotiating child custody agreements. Specific, alternative methods of negotiating agreements in mediation are the focus of Chapter 7. In addition to a general introduction, case histories are used to illustrate various mediation techniques including uncovering hidden positions and brainstorming alternative outcomes.

Research on the process and outcome of custody mediation is considered in Chapter 8, particularly my own studies of families who were assigned at random to either mediate or litigate their child custody disputes. Chapter 9 is a detailed overview of research on children's experience of and adjustment to divorce. The material included in this chapter ranges from demographic information on divorce, custody arrangements, and visitation patterns to psychological research on interparental conflict and postdivorce parenting. This evidence is helpful in shaping such goals as taking a realistic approach to negotiating joint physical custody in mediation and attempting to reduce children's exposure to conflict between their parents. Finally, some issues about divorce, child custody, and mediation are considered in broad social context in Chapter 10.

CHAPTER 2

Renegotiating Relationships I
Separating Marital and Parental Roles

M any parents cannot resolve custody disputes, because they cannot solve the individual or interpersonal conflicts brought about by their marital distress, separation, and divorce. Thus, negotiating a child custody agreement is as much a psychological task as it is a legal one. While emotional distress greatly complicates the negotiation of a custody agreement, it is conversely true that the resolution of custody and other legal issues is an important step toward abandoning past conflicts and redefining future family relationships. Thus, the negotiation of a custody agreement is inseparable from the renegotiation of family relationships following separation and divorce.

The renegotiation of family relationships begins before the marital separation, and it continues to evolve long after the legal divorce. The necessity of adopting such a developmental perspective on divorce is apparent in the findings of longitudinal research (e.g., Hetherington & Clingempeel, 1992; Hetherington, Cox, & Cox, 1982; Wallerstein & Kelly, 1980). Divorce is a process, the unfolding of a series of partially predictable events and emotions over a substantial period of time.

Despite a considerable body of research, however, there still is no widely accepted conceptualization about what the divorce process entails. This circumstance is problematic both theoretically and practically. A clear conceptual view is needed to organize and direct the large and diverse body of research on divorce (Emery, 1988). It also would help practitioners and divorced family members to understand and organize their interventions and experiences.

Some of the most useful and frequently articulated perspectives on the divorce process emphasize either the psychological tasks of divorce (e.g., Wallerstein, 1983) or the various social, psychological, legal, and economic components of divorce (e.g., Bohannon, 1970). Others adopt general models of grief (e.g., Kubler-Ross, 1969) and apply them to the divorce context. Each of these approaches has value, and some details of these various perspectives are discussed in this chapter.

The purpose of this chapter, however, is not to review existing theories. Instead, the goal is to present my family systems model of the divorce process. The model offers an integrated yet extensive view of the psychological and interpersonal processes of divorce. At its core, the model asserts that divorce requires the renegotiation of individual, dyadic, and triadic boundaries in the system of family relationships. Individual issues and the renegotiation of the former marital relationship are discussed primarily in this chapter, while the renegotatiation of parent–child relationships and the parent–child-parent triad is discussed primarily in Chapter 3. As noted, it is essential for mediators and others involved in the legalities of divorce disputes to understand these dynamics of family reorganization, both because relationship issues can impede legal settlements and because legal settlements help to redefine relationships.

RENEGOTIATING RELATIONSHIPS: SOME CONCEPTS

Many of the interpersonal and emotional processes involved in divorce can be conceptualized in terms of the family's need to renegotiate their relationships. Of course, one major change that parents must renegotiate involves their relationships with their children. How and when each parent now will spend time with the children is an obvious way in which parent–child relationships must be redefined, but parents also must negotiate new rules about affection, discipline, and household responsibilities. This is true irrespective of parents' strong desire to maintain consistency for their children.

In addition to reworking their relationships with their children, separated and divorced partners also must renegotiate their relationship with each other. Many people find this observation ironic, because at least one partner apparently does not *want* a relationship with the other. It is true, however, that partners who are also parents can never fully divorce. Former spouses must have some form of a continuing relationship when children are involved in a divorce. On an ongoing basis, the parents must determine practicalities such as how to exchange the children or how to share basic information about them. This is true even when exchanges are highly structured, or when contact with one of the parents is very infrequent. Ultimately, parents also must renegotiate the degree of closeness or distance in their relationship with each other. A highly conflicted relationship is still a relationship, and, in fact, it is suggested here that intense parental conflict is a sign of an overly involved relationship between former partners, not of an overly distant one.

The triangle formed by the two parents and the children is another relationship that the divorced family must redefine. Marriage and parenting are inextricably linked in two-parent families, and parent–parent and parent–child relationships remain tied together in divorce (Emery & Tuer, 1993). The second parent is psychologically present even when physically absent, thus the triadic relationship persists even when parents live in different households. This psychological presence is obvious in the questions that parents ask children about the other parent, in the messages that children are told to carry back and forth, or simply by what is not discussed about one parent in the presence of the other. A major goal for successful parenting following divorce, however, is to make the quality of parent–child relationships less closely tied to the quality of parent–parent relationships.

The reason why relationships must be renegotiated following a marital separation is that the divorced family is a family. The divorced family is not defined by a shared residence. Instead, it is defined by shared relationships. Conceptually and practically, the feelings, thoughts, and actions of individual family members cannot be understood apart from this broader family system. In fact, most children from divorced families list both parents as being members of their families, even though their parents rarely include the former spouse in the list (Peterson & Zill, 1986).

Boundaries in Family Systems

Family systems theory, particularly the structural family therapy perspective (P. Minuchin, 1985; S. Minuchin, 1974), offers some valuable concepts for describing how relationships are renegotiated in divorce. The concept of *boundaries* is particularly useful for the present analysis. Boundaries are the stated or unstated rules of relationships. Boundaries in families are akin to the boundaries that divide the territory of two nations. They define the psychological territory of an individual or of a relationship. However, interpersonal boundaries are by nature much more subtle, flexible, and complex than international boundaries.

The boundary of interpersonal space is a straightforward example of an interpersonal boundary that can be readily envisioned.

Unstated social rules dictate acceptable physical proximity in social interaction. (In fact, subtly different rules about physical proximity apply to different relationships and across different cultures.) As with other psychological boundaries, the boundary of interpersonal space is not apparent until it is violated. Discomfort is immediate when a stranger stands too close, revealing the existence of the psychological territory.

More subtle rules of relationships similarly become obvious when the boundaries that define them are crossed. For example, the boundary around a typical marital relationship is defined in part by the topics that parents are unwilling to discuss in front of their children (e.g., sex, personal conflicts). The boundary is not established explicitly, but its existence becomes obvious when it is violated as a result of an argument or an accident. Everyone becomes uncomfortable as they recognize that a line has been crossed. Other examples of conversational boundaries include topics that lie within a child's area of autonomy. When parents ask a teenager detailed questions about a boyfriend or girlfriend, for example, they soon learn that they have crossed an impregnable line.

There are many important boundaries that define the contours of the relationships between the members of separated or divorced families. One obvious example is the schedule that each parent has for spending time with the children. As with other psychological boundaries, the significance of a schedule becomes clearer when it is violated. A father who fails to pick up his children according to the pre-arranged schedule violates an essential boundary in his relationship with his children. Similarly, parent–child boundaries are violated when a mother pops in for a spontaneous, unscheduled visit during her children's time with their father. Of course, both of these actions also are transgressions of boundaries in the relationship between the former partners.

Thus, a visitation schedule explicitly defines some boundaries in the relationship between parents and children, and it also helps to define boundaries in the parents' relationship as well. Other rules for the relationships between the members of the divorced family remain unclear, however, even after a formal divorce. In fact, a central thesis of the present conceptualization is that the lack of clear boundaries is one of the major sources of conflict and distress in the relationships between members of the divorced family system. Thus, an overriding goal of renegotiating relationships in divorce is to establish new and clear interpersonal boundaries, particularly in the relationship between the former spouses.

Intimacy and Power

Systems principles such as boundaries are essential concepts in understanding the process of interaction in families, but they fail to specify which issues comprise the most important areas of interaction. That is, complexities in interactional processes are outlined in richly descriptive terms, but family systems theory is not clear about which dimensions comprise the key contents of family interaction. Nations draw boundaries around geographical territory, but family systems theory is not explicit about what constitutes psychological territory. I have argued elsewhere, however, that intimacy and power are the two major dimensions that comprise the core contents of family relationships (Emery, 1992). That is, I assume that intimacy (or love) and power are the issues around which family members draw their psychological boundaries.

The emphasis on intimacy and power as basic relationship dimensions may seem unique to the reader at first, as it did to me when I first conceived this scheme. In fact, however, this emphasis is pervasive throughout different subdisciplines of psychology. Ethologists discuss dominance (power) and affiliation (intimacy) in describing the basic dimensions of relationships between social animals (Sloman, Gardner, & Price, 1989). Ego psychologist Harry Stack Sullivan (1953), interpersonal theorist Timothy Leary (1957), and their followers (Benjamin, 1974; Wiggins, 1982) constructed an entire theory of personality around these dimensions. A metaphorical interpretation of Freud's basic intrapsychic instincts of sex (intimacy) and aggression (power) yields the same two relationship domains (Cameron & Rychlak, 1985). Finally, the dimensions of intimacy and power form the foundations of the most widely accepted classification of parenting styles used by developmental psychologists (Baumrind, 1971; Maccoby & Martin, 1983).

As used here, the terms "intimacy" and "power" are intended to have broad meaning (Emery, 1992). Intimacy refers to emotional closeness in general. It applies to businesslike relationships that are low on intimacy, as well as to relationships between lovers and spouses that are highly intimate. It should be noted that the present definition of intimacy differs from that adopted by Sullivan and his followers. Sullivanian theorists placed love and hate at opposite poles of a continuum of intimacy. For reasons that are elaborated shortly, the present analysis places love and hate next to one another at one end of the continuum of intimacy, and it defines disinterest as the polar opposite of both of these intense feelings (see Figure 2.1). Thus, the

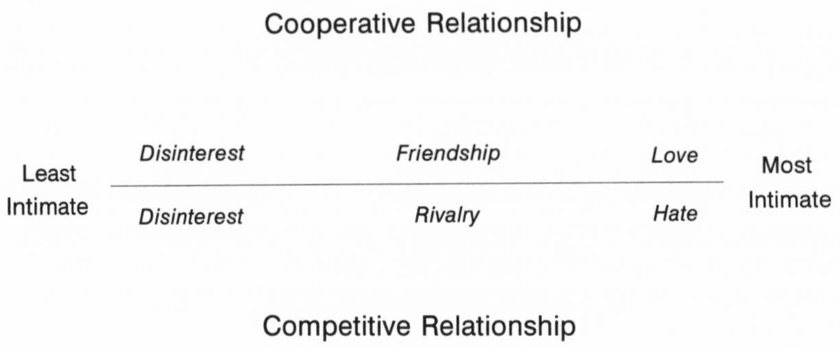

Cooperative Relationship

	Disinterest	Friendship	Love	
Least Intimate				Most Intimate
	Disinterest	Rivalry	Hate	

Competitive Relationship

Figure 2.1. A continuum of intimacy in relationships. Note that love and hate are located on the same pole of intimate involvement, unlike in theories in which they are polar opposites.

key to the present definition of intimate involvement is emotional intensity, not emotional valence (Emery, 1992).

Power refers not only to designated authority but also to actual social influence. A forceful husband holds much power in a family, but so does a man who is chronically depressed, complaining, and manipulating. In the absence of conflict, interpersonal power is defined similarly to the concept of dominance: holding uncontested privileges that are not held by others. During conflicts, power is defined by winning, or more broadly, by having control over the outcome of disputes. In dyadic conflict, power always involves winning and losing. In triadic conflict, however, the third party who directs the dispute resolution may be the most powerful (e.g., a judge, a mediator). Thus, a child who mediates parental disputes is in a powerful (and developmentally inappropriate) position in the family (Emery, 1992).

Surface and Deeper Meanings of Conflict: Power and Intimacy Struggles

Family members usually do not explicitly define their conflicts in terms of love and power. Instead, they focus on specific issues. A child needs to have a bedtime enforced, not to engage in a discussion of parental authority. A former spouse needs to know that it is unacceptable to make telephone calls in the middle of the night, not to hear seemingly vague complaints about violations of the partner's boundaries.

As specific problems are resolved at the surface level, however, the nature of their resolution helps to define love and power boundaries at a deeper level of analysis (Emery, 1992). That is, in addition to getting their youngsters to sleep at a proper hour, parents who enforce bedtime schedules communicate to their children that they will exercise their parental authority. Similarly, when a divorced partner refuses to speak to a former spouse on the telephone except during scheduled hours, at one level they are simply avoiding annoying interruptions. At another level, however, they are redefining the boundary of intimacy in their relationship. In so doing, they communicate that their relationship now is more formal, and their privacy must be respected.

Thus, when divorced family members and the practitioners who work with them focus on the specifics of a dispute, they are also addressing its more general meaning. Irrespective of the specifics, the deep meaning of conflict and its resolution always is a meta-communication about intimacy and/or power boundaries in the relationship. That is, all family conflicts involve either power struggles or intimacy struggles at this deep level of meaning (Emery, 1992).

The discussion of boundaries and of the central roles of intimacy and power in relationships leads to a succinct statement of the fundamental view elaborated on in this book. That view is that divorce entails *the renegotiation of intimacy and power boundaries in the system of family relationships*. This chapter focuses on the renegotiation of intimacy and power boundaries in the relationship between former spouses. In Chapter 3, the dyadic relationships between children and their residential and nonresidential parents are discussed, as is the renegotiation of love and power boundaries in the parent–child–parent triad. Prior to discussing these relationships, however, the major intimacy and power issues in divorce are addressed from the perspective of the individual, particularly the individual partner/parent.

INTIMACY, POWER, AND THE INDIVIDUAL: GRIEF AND IDENTITY CONFLICT

Interpersonal conflicts that arise from ill-defined boundaries of intimacy and power in the divorced family are accompanied by intrapersonal conflicts. Both parents and children grapple as individuals with various concerns related to love and power. Two of the most important tasks involve coping with loss and coping with challenges to one's sense of self. Specifically, these are issues of grief and of identity conflict.

Grief in divorce is very much like the grief experienced following the death of a loved one, with one major exception. Nothing is ever final in divorce. For many former partners and for their children, the possibility of a reconciliation always remains. This is so even after the legal divorce is final, even after one partner remarries, and even after many years have passed. In contrast to bereavement following the death of a loved one, this means that the experience of grief in divorce is more likely to be repeated, prolonged, and unresolved.

The necessity of identifying oneself as a divorced woman or man rather than as a wife or husband is one specific example of identity conflict and the need for redefinition of self in divorce. Children also somehow need to incorporate the idea that their parents are divorced into their sense of self. More broadly, however, new identities must be adopted as divorced family members actually change their life roles, for example, when a woman who has been a homemaker must return to the workforce. Not surprisingly, identity conflict is more intense for people who have derived their primary identities from family roles and who have to master new and challenging roles as a result of divorce.

Different individuals and different families do not confront identical grief and identity issues, of course. There are many individual differences between people and between families in what they experience and how they cope with separation and divorce. In fact, there are many essential differences *within families* in how parents and children in the same family experience grief or identity conflict. As noted in Chapter 1, these differences in intraindividual experience are essential to custody mediation, because the misunderstandings that result can create interpersonal conflict and lead to insensitivity to children's experiences.

Grief in Divorce

Divorce is a loss, regardless of whether or not it also is a relief. Divorce involves the loss of one's mate, the loss of time with one's children or parents, and the loss of cherished possessions. Divorce is a loss of dreams, of shared goals, and of life roles. Divorce creates a loss of control, a loss of trust, and a loss of security. These multiple losses mean that divorce also is a time of grief.

Grief is a common, familiar, and acceptable reaction to loss. Many rituals, particularly those surrounding death and bereavement, attempt to encourage and support grief. A problem with grief in divorce, however, is that many family members do not recognize and label their feelings as a part of the grieving process. Others may identify the feelings correctly but, when dealing with divorce, attempt to squelch their grief as a means of protecting themselves or others in their family. Yet another difficulty is that friends and relatives may not recognize the grief experienced by divorced family members, or they may not know how to cope with it. Grieving is a normal, healthy response to loss, but there is no ritualized means of supporting and encouraging grief in divorce.

Stage Theories of Grief

The experience of grief has been described by many, but the work of attachment theorist John Bowlby clearly is the leading contribution. In his trilogy on attachment, separation, and loss, Bowlby (1969, 1973, 1980) articulated his theoretical views on the topic, and described a stage theory of grief. According to Bowlby (1979), the experience of grief involves four stages: (1) numbing, (2) yearning and protest, (3) disorganization and despair, (4) reorganization and detachment. That is, according to attachment theory, children and adults initially are numbed by a loss; they next try to bring about reunion with angry protest; failing this they fall into a state of depression and confusion; and finally the despair is resolved by becoming detached. The special bond with the former attachment figure is lost, and the bereaved individual moves on with life alone.

A similar stage theory of bereavement has been described by Kubler-Ross (1969). Kubler-Ross' familiar stages proceed from denial to anger to bargaining to depression to acceptance. With the exception of bargaining, the content and sequencing of the stages is very similar to Bowlby's. This is true despite the much more elaborate details of attachment theory, and the fact that Bowlby's audience was largely a professional one, while Kubler-Ross has received more popular interest.

Not surprisingly, these strongly articulated theories of grief have been challenged. One valid criticism is that there is no single, "right" way to grieve. It is not necessary, for example, for all bereaved individuals to express intense emotions in order to cleanse themselves through grief. In fact, some people apparently benefit from "suffering in silence" (Wortman & Silver, 1989). Another common critique is that grief does not follow in stages that are as neat as their descriptions imply. Descriptions of grief in terms of stage theories can be of practical value, because their simplicity makes them easily understood, they convey a sense of organization and control, and they imply that grief should be time-limited. Real experiences of real grief do not necessarily proceed in tidy stages, however. Neither Bowlby nor Kubler-Ross asserted that their stages were immutable, but neither did they emphasize the constant cycling back and forth that seems to characterize many people's experience of grief.

A Cyclical Theory of Grief

I have developed a somewhat different model of grief in divorce in order to address some of these shortcomings. In contrast to the theories of Bowlby and Kubler-Ross, the present model of grieving highlights (1) the central role of affect (particularly the feelings of love, anger, and sadness), (2) the constant cycling back and forth between these conflicting emotions, (3) the need to integrate apparently contradictory feelings over time, (4) differences in the experiences of the partner who leaves the marriage and the partner who is left behind, and (5) the interpersonal consequences of the partners' conflicting experiences of grief in divorce. The first three aspects of this model are discussed in the following sections, and the latter two are described later in the chapter.

Love, Anger, and Sadness

Some of the basic assumptions of the cyclical theory of grief in divorce are portrayed in Figure 2.2. The most prominent aspect of the model involves the three different emotions that comprise the major affective components of grief: love, anger, and sadness.

As used in the present context, these terms should be construed broadly. "Love" retains all of its usual, elusive meanings, but it includes the intense longing that follows separation from a loved one. "Love" also includes vague hopes for reconciliation, guilt-ridden concern, and related emotions that cause one person to want to move closer to another. "Anger" refers to a variety of related affective states that includes feelings of frustration and resentment, as well as the far more intense fury and rage that is commonly experienced in divorce. Anger typically is felt toward the former spouse or the spouse's life circumstances, but it is not necessarily accompanied by conflict. "Sadness" refers to a constellation of associated feelings including loneliness, depression, and despair. Unlike anger, these feelings are directed inward toward the self, rather than outward toward the other. When it is most intense, sadness may be experienced as being physically painful, and in the midst of their grief, many people refer to their feelings of hurt and pain rather than sadness and depression.

The emotions of love, anger, and sadness can be construed as affective components of the well-known behavioral patterns of moving toward, against, and away from others as described by ego psy-

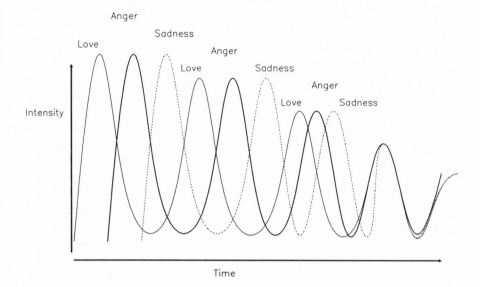

Figure 2.2. A representation of cycles of love, anger, and sadness in grief. Note that the emotions diminish in intensity over time, as they come into phase.

chologist, Karen Horney (1939). The emotions also have obvious similarities with various stages found in the theories of both Bowlby and Kubler-Ross. A notable difference, however, is that the present model includes swings back to loving/hopeful feelings that are not found in the other two theories, although Bowlby's theory clearly assumes that love or attachment is a precondition for grief.

One reason why a stage comparable to "love" may be absent from these theories is that Kubler-Ross and Bowlby were primarily concerned with irrevocable losses, whereas the present model includes the possibility of actual reunion, however unrealistic the possibility may be. The failure to include the possibility of reunion also may reflect a general disadvantage of stage theories. The stages can proceed only in one direction, and because both theories assume that grief begins only after love is lost, this central emotion is not revisited.

Emotional Cycles

The explicit focus on emotional cycling also distinguishes the present model of grief from stage theories. An essential aspect of the model of grief portrayed in Figure 2.2 is the tendency for one emotion to predominate at any given point in time, especially early in the grieving process. For example, while individuals are feeling extreme anger, they do not experience the sadness or love that also might be felt at some deeper level within. The existence of the hidden emotion becomes apparent, however, when it subsequently surfaces to the exclusion of the two other feelings. Not infrequently, this swing of emotions happens within a very short period of time.

Although grief involves the cycling between feelings of love, anger, and sadness in the present model, many individuals apparently get "stuck" on one of the emotions of grief. That is, feelings of love, of anger, or of sadness often form the predominant emotional style with which they cope with the loss. The missing emotions are felt, but they are of lesser intensity and only last for a relatively brief period of time, at least in terms of the individual's conscious experience.

Thus, three problem styles characterize individual difficulties in coping with loss in divorce. Some people get stuck on love, and they seem to deny reality and endlessly hope for a reconciliation. Others get stuck on anger, and they relentlessly pursue vindication or revenge. Finally, many separated or divorced adults get stuck on sadness, and they become depressed as they blame themselves for all of the failures of the family.

All three patterns may be particularly likely to occur among people who did not want or cannot accept a separation or divorce. Those who accept the loss as an irrevocable one are more likely to move through the cycles of grief more rapidly. It also should be noted that the cycling of emotions and the three styles of coping with grief describe patterns that can be found among children, as Bowlby so aptly observed.

Integrating Emotions

The tendency to experience only one emotion at a time suggests a necessary step in proceeding through the emotional cycles of grief in divorce. The "missing" emotions need to be experienced. When anger predominates, it is time to search for hidden sadness and caring. When sadness takes center stage, unexpressed hopes and anger must be brought to the fore. When unrealistic reunion fantasies form the major feeling state, there may be a need to uncover hidden anger and sadness. Simply put, the task is to cut across the grain of the surface emotion and to seek out and experience the underlying affects.

This idea forms a third, core assumption of the present model of grief. As illustrated in Figure 2.2, conflicting emotions tend to come into phase and diminish in intensity over time. As time passes, the cycling between love, anger, and sadness does not disappear, but each feeling becomes less intense and the swings of emotions become less dramatic and less frequent.

An important aspect of the diminished emotional intensity is the individual's increasing recognition of the conflicting emotions over time. When a husband's anger over his wife's rejection arises once again, for example, he gradually develops increased awareness that he simultaneously feels lonely. At the same time, he comes to recognize that he also vaguely longs for a return to an earlier point in the marriage, or at least to fantasies of what might have been. A single emotion no longer predominates in his experience of grief.

In fact, grieving can be assumed to be complete (or as complete as it ever will be) when individuals can simultaneously recognize and experience all three core emotions. They are saddened by the loss of their marriage. They are angry about all that has happened. Yet, they still have some warm memories about the past and regrets about what might have been in the future.

Although some awareness of the conflicting, underlying emotions may come from therapy or from the direct advice of friends, time does heal. However, coping with grief is an emotionally intense task that is often prolonged in divorce because of the potential impermanence of a separation, occasional sexual reunitings, or actual, if temporary, reconciliations. Even after a divorce is final, fantasies of reunion may live on, and actual reunitings apparently occur with some frequency.

Identity Conflict and Role Redefinition

An equally intense and long-lasting task that each individual must accomplish in divorce is a redefinition of self. In contrast to grief, this task is essentially an issue of power, or more specifically, of feeling efficacious in one's identity in various life roles.

The extent to which divorce creates identity conflict and necessitates a redefinition of roles depends both upon the individual's roles in the marriage and on the magnitude of change brought about by the divorce. Divorce can be expected to result in more identity conflict when the transition entails more financial pressures, loss of contact with the children, diminished social support, or similar upheavals. In addition, the more closely an individual's roles and role identities have been tied to the marriage, the more a divorce challenges the sense of self. A woman who has viewed her primary roles in life as being a wife, mother, and homemaker, for example, will go through considerable redefinition of self as a result of divorce. In contrast, a woman who has had other central role identities, for example, as a friend, daughter, and teacher, will have more stability in her sense of self. The continuity in these identities can modulate the changes that divorce necessitates in other life roles.

In conceptualizing the redefinition of self, it is necessary to elaborate briefly on the concepts of identity, roles, and self-efficacy. As used here, the meaning of the term "identity" is in accord with Erikson's (1959) rich descriptions of the construct. Identity is one's sense of self, the composite answer to the question, "Who am I?" Erikson's (1959) ideas about the adolescent identity crisis also are relevant to the present context. Divorce often forces adults in midlife to redefine who they are, much like they once grappled with forming an identity during the transition to adulthood. Many psychosocial tasks can create identity conflict during divorce, ranging from more simple issues such as coming to grips with being divorced to much more complex challenges such as assuming major new roles in family, social, and work life. To paraphrase Erikson, the central identity question becomes, "Who am I . . . now?"

Multiple Role Identities

One departure from Erikson's views is that the present conceptualization assumes that people have multiple identities which correspond to their various life and social roles. In this sense, the idea of a single identity is an illusion, as each individual has many identities. This assumption directly implies that identity is fluid rather than fixed. One's identity changes throughout life as old roles are abandoned and new ones are assumed.

This view of identity also focuses at least as much on life roles as on the individual's role identity. Part of the reason why it is difficult to integrate the idea of being a divorced woman or divorced man into one's sense of self, for example, is because this idea is dissonant with earlier definitions of oneself and with one's dreams of a life trajectory. Another part of the reason for identity conflict, however, comes from difficulties in assuming new life roles. Much of the difficulty in feeling pride about being a competent single parent, for example, comes from the struggles involved in competently parenting alone.

A large part of identity conflict therefore stems from the fact that it is not clear how, or if, people are supposed to act differently following separation or divorce. Dating provides a clear example of role and identity conflict. Dating would seem to be a normal part of being divorced, but it is greatly complicated by emotional, interpersonal, practical, and legal considerations. Thus, it is unclear when, how, and with whom separated and divorced partners are to socialize. Moreover, stereotypes about dating among divorced adults hardly are positive ones. These social uncertainties can combine to cause severe doubts about an identity issue that many adults thought was resolved once and for all when they were married.

It is also true that many roles that are assumed informally can become vital to identity. People identify themselves, in part, based on unstated roles in their families or in other key relationships. They may be or have been "the smart one," "the pretty one," "the caring one," or "the reliable one." An individual's overall sense of self may be strongly dependent upon such specific, but subtle, role identities, and these too can become a source of identity conflict. For example, it can be a tremendous struggle to integrate a decision to leave one's marriage with the life-long identity (and role) of being "the responsible one" in relationships.

Self-Efficacy

Self-efficacy has been defined as the sense of feeling able to control outcomes (Bandura, 1977), a definition which highlights feelings of competence or power and is central in the present view of identity. It not only is important to have multiple role identities, but it is essential to have a sense of efficacy in at least some of these roles. Thus, a sense of efficacy is vital to a healthy self-concept. Because individuals may feel and be more or less efficacious in different life roles, the key to withstanding distress successfully may be to have several areas of competence. That is, one might wish to feel efficacious in multiple role identities. Since events like divorce can dramatically alter important life roles and undermine associated role identities, one definition of positive mental health is feeling efficacious in multiple role identities, each of which is significant, but none of which is paramount in importance.

Of course, certain role identities are more important than others to some people. These core identities often are associated with roles that are expected to be relatively stable across adult life, such as those roles related to family and work. It therefore may be impossible to protect one's sense of self completely against major transitions such as divorce.

Intrapersonal and Interpersonal Conflict

The individual's various intrapersonal conflicts sometimes are responsibile for interpersonal disputes. As was noted in Chapter 1, the two partners' differing experiences of grief can cause much of the conflict between them. Identity issues also can play a significant role in divorce disputes. Some difficulties in reaching settlements are partially attributable to one or both partners' difficulties in assuming new roles or in integrating these roles into their sense of self. Individuals may contest custody not only because they want the children with them, but also because it is incompatible with their sense of self to admit that full-time custody is not what they want. Remarriage and other changes in life roles also can greatly alter both the remarried and the unremarried partners' sense of self, as well as their views of their relationships with their children and the former spouse.

One reason why it is valuable for mediators and legal professionals to be aware of these intra-individual conflicts is that interpersonal conflicts can be more readily settled when intrapsychic struggles are resolved. The more parents/partners are able to accept a divorce, the more they will be able to stand firm where they feel most strongly and to compromise on issues of lesser importance. Even though the focus of mediation is on the parental relationship, and more specifically, on negotiating a separation agreement, sensitivity to these individual concerns can help the negotiation process to move forward. At times, an empathic statement that conveys an understanding of one partner's grief may help to refocus a discussion back on issues and away from painful emotions. In other cases, a referral for individual therapy may be necessary before mediation can continue in a productive manner.

It also is important for mediators to be aware of family members' potential grief and identity conflicts, because everyone benefits as other family members adjust to their dramatically changed circumstances. In particular, better mental health among parents is associated with better mental health for children, as parents who have coped with their own emotions can be more sensitive to the children's needs. This is particularly important because the children's needs differ from those of the parents. The nature and pacing of the children's struggles with grief and identity do not necessarily follow those of their parents.

The quality of parent–child relationships is of ultimate concern to mediators because the potential to serve children's best interests in divorce is one of the most compelling rationales for custody mediation (Emery & Wyer, 1987b). Children's best interests, as indexed by their own mental health and the quality of parent–child relationships, are closely linked with the relationship between the parents themselves. In fact, a considerable body of research points to parental conflict as one of the most consistent predictors of postdivorce adjustment problems among children (Emery, 1982, 1988; see also Chapter 9).

The relationship between the former partners may be the most important to renegotiate, but ironically the fact that this relationship continues following separation and divorce has long been overlooked.

THE PARENTING ALLIANCE: DISENTANGLING MARITAL AND PARENTAL ROLES

Parents do not divorce their children, and because of this, they can never completely divorce each other. Children form a continuing tie between former spouses, who remain parents throughout their lives. Thus, former partners must struggle to disentangle their continuing role as parents from their past role as spouses. In order to do this, they must redefine the boundaries of intimacy and power in their relationship. There are many ways in which the new relationship can be defined, but all take time and effort to negotiate.

Renegotiating the Boundary of Intimacy between Former Spouses

In many cases, the key to the successful renegotiation of all family relationships following separation and divorce lies in redefining the boundary of intimacy between the former partners. Of course, it is obvious that the loving relationship between husband and wife changes when they separate and divorce. What is less obvious is that the new boundary of intimacy is not automatically defined by the marital separation, the legal divorce, or even by such dramatic changes as the remarriage of one of the former spouses. The decision to divorce typically is accompanied by much ambivalence and uncertainty, even on the part of the individual who initiated the action. Thus, the renegotiation of intimacy boundaries may take years to complete. Common attempts at redefining the relationship range from cutting off all communication, trying to "be friends," provoking jealousy, and occasional sexual reunitings.

The Leaver and the Left

The fact that most divorces are not mutually agreed upon is a basic reason why it is so difficult for separated and divorced partners to renegotiate their boundary of intimacy. Typically, one person is leaving the marriage (the leaver), and the other is left behind (the left). One party wants out of the relationship, but the other wants it to continue. This simple and easily overlooked fact means that each partner is likely to want a very different boundary of intimacy around their relationship.

The leaver typically is more disengaged from the relationship, at least shortly after the initial separation. The leaver may want the marriage to end, but he or she commonly wants to preserve other aspects of the relationship. In particular, the leaver may hope to "be friends." This desire may be motivated by guilt over the decision or by concerns about the children's well-being. The partner who leaves may have completed his or her grief and may genuinely care for the former spouse, or the leaver may simply want to be friendly so that the legal negotiations will proceed smoothly and quickly.

The problem, of course, is that the partner who has been left is unlikely to want to "be friends." The left partner typically has had little time to prepare for the end of the marriage, and if he or she had some warning, this time might have been used in an attempt to repair the relationship, not to cope with its loss. Because of personal hopes and volatile emotions, the left partner therefore is apt to interpret the former spouse's friendliness either as a sign that he or she still loves them, or as a glib rejection of the former relationship. "Love and hate are not far apart," and the partner who was left may face an emotional choice between being lovers or being enemies.

The Pursuer and the Pursued

A result of these differing feelings and desires is that neither partner is likely to be satisfied with the intimacy boundary that the other attempts to draw. The leaving partner suggests having dinner to keep communication open, but the left party views this as a date and hopes for a nightcap. When this secret hope becomes clear, the leaver lets it be known that he or she is interested in being "just friends." If the left partner refuses the next invitation to dinner as a result of this rejection, the leaver fears the loss of everything, including the desired friendship. As a result, the leaver pushes for dinner at another time, another place, or at least lunch.

In short, the interaction between former spouses often takes on the characteristics of a "pursuer–pursued" relationship, a common pattern found when intimacy boundaries are poorly defined (Emery, 1992). The pursuer chases and the pursued partner distances. When the pursuer gives up and moves away, however, the pursued party is threatened. He or she may not want to be intimate with the pursued partner but does want some form of a relationship. Thus, the partners reverse roles, and the pursued becomes the pursuer.

Conflicts frequently erupt as a result of a pursuer–pursued

relationship, and more generally, from ill-defined boundaries of intimacy between former spouses. The conflicts may be direct and focus on issues such as spending time together, attempting a reconciliation, or dating others. Because of each partner's fears and uncertain feelings, however, the conflicts often will be indirect. Not surprisingly, the children are a frequent focus: The children are a continuing link between the partners, and a topic of dispute that can arouse many strong feelings. Thus, a conflict that appears to be about the children on the surface actually may concern an ill-defined boundary of intimacy between the parents.

Enmeshment

In considering the potential for such underlying conflicts, it is essential to recognize that winning is *not* the key to an intimacy struggle (Emery, 1992). Rather, the central issue is discovering the extent to which the other partner still cares. The overriding question is, "Is he or she still 'hooked'?" This question is answered by the intensity of the other's emotional response to provocation, irrespective of the valence of the affect. The more intense the emotion, the more the other still cares, even when the intense emotion is anger (Emery, 1992). For example, when a young woman breaks off a relationship, her boyfriend's response, "You can't do this to me!" conveys far more intimate involvement than does the answer, "OK. If that's what you want." Similarly, when a rejected man fights with his former spouse about the children, he may have legitimate concerns, but part of what he may be looking for is a reaction from his former wife.

This is one reason why highly conflictual former spouses are said to have an enmeshed relationship (S. Minuchin, 1974), not a disengaged one. Even though many separated and divorced partners vehemently deny harboring any feelings for their former spouses, clinical observation and some research indicate that the problem among contentious divorced couples is *not* that they need to be more friendly, communicate more frequently, and be less distant. Rather, the opposite seems to be true. The partners need to be less friendly, communicate less frequently, and be more distant.

This observation is obvious to some people, but others are oblivious to the enmeshment possibility. In particular, many partners interpret their own anger as a sign of their *lack* of caring and concern for their former spouse, or at least that is what they profess. According to the present analysis, however, intense anger conveys greater not lesser intimacy. Thus, the central problem for separated and divorced partners who find themselves repeatedly embroiled in conflicts is that they are too involved with one another. They need to become associates, not friends. They need to communicate more formally and less often, not more frequently. They need a boundary of intimacy that is both more distant and more clearly defined.

Different Cycles of Grief for the Leaver and the Left

Part of the problem that former partners have in redefining their boundaries of intimacy can be understood in terms of their differing experiences in grieving over the divorce. As noted earlier, grief is characterized by swings between love, anger, and sadness for both the leaver and the left, and each partner needs to integrate these emotions over time. Despite these similarities, however, there are some key differences in the experience of grief for the leaver and the left. These differences often prevent the former partners from understanding each other, despite the fact that they are sharing the experience of grief.

One difference between the leaver and the left is the intensity of the emotions that each feels. In general, the leaver's emotions can be expected to be less intense than those of the left partner, because their grieving typically began long before the separation. The grief of the leaver is akin to bereavement following a chronic illness. The extended period of preparing for the end of the relationship leads to a lessening of the intensity of their emotions. In contrast, the partner who is left usually has had little time to prepare for the loss and experiences intense emotions that are more analogous to bereavement following a sudden and unexpected death.

Differences in the dominant theme of their grief also distinguish the experiences of the leaver and the left, because one partner has chosen to end the relationship while the other has not. In general, this means that the partner who leaves experiences grief that is pervaded with guilt, while a sense of rejection tinges all of the feelings that accompany the grief of the partner who was left. Not only do these two affects distinctively color each partner's experience of grief, but feelings of guilt and rejection underlie much of each partner's cycling between feelings of love, anger, and sadness.

In general, rejection is responsible for the shifts in the left party's feelings from love to anger and from anger to sadness. Hope, the opposite of rejection, accounts for the switch from sadness to love. Specifically, the left party experiences rejection as feelings of hurt and pain, and this turns loving feelings into angry ones. As the left party accepts the rejection for what it is, however, anger turns into intense sadness and self-blame. Fueled by imagined or real encouragement, rejection eventually turns into hope. This converts sadness back into loving feelings, which eventually lead around to hurt and pain, as the grief continues in a relentless cycle (see Figure 2.3).

Although the major feelings of love, anger, and sadness are the same, the emotions that provoke changes in affect differ sharply for the leaver. For the partner who chooses to end the relationship, the theme is one of guilt instead of rejection (Figure 2.3). Guilt turns anger into sadness, and over time, a guilty sense of responsibility converts the sadness and self-blame into feelings of dutiful caring. Loving feelings are transformed into anger when the leaver begins to feel a sense of righteousness, an emotion that is the opposite of guilt. That is, the leaver

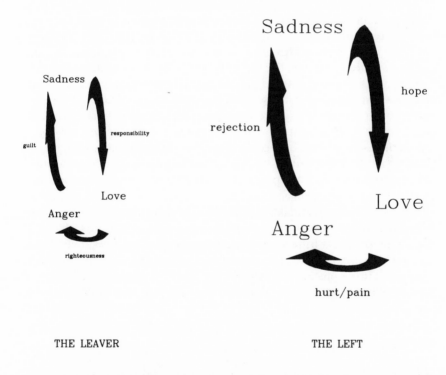

THE LEAVER   THE LEFT

Figure 2.3. Emotional cycles of grief for the leaver and the left. Note the different intensities of grief (indicated by size) and the differences in the feelings that lead to changes between love, anger, and sadness. The leaver's grief is dominated by guilt, while the left party's grief is dominated by rejection.

temporarily believes he or she has been wronged by a spouse or by life. Perhaps as a result of feeling they should have tried harder, or perhaps in response to the suffering of the former spouse, the blame comes to be refocused inward over time. Guilt again dominates, as the leaver's grief, while less intense, pursues a cycle that is no less relentless than the emotional swings experienced by the left party.

Grief and Conflict

One very important aspect of these differing cycles of grief is that the two former partners do not experience the same feelings at the same time. On one level, this leads each partner to question the other's feelings. They do not understand why their former partner does not feel the same way that they feel. The left party sees the leaver as uncaring. The leaving party sees the left partner as unable to cope.

At another level, the differing experiences of grief become a part of the pursuer–pursued relationship, as illustrated in Figure 2.4. As the leaver grows more angry due to a (temporary) sense of righteousness, the left party feels increasingly rejected and depressed. Seeing the other's sadness, however, the leaver's righteousness turns into guilt, and anger turns into sadness. The leaving partner's apparent change of feelings gives the left party some hope, and his or her loving feelings arise anew. These rekindled loving feelings turn to hurt and pain, however, as it is recognized that the leaver's caring is based only on a sense of responsibility. In turn, in response to the left party's anger, the leaver's sense of duty turns back into righteousness. This leads around to renewed hurt and a repetition of the cycles of grief, conflict, and misunderstanding (see Figure 2.4). Thus, the former partners move through an cycle of conflict that tracks each party's cycle of grief.

One important implication of these observations is that the partners' progress in resolving their own grief not only moves them forward as individuals, but also helps to alter the pursuer–pursued pattern. The resolution of grief thereby reduces conflict and facilitates the establishment of new boundaries of intimacy in the coparental relationship.

Renegotiating Intimacy Boundaries

Although each partner's resolution of grief helps to improve their relationship, the former partners still must negotiate a new boundary of intimacy. Intimacy boundaries may be negotiated directly in face-to-face meetings, as they often are in couples or family therapy. Unless professional help is sought and followed, however, separated spouses

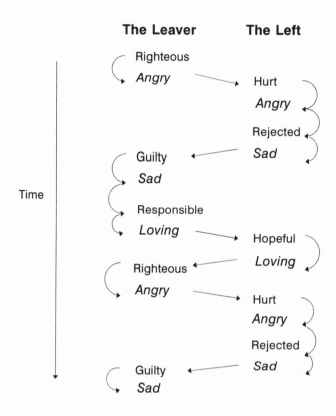

Figure 2.4. The leaver's and the left's differing experiences of grief and cycles of interpersonal conflict. Note that the two partners experience different aspects of their grief at the same time, thus causing conflict and misunderstanding.

rarely negotiate their interpersonal boundaries quite so directly. Rather, they attempt to negotiate or to test a boundary of intimacy through their actions. A telephone call may be made late at night, for example. Such a call serves several purposes. It is a way of finding out whether or not the partner is at home or whether they are alone, and it also is a test of whether or not the former spouse is willing to talk at an inconvenient hour.

An unfortunate circumstance is that many of the parents' boundary conflicts occur in the children's presence or over topics that concern the children. When one partner stops by on a Saturday night for a spontaneous "visit with the children," for example, the children clearly are a secondary consideration. The children are likely to remain the focus when the other partner indicates that such visits are inappropriate, perhaps because they are not in the children's best interests. Rather than discussing (or refusing to discuss) the terms of their own relationship, the former partners get caught up in arguments about the children's well-being and their rights as parents. As suggested by the data presented in Chapter 1, such conflicts over intimacy boundaries can even escalate into formal custody disputes.

Just as intimacy struggles can be enacted in terms of threatened or formal disputes about custody, custody settlements also help to redefine the boundary of intimacy between the partners/parents. A good custody agreement not only spells out boundaries in parent–child relationships by providing very specific information about times and exchanges, but in so doing, it also helps to define the boundaries of the former spouses' relationship. By indicating when the children will be with each parent, a carefully written custody agreement helps to establish each parent's autonomy from the other. A very specific custody agreement also cuts down on the need for communication between the parents, thus removing further opportunities for conflict.

These are some of the reasons why mediators typically write very detailed custody agreements. Among the things that these agreements spell out are specific times that the children will be with each parent, clear methods for exchanging the children, basic rules for consistent parenting in two households, and a structured means for the parents to communicate when it is necessary for them to do so (see Chapters 4 and 7). The terms of a custody agreement can be particularly important, because the resolution of grief and redefinition of self take a considerable amount of time, while some sort of a structured custody arrangement is needed soon after a marital separation.

Renegotiating Power Boundaries between Former Spouses

Just as former partners must redefine the boundary of intimacy in their relationship, they must also renegotiate their power boundaries. In a marriage, power boundaries are defined, in part, by the roles that each partner fulfills. Power is rarely equal in all areas of a relationship, as most couples specialize in their marital roles. A "breadwinner" husband assumes more responsibility and authority for earning income and relating to the external world, for example, while a "caretaker" wife assumes more responsibility and authority for raising the children and managing family relationships. Divorce obviously necessitates changes in these and other marital roles, whether the marriage was traditional or nontraditional. This means that former spouses must renegotiate a second basic aspect of their relationship.

Fortunately, the renegotiation of power relationships typically is less difficult than the renegotiation of intimacy boundaries. One reason for this is that disputes over ill-defined power boundaries usually do not involve the same degree of affective intensity. Conflict over intimacy has the hidden goal of testing the partner's emotional investment in the relationship, and the intensity of the partner's affective reaction is the key to the test. Disputes over power boundaries are more straightforward. The dispute at hand is truly important in a power struggle, and the outcome of the conflict does matter. Power boundaries are defined by winning or losing, not by the other's affective reaction (Emery, 1992).

Conflicts over power boundaries are common in marriage, as partners attempt to define and redefine their marital roles. Spouses maneuver explicitly or implicitly to gain authority over issues (or individuals) that are important to them and to give up responsibility for tasks that are burdensome. The women's movement and related social changes have greatly complicated the negotiation of power boundaries in marriage. The range of expected and socially accepted marital roles has expanded greatly, making power boundaries more ambiguous and the source of considerable marital conflict. As a result, power struggles probably are more common in marriages today than they were in the past, despite the clear benefits of more flexible marital roles for individual autonomy.

Power struggles can and do carry over into the renegotiation of relationships following separation and divorce. Many people view divorce as an opportunity to free themselves from the constrained roles that they adopted in a marriage, and others are threatened by such changes in their partner even following a divorce. Thus, some people continue in their attempts to dominate long after a separation, while others remain locked in a fight to gain the upper hand at last. Such unsettled conflicts over the partners' power boundaries sometimes form the basis for prolonged disputes following a marital separation. The degree of control that partners can exercise over one another is dramatically reduced by divorce, however. Moreover, the much more straightforward nature of the topics that define power boundaries following a separation makes redefining them easier.

Power Boundaries and the Law

In fact, many of the substantive issues related to power in the relationship between divorcing spouses are explicitly addressed in the law.

There are legal guidelines for redefining power boundaries about such important issues as how to divide shared property, and whether and how much alimony or child support is to be paid. Lawyers can easily advocate for a partner who feels powerless about negotiating these relatively straightforward issues, and a judge will eventually render a decision about each partner's power as defined by financial matters. Each parent's power boundaries in relation to childrearing also can be addressed in the law, inasmuch as they fall under the rubric of child custody or visitation.

Because the renegotiation of many power boundaries has a legal focus, most discussion of this topic is deferred until Chapter 4, where an overview of the substantive law in divorce is presented. It can be noted here, however, that many of the decisions made through the legal system are neither simple nor straightforward. Many innovations both inside and outside of the law have complicated the resolution of disputes in divorce, particularly with respect to children and childrearing. As discussed in detail in Chapter 4, one basic problem is that much of divorce law has become indeterminate. That is, the law provides only general, not specific, guidelines on arrangements for postdivorce finances and childrearing. In the terms used to describe the renegotiation of relationships, this means that the law fails to be explicit about where new power boundaries are to be defined in the partners' postdivorce relationship.

A particular problem with childrearing is that it is outside of the scope of the law to address many of the power boundaries in the coparental relationship. There are no laws about how parents are to make necessary, day-to-day decisions about childrearing, and judges are understandably reluctant to get involved even in relatively major parenting conflicts, such as deciding where children should go to school or what their religious upbringing should be. Such reticence is increased exponentially when disputes arise about more minor parenting concerns, such as the parents' standards of conduct in the presence of the children, or such disciplinary rules as appropriate bedtimes or dress.

However, these are real sources of potential dispute among divorced parents, at least until new power boundaries are defined about who has the authority to make these decisions. Financial disputes are decided more clearly and with more finality in the law. Thus, conflicts over power boundaries share one very important feature with disputes over intimacy: both forms of conflict are likely to focus on the children.

Changes in Power Boundaries

The renegotiation of power boundaries or parental roles can be facilitated if certain areas of potential dispute are anticipated and understood. For example, all parents need to learn to accept that one inevitable result of divorce is loss of control over aspects of the children's lives. The reason for this is not that parents become less effective disciplinarians (although they often do), but because they have less influence over each other's parenting. Former partners who remain parents can negotiate a variety of potential new boundaries in regard to their respective childrearing power and the integration of their efforts across households. Some parents rarely communicate about their children, and others talk about them on a daily basis. In both extremes and in all cases in between, however, both parents lose some influence over each other's parenting. The coparental power boundary invariably is defined more sharply than it was in marriage.

Some other general principles facilitate the redefinition of power boundaries following divorce. As with renegotiating intimacy boundaries, power boundaries will be more readily renegotiated if the rules for the coparenting relationship are simple and clear and require little coordination of efforts. It is beneficial if the new rules for the coparenting relationship are rigidly enforced, especially soon after they are first negotiated. In addition, the renegotiation of the parenting roles following divorce can be made easier by following guidelines about more and less healthy parent–child relationships, as is discussed in Chapters 4 and 9.

Confusion between Power and Intimacy Struggles

A basic problem with renegotiating any relationship is that power struggles are often confused with intimacy struggles (Emery, 1992). For example, a wife may complain that her husband frequently works late, but does not call to let her know of his plans. In voicing her objections, the wife may be concerned about intimacy. She may be uncertain about whether her husband wants to be with her, or she may wonder why he does not care enough to call. To the husband, however, power may be the issue. He may feel controlled by his wife and intentionally come home late to prove his independence. In short, the wife may be involved in an intimacy struggle, while the husband is involved in a power struggle.

In fact, the idea that power struggles and intimacy struggles frequently get confused following separation and divorce is a major point of this chapter. Disputes over child custody or postdivorce childrearing may appear to be conflicts about power, but intimacy often is the real, underlying issue. That is, a conflict about the children is used to test the boundary of intimacy between the former spouses. Thus, prolonged, seemingly irrational disputes between former partners may represent struggles about intimacy not power, at least from the perspective of one of the partners.

This basic confusion between intimacy struggles and power struggles underlies a basic point that is repeated throughout this book: An overriding goal for renegotiating relationships in divorce is for former partners to separate their spousal and parental roles. The role of spouse ends in divorce but the parental role does not end. Parents therefore have an obligation to work to separate their common concerns about parenting their children from their angry and uncertain feelings toward one another.

SUMMARY

This chapter presents a conceptual perspective of my family systems view that divorce necessitates the renegotiation of intimacy and power boundaries in the system of family relationships. Separated and divorced families are defined by relationships, not by households, but changes in the family require the creation of new rules or boundaries in their relationships. Ironically, the need to redefine power and intimacy boundaries between former partners who remain parents is the single most important task for separated or divorced families.

In order to renegotiate their relationship, individual family members must cope with grief over multiple losses and with identity and role conflicts that challenge their sense of self-efficacy. Specific rules for relating also must be negotiated between the former spouses, either formally in mediation or informally through their interactions over time. Broadly speaking, the task for the divorcing partners is to separate their marital and parental roles—roles that are bound together in marriage but that must be disentangled in divorce.

CHAPTER 3

Renegotiating Relationships II
Children in the Divorced
Family System

The renegotiation of the coparental relationship is central to achieving the ultimate goal of both legal and psychological intervention in separation and divorce: redefining family relationships in a manner that will best promote children's well-being. It is not necessary for parents to have an integrated, highly cooperative relationship in order to achieve this goal. Rather, parents only need to establish a relationship in which their anger and conflict is contained. That is, the parents must only develop a relationship that is more formal and disengaged, not necessarily one that is friendly.

Such a disengaged relationship, or even a highly cooperative one, does not guarantee a smooth transition for children, however. Separated and divorced parents still must renegotiate their individual relationships with their children. This is true despite many parents' strong desire to maintain stability. The practicalities of a custody schedule require parents to redefine how and when they will spend time with their children. This is true even when joint physical custody is maintained, and even for a parent with whom the children spend most of their time.

The challenges of parenting alone also test each parent's ability to discipline the children. Single parents often must develop new approaches to setting limits, and some must master a new role as the disciplinarian in the family. Discipline can be a particular struggle for residential parents, who have an added weight of responsibility in their children's day-to-day activities and management. Of course, the distress that children feel adds considerably to this task, as their behavior can be expected to be more angry, erratic, and challenging during this difficult transition.

Perhaps the most basic change in parents' relationships with their children involves the triangle formed by the child and each parent. The relationship between former spouses is changed dramatically by separation and divorce, no matter how cooperative or disengaged it may be. The conflict or distancing in the former marital relationship unbalances the broader system of family relationships in a manner that usually begins well before a separation and continues for varying lengths of time afterward. Children are faced with the dilemma of loving two parents who do not love (or who actively hate) each other. Because the system is out of balance, parents and children must renegotiate their relationships with each other as part of the attempt to achieve a new homeostasis in the divorced family system.

The renegotiation of the coparenting relationship, of parent–child relationships, and of the continuing triadic relationship between both parents and the children can be facilitated by guidelines about what constitutes more and less adaptive boundaries for children's mental health in the divorced family system. As reviewed in detail in Chapter 9, research substantiates the concept that particular types of family relationships are linked with more or less adequate adjustment. In this chapter, these rules for healthy parenting are discussed conceptually from the perspective of renegotiating intimacy and power boundaries in parent–child relationships following separation and divorce.

AUTHORITATIVE PARENTING

Parent–child relationships can described in terms of intimacy and power, much as the relationship between parents can be described in terms of these two dimensions. In fact, the most widely accepted classification of parenting styles constructed by developmental psychologists is based on a combination of intimacy and power (Baumrind, 1971; Maccoby & Martin, 1983; see Figure 3.1). Authoritative parents are warm and loving, yet they are strict but fair in disciplining their children. Authoritarian parents also are strict in discipline, but they are autocratic and offer their children relatively little love, understanding, and support. Indulgent parents are the opposite of authoritarian parents. They give their children much love, but they provide them with little in the way of discipline. Finally, neglectful parents offer their children little in the way of either affection or discipline. They show little concern for their children and have scant interest in parenting (see Figure 3.1).

These four parenting styles have been related to children's mental health in a number of studies. Children of authoritative parents have been found to be independent, responsible, and self-confident, while

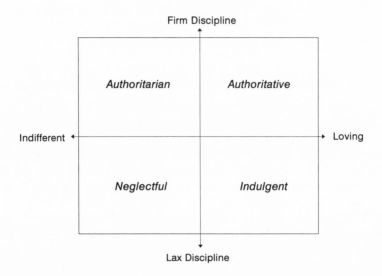

Figure 3.1. Four styles of parenting created by dichotomizing and crossing the dimensions of intimacy and power. Adapted from Maccoby and Martin (1983). Copyright 1983 by John Wiley & Sons, Inc. Adapted by permission.

children of indulgent parents are likely to be self-confident, but they also are selfish and impulsive. The children of authoritarian parents tend to be less self-assured and socially competent than the children of indulgent parents, even though they are better behaved. Neglectful parenting appears to be most strongly related to children's distress. This parenting style is common among parents in families with extreme problems such as child abuse and juvenile delinquency (Lamborn, Mounts, & Steinberg, 1991; Maccoby & Martin, 1983). Although parenting hardly accounts for all of children's psychological difficulties and some parenting difficulties are a reaction to dealing with a troubled child, the numerous benefits of authoritative parenting are clear nevertheless.

For a number of reasons, however, both residential and nonresidential parents commonly have difficulties with maintaining authoritative childrearing following separation and divorce. This may be the result of inevitable changes in the amount of time they spent with children, each parent's own emotional problems, difficulties in the parents' relationship with each other, or a variety of other influences. Even parents who maintain joint physical custody face the prospect of less effective parenting, despite the greater similarity of this arrangement with parenting before divorce. To put these challenges into the terms used in this book, the boundaries of both intimacy and power in the parent–child relationship are likely to be threatened.

Residential, Nonresidential, and Joint Parenting

Even once new boundaries have been defined or a new homeostasis is reached, a number of challenges make it difficult to achieve or maintain authoritative parenting following separation and divorce. The challenges encountered by residential, nonresidential, and joint custody parents can differ dramatically, however. Residential parents are likely to be overburdened, overwrought, and overwhelmed with the tasks of single parenting. Nonresidential parents, in contrast, are likely to feel cut off from the children and helpless, isolated, or detached in their parenting. Parents with joint physical custody experience both of these sets of problems to a lesser extent, but they face the added struggle of coordinating parenting schedules and practicalities with their former spouse. As a result of these differing circumstances, nonresidential parents and their children tend to have more difficulties in redefining boundaries of intimacy or love, while residential parents have more of a struggle reestablishing boundaries of power or discipline. The redefinition of the parent–child–parent triad often is the biggest task for joint custody families.

A detailed overview of research on custody arrangements is presented in Chapter 9, along with other evidence on postdivorce parenting and children's mental health. At present, the renegotiation of parent–child relationships is considered from the family systems perspective already outlined. In the discussion that follows, residential parents are frequently referred to as mothers, nonresidential parents are referred to as fathers, and joint physical custody is given relatively little attention. This is done both for convenience, and because this usage reflects the most common demographic patterns in custody arrangements (see Chapter 9). Alternatives to these normative circumstances are readily acknowledged and are considered more briefly in the following discussion and elsewhere in this book.

PARENTAL LOVE: REASSURANCE, CLARITY, AND CONSISTENCY

Parents' consistent demonstration of love for their children is one of the ideals of healthy family relationships. As children become aware of their parents' doubts about their love for each other, however, they often question their parents' love for them. Some of children's insecurity and uncertainty stems from realistic changes in parent–child relationships. Children are likely to spend less time with one or both of their parents as a result of separation and divorce. Moreover, when children are with their separated or divorced parents, the love, affection, and support they receive may be diminished as a result of the parents' preoccupation with their own concerns.

Other doubts that children have about each of their parent's love for them can stem from their own fantasies and concerns. The limited cognitive capacities of preschoolers, for example, may prevent them from comprehending the reasons for and meaning of a separation. As a result, young children may openly or secretly fear that both of their parents will abandon them. While perhaps more prevalent among preschoolers, such fears are not limited to this early age. Evidence indicates that many school-age children fear abandonment by both of their divorced parents (Kurdek & Berg, 1987), and even adolescents may harbor such unrealistic fears despite their rational understanding that their fears are irrational.

Because of such realistic and fantasized threats to children's security in their parents' love, at a minimum, separated and divorced parents need to offer extra reassurance to their children about their unconditional love for them. In many circumstances, parents also must develop practical new boundaries of love and affection with their children. In so doing, the overriding goal is to be clear and consistent in offering support and expressing affection.

Visitation Schedules

The most obvious renegotiations of parent–child relationships following separation and divorce involve the changes that take place in the boundaries of intimacy between children and their nonresidential parents. By definition, nonresidential parents spend less time with their children following divorce. In a surprisingly large number of cases, the reduction in contact is dramatic. According to the reports of divorced mothers in one recent study, 32% of divorced fathers had not seen their children at all or only a few times in the past year; 22% saw them several times a year; and 21% saw them up to three times per month. Only 25% of divorced fathers saw their children every week (Seltzer, 1991; see Chapter 9).

Contact between nonresidential parents and their children is higher soon after the marital separation, but it lessens over time. Still, the immediate reduction in contact often is dramatic, and this can lead to distress and grief among children. Children who are separated from an attachment figure demonstrate periods of protest and despair before becoming detached or accepting the loss (Bowlby, 1973, 1980), much as parents move through cycles of love, anger, and sadness as they grieve the end of their marriage. Also similar to their parents' experience, ambivalence, ambiguity, and uncertainty about the permanence of the separation often cause children's grief to be repeated and prolonged.

An added problem is that the dramatically altered relationship with the nonresidential parent comes at a time when children are likely to need more, not less, reassurance and stability. Alternative sources of security can help to ease children's experience of separation and loss, but these too may be disrupted by divorce. Children may fear (or experience) loss of contact with their residential parent as well as their nonresidential parent, and financial and practical arrangements may take children away from other essential sources of the children's security, such as the family home, their school, and their friends.

The grief of separation hurts, but research indicates that children can cope with the loss even when the new boundaries of intimacy with their nonresidential parents are distant (see Chapter 9). The process of grieving can be painfully prolonged, however, when the new boundaries of the nonresidential parent–child relationship are unclear or inconsistent. If they know when and how they will see the parent again, children can eventually accept less frequent contact with their nonresidential parent, even dramatic reductions in contact. When the boundaries of the relationship are uncertain, however, so are children's expectations. This is a particular problem shortly after the separation when the parents may not have agreed on a schedule for sharing time with their children. Thus, an issue that frequently arises in mediation is that the parents need to work toward a clear agreement about a schedule, even if it is only a temporary one.

Flexible Visits

When a schedule is agreed upon, it is essential to follow it religiously. A host of problems can develop around visitation when a schedule is unclear, overly spontaneous, or too flexible. For example, to the visiting parent, unscheduled visits may seem spontaneous and natural. However, from the child's perspective they add uncertainty to the relationship, and unplanned visits clearly violate a boundary in the new relationship between former spouses.

Visits that are scheduled but are late or never occur at all are equally problematic. An hour or two may seem like a short amount of time to a parent, but this can be an eternity to a child. Young children especially have much shorter time horizons than adults, and when time moves more slowly, it takes on added importance. This is especially true when a child has looked forward to a visit for a week or more. Thus, it is wise to follow a schedule strictly, at least until a clear pattern of visitation is established. Flexibility can come later, but even then, parents would do well to remember that what may seem like flexibility to them may feel like instability to their children.

Because of their more narrow time horizons, younger children, especially infants and toddlers, may also benefit from visits that are more frequent but of shorter duration. For preschoolers and early school-aged children, calendars that clearly mark the schedule for the coming weeks can help them to understand the abstraction of time, which suddenly takes on tremendous importance in their lives. Older children can more easily grasp the mechanics of a schedule, as can adolescents whose biggest problem often is coordinating their own social life around household changes. Despite their apparent or stated disdain, even teenagers need a clear and consistent boundary of parental love.

As noted, a parent who fails to follow through with a visitation schedule not only violates the boundary of intimacy with their children, he or she also violates a power boundary with the residential parent. Residential parents make plans for times that the children are to be away, and for many overburdened parents, this is not a time for fun but a time for finishing previously unattended chores. Thus, there are several reasons for working toward clear and consistent visitation schedules. Courts may award "liberal rights of visitation," but children's need for reassurance, predictability, and consistency—and the coparent's legitimate desire for the same—reaffirm the importance of clearly renegotiating relationships following separation and divorce.

Under- or Overinvolvement with Residential Parents

While changes in the relationship with the nonresidential parent are obvious and sometimes dramatic, children's boundaries of intimacy with their residential parents also are likely to be strained. This is particularly likely shortly after the marital separation. At the same time that children need extra attention and reassurance, residential parents are likely to be preoccupied with concerns of their own. Residential parents often find themselves overwhelmed with the burden of parenting alone, a burden made heavier by their grief and loss of confidence in their role as a parent or a partner. Various practical burdens such as financial worries also may preoccupy single parents, and the coparental relationship often exacerbates rather than alleviates these concerns. For a variety of strategic or emotional reasons, the parents may intentionally subvert rather than support each other's parenting.

As a result of these multiple stressors, residential parents often find that they simply have less time to spend with their children. Financial pressures may mean that they spend more time at work, and the children spend more time in child care. New social activities such as dating also may take residential parents away from their children. Thus, children's relationships with both their residential and nonresidential parents can become more distant and erratic as a result of separation and divorce.

Role Reversal

While such changes frequently have been documented in research (see Chapter 9), there also is a potential for a very different kind of problem concerning parental involvement with children. Some parents, particularly residential parents, may become overinvolved or dependent upon their children following a marital separation. Often this leads to a reversal of roles, so that the child becomes the caretaker for the parent's emotional needs. A preadolescent child may be encouraged to sleep with the parent, for example, or a teenager might be treated as a peer and confidant. In these and other circumstances, the central problem is that the parent's emotional needs take priority over the child's.

This circumstance is distinct from the situation where children assume increased responsibilities at home as a result of separation or divorce. Increased demands for completing chores and helping out around the house is a discipline (or power) issue. These added responsibilities may cause children to have to "grow up a little faster" (Weiss, 1979a), but the household tasks typically are manageable and appropriate. Same-age peers in two-parent families may have the same or similar responsibilities, especially if both parents are employed, or if the children are the oldest of several. In contrast, the child takes on the developmentally inappropriate responsibility of caring for the parent in a role reversal circumstance.

The potential problems with role reversal are numerous because it is an unfair emotional burden for a child to assume responsibility for an adult's psychological well-being. In the normal course of child development, parents are stable sources of support for their children. From infancy through adolescence, parents offer children a safe base from which they can explore the world. In role reversal, however, the child is the parent's safe base. The child becomes the parent's source of security.

Thus, even as residential parents have the opportunity to maintain more stability in parenting, they too must renegotiate their boundaries of intimacy with their children. Children are challenged by the process and uncertainty of change, and to the extent that residential parents can offer clarity and consistency in their affection and support, this source of stability can ease the difficult transition of separation and divorce. Despite their own struggles, many residential parents do succeed in quickly establishing new boundaries of intimacy with their children. As long as parents are responsive to the children's needs, they are not likely to be able to love their children "too much."

DISRUPTIONS IN DISCIPLINE

Authoritative parents are not only loving, but they are also firm (and democratic) in disciplining their children. For a time following separation and divorce, however, discipline often becomes problematic. The parents' guilt about the effects of their marital problems on the children can make discipline difficult to enforce, as can each partner's doubts about their parenting efficacy. In addition, separated parents may not readily consult each other about appropriate standards of conduct, and they have no immediate ally who will help in enforcing rules.

Disruptions in discipline create an added problem, because children may already behave more erratically as a normal result of the distress of divorce. Children sometimes test the boundaries of discipline out of anger, and sometimes they test them as a way of seeking parental attention or love. Children may act more erratically because they are distraught and confused, or they may have more selfish motivations when they push the limits of acceptable behavior. Because residential parents spend much more time with their children, they inevitably encounter more difficulty with discipline.

Residential Parents

The cliché, "Just wait until your father gets home," conveys a basic difficulty that many residential mothers face in disciplining their children alone. The option of deferring discipline obviously is no longer available. Single mothers (and fathers) must redefine their relationships with their children, and sometimes they must master a new parenting role. For parents who relied on their partner to be the disciplinarian, mastery of this new role often is a struggle, especially given their own distress.

Other struggles also may make it difficult for residential parents to reestablish clear and firm boundaries of parental power. The emotional and practical burdens faced by residential parents often necessitate a decrease in parental monitoring and discipline, as well as a decline in the love, affection, and attention that they can give to their children. As a result of their assumption of new household responsibilities, children also may be given increased independence from former family rules. Growing up a little faster can be beneficial, but not all children are capable of adequately exercising autonomy at an earlier age.

Parental Guilt and Coercive Interactions

Perhaps the most thorny problem with discipline in separation and divorce, however, stems neither from lack of experience nor from the exhaustion of parenting and living alone. A parent's biggest problem with discipline often stems from his or her own guilt, uncertainty, and self-doubt. Because of their own feelings and fears, parents often mistakenly attribute their children's misbehavior to the divorce or related causes, rather than to more normal influences. Young children's fears of the dark, for example, may no longer be seen as normal worries that need to be gradually conquered, but instead are viewed as signaling deep-seated insecurities. Standard bedtime practices thus are disrupted, and overcoming normal fears becomes a tricky task. The parent's guilt, which often is exacerbated by popular and professional writing about divorce, undermines their usual parenting practices.

As a result of the parents' self-doubt and the children's demands, parents and children may get caught in a coercive cycle (Patterson, 1982). Children may be positively reinforced for misbehavior that would have been punished previously, and parents are negatively reinforced for giving in to their children's demands. The child pushes the limits, and the parent begins to assert them. Before long, however, the parents' doubts undermine their determination to be firm, and they give in to the action they were attempting to control. Thus, the lesson learned by children is that they will get their way if they persist in their misbehavior, while the parent learns that the child will (temporarily) stop testing the limits if the parent gives up the attempt at control. The child's positive reinforcement for obnoxious behavior and the parent's negative reinforcement for capitulation ensure the continuation of such coercive interactions (Patterson, 1982).

As a result of the success of coercive exchanges, children learn to provoke parental guilt with startling rapidity, and they often use their newfound powers with alacrity. Children will freely remind one parent how much better things are with the other, or say whatever else might "push a guilt button." As parents slowly become aware of the coercive cycle, they often assume that the children's motivation in provoking their guilt has been malicious. From a therapeutic distance, however, the children's intent seems wonderfully and purely manipulative. A child's job is to get through life in the easiest way possible. A parent's responsibility is to ensure that the easiest path is the most adaptive path.

Thus, the appropriate focus of renegotiating boundaries of power in residential parent–child relationships often is not to examine children's motivations, but to increase parents' confidence in developing and enforcing rules of conduct. As with redefining other boundaries in the system of family relationships, clarity and consistency are the keys to reestablishing effective discipline after a separation or divorce. Specific rules are not of paramount importance. Rather, what is essential is that there are rules, and that these rules are consistently enforced.

Nonresidential Parents

The major difficulty that nonresidential parents have in redefining power boundaries in their relationship with their children is the same as for residential parents: the tendency to discipline less often and less effectively. In fact, many nonresidential parents discipline their children very little or not at all. These "Disneyland dads" (or "merry-go-round moms") design visits with their children that are a trip into fantasyland. Everything is always fun, too much is never enough, and nothing is ever wrong.

Such hectic visits often can be seen as a parent's attempt to substitute intense quality time for a lack of quantity time. Nonresidential parents understandably try to compensate for their limited contact with their children by making the very most out of the time that they do have. Many nonresidential parents desperately want to have a normal relationship with their children, but fantasyland visits are not normal. Most fathers and mothers do not endlessly entertain their children on a routine basis, and parents often need to be reminded of this seemingly obvious fact. If nonresidential parents want a normal relationship with their children, then they need to reestablish a relationship that includes more "down time" and more discipline.

Thus, clarity and consistency are not necessarily the primary concerns for discipline by nonresidential parents. Rather, the principal concern is establishing a boundary of parental authority—and then making it clear and consistent. Not only do children stand to benefit from the development of a more normal relationship with the non-residential parent, but the relationship between parents may well improve as both of them take an active hand in discipline. Many residential parents feel cheated because they do all of the work, while the nonresidential parent has all of the fun. The goal for both, however, is to reestablish their roles as authoritative parents, parents who offer their children both love and discipline.

Joint Physical Custody and Other Parenting Arrangements

The discussion of the renegotiation of intimacy and power boundaries in parent–child dyads has focused on residential/nonresidential parenting after separation and divorce, but it is important to acknowledge alternatives to this arrangement. The involvement of other parenting figures such as relatives and stepparents is one important alternative that has not been discussed.

In many families, a relative, particularly the maternal grand-mother, may serve an important role in rearing children after separation or divorce. This is found with particular frequency among African-American families (Emery & Kitzmann, in press; Wilson, 1989). Such relatives can be an extremely important source of support. They may offer childcare while the biological parent is working, serve as a consultant and ally in disciplining a child, and provide a secondary source of security both for the parent and for the child.

Remarriage and stepparenting is another essential reality of family life after divorce. Intimacy and power boundaries in both the divorced family and the stepfamily must be renegotiated once again following remarriage. The remarriage may rekindle jealousy in the former spouse or among the children, or it may destroy fantasies of reconciliation. All of the new boundaries that have been established in the divorced family may be challenged as a result.

Of course, new boundaries between the stepparent and the children, the new spouses themselves, and the parent–child–stepparent triad also must be negotiated following remarriage. The complexity of these issues is beyond the scope of the present chapter, but one basic observation can be made. In general, stepparents are more successful if they first establish a relationship as a friend to their stepchildren. They can assume the role of disciplinarian later. That is, stepparents wisely work first to establish a boundary of intimacy with stepchildren, while following the biological parent's lead in enforcing boundaries of discipline (Hetherington & Clingempeel, 1992). This pattern, in fact, recapitulates parent–child relationships with biological parents: The formation of an attachment in the first year of life precedes the establishment of firm discipline during the second and all subsequent years of child development.

The present discussion of grandparents and stepparents is brief, especially given the vital roles that these substitute parenting figures often play in children's lives following separation and divorce. The emphasis on biological parents is justified by one essential assumption made in the present approach to custody mediation—that biological parents hold both the right and the responsibility to determine the parameters of their children's relationship with these alternative parenting figures. In fact, many problems that arise with grandparents and stepparents appear to result from the biological parent's failure to assume authority in rearing their children.

In terms of the coparenting of the biological parents, joint physical custody, in which children spend approximately equal amounts of time with each parent, is a major alternative to residential and nonresidential parenting. As noted earlier, parents with joint physical custody share many of the struggles faced by both residential and nonresidential parents, both in terms of renegotiating their relationships with each other and with their children. Thus, all of the issues discussed in terms of residential/nonresidential parenting also apply to parenting in joint physical custody.

Parents with joint physical custody are especially likely to encounter difficulties in renegotiating the parent–child–parent triadic relationship. Joint physical custody appears to benefit children when the parents' relationship is cooperative, but when conflict continues, children in joint physical custody apparently suffer because of their more extensive involvement with both of their parents (Maccoby & Mnookin, 1992; see Chapter 9). Thus, the final topic considered in this chapter is particularly relevant to parenting in joint custody families.

THE PARENT–CHILD–PARENT TRIAD: BALANCING LOYALTIES AND ALLIANCES

The importance of triadic or systemic relationships irrespective of a custody arrangement (and irrespective of marital status) has been consistently demonstrated by research documenting that conflict between parents is a potent predictor of children's adjustment (Emery, 1982, 1988; see Chapter 9). In a well-functioning, married family, the parents are the most powerful individuals, and the spousal relationship is the most intimate and powerful dyad. Relationships between each parent and the children therefore are greatly influenced by the relationship between the spouses. As has been discussed, however, former partners experience many difficulties in renegotiating their relationship following separation and divorce. In particular, recent evidence points to the children's feeling of being "caught in the middle" of their parents' disputes as a key component of triadic conflict in divorce (Buchanan et al., 1991).

The Parenting Alliance

Some partners are able to preserve the parenting alliance that they formed in marriage, even as they lose their relationship as intimates and friends. That is, the coparental relationship remains the most powerful dyad in the family, even as it becomes the least intimate relationship. For other former spouses, however, the opposite is true. Their inability to renegotiate or accept changes in their lost role as spouses continually undermines their ongoing relationship as parents. Because of this, the most complex and unstable boundaries in the divorced family system involve the triangle formed by the two parents and the children. Children continually find themselves triangulated into the middle of a conflicted relationship between their parents.

Loyalties and Alliances: Intimacy and Power in Triads

Intimacy and power remain the major issues around which family members must renegotiate the parent–child–parent triad. Elsewhere I have used the term *loyalty* to refer to intimacy conflicts in triadic interactions, while the term *alliance* describes triadic power struggles (Emery, 1992). For example, power may be part of the issue when two family members side together against a third. They form an alliance; two less powerful family members sometimes can dominate a third who has more power than either alone. Siding together also is a demonstration of loyalty, however. Taking sides carries meaning about who a third party "likes more" (Emery, 1992).

Alliances and loyalties are issues in many relationship systems, not just in divorce. A boy who complains about his mother's favoritism toward his younger brother, for example, is arguing about both loyalties and alliances. Part of his concern is about losing a battle, but his complaints also may reflect his fears and uncertainty about whether his mother likes his sibling more than she likes him. Similarly, when only one of two "best friends" gets asked to play at a third friend's house, part of the neglected child's concern is not getting to play (a power issue). A bigger part of their concern, however, is likely to be that they may not be the best "best friend."

As in dyadic relationships, the person who controls an outcome has more power in triadic relationships. Winning or losing is not the only means of controlling outcomes in triads, however. A third party who directs the process of dispute resolution (e.g., a mediator or a judge) also holds a great deal of power. Thus, powerful positions are held both by the parent who decides which sibling gets a toy and by the friend who decides which "best friend" can come over to play. Similarly, a child who mediates between two warring parents is in a powerful, if difficult and developmentally inappropriate, position in the family.

Like power, intimacy also is indexed differently in triads than in dyads. The critical outcome that conveys greater intimacy in triadic relationships is who a third person "sides with," or whether they side with anyone at all. (Recall from Chapter 2 that the intensity of expressed affect is the key signal of intimacy in dyads.) This means that intimacy is always relative in triadic interaction.

Divided Loyalties

One unavoidable, triangular dilemma that divorce creates from the child's perspective is a loyalty conflict. The parent–child–parent triangle is unbalanced. Even when the parenting alliance is preserved, children confront the conflict of loving two parents who do not love each other. Loyalty to one parent feels like disloyalty to the other, and children often feel pressure to take sides and show who they "like more" as a result.

The discomfort that this middle position causes can take a number of forms. Anxiety, anger, and sadness are some of the most common affective reactions that children report when they are exposed to conflict and anger not directed at them (Cummings, 1987). If parents allow the children to have separate relationships with each of them, these emotions can dissipate over time, and children's relationships with both of their parents can be maintained without inordinate, ongoing effort. Over time, the quality of parent–child relationships become less closely tied to the quality of the relationship between the parents.

For many children, however, loyalty dilemmas are real and lasting. The problem for these children is not that their parents no longer love each other. The problem is that they apparently hate each other. Some parents share their scorn for a former spouse with their children and directly deride any real or perceived disloyalty. Other angry parents act hurt when their children are with the other parent, especially if they seem to have enjoyed the time together. The loyalty dilemmas that such parents create for their children are anything but subtle, as frequently becomes clear during custody mediation.

Thus, new boundaries of intimacy need to be negotiated in the parent–child–parent triad, just as they are in the dyadic relationships between parents and between parents and children. Many loyalties are defined by obvious issues, such as the amount of time each parent spends with the children, what the parents say about each other to or in front of the children, and whether the parents fight in the presence or within earshot of the children. Other triangular issues are more subtle, but no less troubling to children. For example, children may not be allowed to talk about their time with the other parent, they may be quizzed about their activities, or they may be forbidden to bring their "stuff" back and forth between households. In short, the children's relationship with one parent becomes a test of their loyalty to the other.

Balancing Divided Loyalties

When children are caught in the middle of a loyalty dilemma (or any conflict between their parents), there are a handful of ways in which they can attempt to resolve their predicament. In a happily married family, relationships are balanced. The positive marital relationship is consistent with two positive parent–child relationships. As noted, however, conflict in the core relationship between the parents disrupts the family's homeostasis, thereby threatening parent–child relationships. One possible solution to reestablishing homeostasis is balancing. The child can attempt to maintain a separate but approximately equal relationship with each parent. This is a workable resolution when the parents' relationship is disengaged, and each parent allows the children to have a relationship with the other (see Figure 3.2). Balancing becomes burdensome and anxiety-provoking, however, when the parents continue to compete over their children.

When their parents' competition and conflict are uncontrolled, children may turn to other tactics in search of homeostasis. Resolving the parents' problems is one possibility, as some children become mediators themselves. They act as go-betweens who try to solve their parents' problems directly. Mediators carry messages back and forth between parents, sometimes distorting them in order to soften the blow. In a manner analogous to a professional mediator, they also may encourage the parents to "be nice" or otherwise improve their communication (see Figure 3.2).

Some children might take the direct approach of attempting to mediate a resolution, but a more common strategy is for children to attempt to distract their parents from their disputes (Vuchinich,

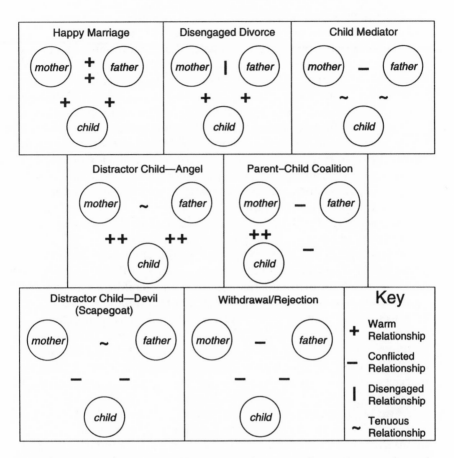

Figure 3.2. Possible triadic relationship structures in separated and divorced families. Note the comparison with family relationships in a happy marriage, and the similarity between parent–child relationships in this family and in the disengaged divorce where the parenting alliance is maintained.

Emery, & Cassidy, 1988). Intentionally or unintentionally, children try to distract their parents' attention away from parental conflicts and onto themselves. Some "devils" become scapegoats who distract by bringing their parents together in their common anger or concern about the child's problems (see Figure 3.2). The scapegoat's function is analogous to that served by common enemies in international politics. Common enemies can make allies out of nations who would oppose each other in more normal times.

Although some children use their problems to refocus their parents' conflict, it is probably true that more children distract parents from their conflict by redirecting parental attention onto the child's achievements (see Figure 3.2). Such "angels" function as a source of common pride and purpose, rather than as a common enemy. Irrespective of their tactics, however, both "angels" and "devils" are likely to feel the burden of responsibility for their parents' relationship.

Other methods are available to children when parents fail to contain their conflicts themselves, or when children are unsuccessful in mediating or distracting. A straightforward way in which children can resolve loyalty dilemmas is simply to pick sides and form a coalition with one parent against the other (see Figure 3.2). The parent–child loyalty and alliance incurs the loss and potential wrath of one parent, but the love and protection of the other parent is firmly gained. Such coalitions are understandable when one parent abandons the children, but it is unfortunate when children have to choose sides between parents who both want to have an authoritative relationship with them.

The most unfortunate manner in which children can resolve loyalty dilemmas is by retreating from both of their parents (see Figure 3.2). Retreaters may cut off contact emotionally and withdraw into themselves, or they may physically withdraw from their parents. Such attempts at escape from parental conflict explain some of the preoccupation with friends or lovers, running away from home, and early marriage that are more common among children from divorced rather than married families (see Chapter 9).

The key to balancing loyalties in a manner that is least stressful to the children is to renegotiate the relationship between the parents themselves. Unfortunately, the redefinition of boundaries in the coparental relationship that is least stressful for children is *not* likely to be the least stressful arrangement for the parents. As noted in Chapter 2, anger is a natural part of grief, and getting as much distance as possible is the typical way that romantic relationships are redefined after a breakup. That is, anger following the breakup of a marriage often can be healthy for the former partners, both in terms of their individual experience of grief and in terms of helping them to set new, distant boundaries in a relationship that has ended.

Despite the fact that the partners' anger is understandable and potentially adaptive, the same anger is maladaptive for the child. This is perhaps the central dilemma in renegotiating family relationships following separation and divorce. Parents who succeed in recognizing their children's perspective must learn to repress some of their own legitimate feelings for their children's sake. In order to minimize the difficulties that divided loyalties create for children, however, it is not necessary for the parents to be friends. Although a cooperative relationship is desirable, rather than continuing in conflict, parents can help by establishing a disengaged relationship that leaves the children out of the middle of disputes and free to pursue a relationship with each of them (Maccoby & Mnookin, 1992).

Inconsistent Discipline

Whether they are married or divorced, it is important for parents to be allies irrespective of the degree of intimacy in their relationship. Parents who present a "united front" offer their children rules that are more clear and consistent, and as a result, they are more likely to be successful in enforcing them. Separated and divorced parents often have difficulty working together, however. That is, they have difficulty preserving the parenting alliance. When two parents attempt to define boundaries of discipline that are in conflict, the children are unlikely to respect either set of rules. In fact, when discipline is inconsistent, children frequently learn to gain power over their parents by dividing and conquering.

Defining Boundaries of Authority between Parents

Some of the inconsistent discipline between separated or divorced parents simply requires defining boundaries of authority in their coparenting relationship. Immediately after the initial separation, it may not be clear what rules of discipline will be the same or different in each parent's household, which parent has the authority to make what decisions, or how the parents will communicate about the children when they need to do so.

As discussed in more detail in Chapter 4, some of these problems can be alleviated by a clear custodial agreement. In particular the meaning of the term "legal custody" must be defined in detail, whether legal custody is held solely or jointly. Because of the likelihood of strains in their coparenting relationship, it is wise to maximize each parent's authority when they are with their children and to minimize the need for communication and cooperation between the two parents. Thus, the decisions shared even in a joint legal custody agreement often include only major issues, such as religious upbringing, education, and elective medical care.

Communication between Parents

Because many day-to-day or week-to-week issues cannot be addressed in advance in a custody agreement or parenting plan, it is important for parents to have some means to communicate with each other. A child may be taking prescription medication, for example, which needs to be continued over a weekend. Some degree of communication between parents also is necessary in order for them to enforce rules consistently. Without this, children quickly learn to play parents off against each other. They may make independent requests of each parent, a wise technique that doubles the child's chances of getting what they want. Such a tactic may be distasteful, but the problem is not a malicious child. It is the parents' responsibility to teach their children, and some lessons can only be taught when parents work together.

As with the smooth working of other boundaries in separated or divorced families, structure is crucial to communication. For example, a telephone call may be planned for at a set time on the night before the child is exchanged between households. Depending upon the complexity of the physical custody arrangements, this may be the only communication between the parents that is necessary. Effective parenting is the only goal of such conversations, and structure and formality help to minimize boundary conflicts when coparents engage in their necessary communications.

Deliberate Subversion

Unfortunately, many problems with inconsistent discipline between parents are not simply a matter of unclear authority or the lack of structured communication. Many separated and divorced parents deliberately subvert each other's discipline. It is distressing how many parents use children as conduits or spies in their triadic power struggles. Children may be asked questions about the other parent's "close friends," or they may be told to deliver messages about inappropriate topics such as child support payments. In short, many children are used as pawns in the battle between the parents.

The reasons for such deliberate undermining of the parenting alliance obviously have little to do with the children and everything to do with the parents. Sometimes a parent's subversion is an attempt to win a child's loyalty. Other times it is a means of punishing a former partner. In some circumstances, subversion simply is a means of demonstrating one parent's power over the other. In all cases, the problems in the parent–child–parent triad can be traced to problems in the parents' relationship with each other, a pattern commonly noted by family systems theorists (S. Minuchin, 1974).

Before they can redefine clear and consistent boundaries in the triangle that includes their children as well as themselves, parents must renegotiate their relationship with each other. Parents must learn to separate their angry feelings about past failures as spouses from their present and future interactions as parents, as discussed in Chapter 2. If they fail to separate their marital and parenting roles, divorced parents run the risk that their pain, hurt, and anger over the loss of one, crucial family relationship eventually will destroy the remaining ones.

SUMMARY

A goal of postdivorce parenting is to maintain authoritative parent–child relationships. Just as parents must renegotiate their own ongoing relationship, the boundaries of intimacy and power in each parent–child relationship must be reaffirmed or redefined following separation and divorce. Residential, nonresidential, and joint custody parents all face difficulties maintaining the warmth and discipline that combine to form authoritative parenting. However, as a result of infrequent contact with their children, nonresidential parents typically have more problems establishing new boundaries of intimacy. In contrast, residential parents struggle more with the discipline that defines the boundaries of power in parent–child relationships. Parents with joint physical custody confront both of these problems, but balancing the triadic relationship between the child and the two parents is perhaps the family's major task under this custody arrangement.

Irrespective of the parenting arrangement, all families must redefine loyalties and alliances in the parent–child–parent triad as a result of separation and divorce. Relationships may be restructured in several more or less adaptive ways as a new homeostasis is achieved following separation and divorce. Even under the best of circumstances, however, children confront the loyalty dilemma of loving two parents who do not love each other. At the same time, parents must grapple with finding ways to make discipline consistent between two households, while keeping contact and communication between themselves to a minimum.

CHAPTER 4

Divorce and Custody Law
Perfect Problems, Imperfect Solutions

P arents turn to the legal system for direction and protection
when their failure to renegotiate their relationship crystallizes
into a dispute over custody of their children. For many people,
this is their first contact with the legal system, and the result is
confusion and a sense of lost control. The latter feeling often can
be traced to legal procedures. Parents may feel they have little
control over their attorneys' negotiations, independent custody
investigations, or courtroom proceedings, as discussed in the
review of procedural law in Chapter 5.

Attempts to learn about the substantive law often are one source of
confusion. The terms custody and visitation are loaded with symbolism,
but their legal implications are unclear. Because the terms are so general
and increasingly have taken on negative connotations, they are avoided
by some lawyers and more mediators, and they have been altered in
some state statutes. As a result, parents instead may learn about "legal
and physical custody," "parental rights and responsibilities," or more
simply, "residence and decision-making." Terminology aside, the two
major childrearing issues that parents must negotiate are (1) where the
children will live at what times and (2) how the parents will jointly or
independently make decisions concerning their children's lives.

Parents also encounter the substantive law relating to child support, spousal support, and property division. Because disputes over
children often become intertwined with conflicts over these financial
issues, it is essential that mediators be familiar with divorce economics.
Familiarity with financial matters also is important because some
practitioners negotiate financial agreements in mediation. Thus, legal

66

issues related both to childrearing and to finances are included in the overview of substantive divorce law in this chapter.

LACK OF SUBSTANCE IN SUBSTANTIVE DIVORCE LAW

A major problem with the substantive law in divorce is that it is indeterminate (Mnookin, 1975). That is, legal principles offer few specific guidelines as to how divorce disputes should be settled. As parents turn to attorneys for legal guidance, they therefore are likely to get answers that are far from definitive.

The law offers only a very general principle for determining the outcome of child custody disputes, for example. The prevailing "best interests" standard indicates that judges should make custody determinations based solely upon what will be in a child's future best interests, a directive that is subject to a variety of interpretations. In fact, one could argue that the best interests standard simply impels judges to make good and fair custody decisions, whatever those decisions may be. The difficult task of deciding how to make custody determinations is left to the discretion of individual judges (Mnookin, 1975).

Similarly vague principles guide property division and the payment of alimony upon divorce. In theory, such indeterminate laws give the judiciary flexibility in deciding equitable settlements for individual families. In practice, however, they have a number of undesirable consequences: litigation is encouraged because judicial decisions are difficult to predict; acrimony is increased because virtually any damaging evidence may be deemed to be relevant to the proceedings; bias may accompany the exercise of broad judicial discretion; and appellate review is limited because the criteria for evaluating judicial decisions are unclear (Mnookin, 1975). Perhaps the biggest problem created by indeterminate regulations, however, is that many divorced adults feel that they are being treated unfairly because the state's conception of their marriage contract, as communicated by the terms of the divorce settlement, does not match their own.

Pluralism and Amorality

Another way of considering the problem of indeterminacy is to note that the law lacks morality (Schneider, 1985). Morality, in this case, must be construed in its broadest sense as the absence of a directive regarding how people should behave. The likelihood that some would call contemporary family law *im*moral reflects a desire to promulgate a particular moral code, but our concern here is with *a*morality. In contrast to American law prior to the 1970s (Grossberg, 1985; Halem, 1981), contemporary family law is amoral in that it does not offer a clear, prescriptive code for how a family's affairs should be ordered when divorce occurs.

Rather than being moral, contemporary family law is pluralistic. It attempts to accommodate the diverse practices of individuals and subgroups within our society by intentionally avoiding determinate prescriptions. In part, this pluralism is an outgrowth of a long history in American law of valuing and preserving family privacy and autonomy (Grossberg, 1985; Halem, 1981). More recently, the women's movement and recognition of ethnic diversity in family forms clearly have encouraged further pluralism by introducing the concepts of gender neutrality and cultural relativity into family law.

Irrespective of its historical antecedents, pluralism creates problems in applying family law to individual cases. Judges are supposed to apply general principles to specific cases, but the rules for making divorce determinations offer scant explicit guidance. As a result, many judges develop their own, individualized rules in order to be consistent across cases. In so doing, individual judges become local agents of family morality. They make rules for deciding custody based on principles about which a social consensus is lacking.

Substance and Procedure

Mediation is at least a partial solution to the dilemma posed by the necessity of deciding individual cases based on laws that offer scant guidance. The inevitability of introducing morality through judicial decision-making is avoided if former partners order their own affairs in mediation or elsewhere.

Mediation is a procedural answer to the substantive vacuum in divorce law, but there would be little furor over procedure if substance was clear. Dispute resolution procedures would be far less important if the law clearly told partners how their affairs should be settled when they separate and divorce. Given the indeterminacy of divorce law and the absence of a consensus about family morality, however, many have argued that divorce disputes increasingly should become a matter of private ordering. It is argued that separated and divorced parents, not judges, should make decisions about how to resolve their disputes, especially those disputes that involve their children (Emery & Wyer, 1987b; Mnookin, 1975).

In fact, judges often are among the most staunch advocates for giving former partners not only the right to resolve their own disputes, but also the responsibility to do so. Pluralism aside, judges find it difficult if not impossible to make unambiguous determinations about the complex issue of how children are best raised by their separated or divorced parents. If parents make these decisions themselves, judges are relieved of the trying task of making the decisions for them.

Less Regulation but More Litigation

Ironically, however, vague laws and rising divorce rates have conspired to increase, not decrease, family court caseloads. Approximately half of all civil cases in the United States involve divorce actions (S.C. Bowman, 1990), and private dispute resolution in divorce has been encouraged so as to uncrowd busy court dockets. In fact, reducing the number of court hearings is an explicit or implicit goal of most court-based mediation programs, and this is another reason why mediation often is viewed favorably by the judiciary.

A potential concern about court mediation programs, however, is that too much pressure can be placed on mediators to get agreements. Although mediation's benefits in reducing litigation are clear, there are numerous reasons why "getting agreements" is not the best index of the success of mediation. Alternative dispute resolution should be encouraged, but access to the courts must not be denied. The appropriate goal of mediation, moreover, is to negotiate fair, appropriate, and acceptable agreements, an outcome which cannot always be achieved. This means that *not* getting an agreement may be an index of success for some mediation cases.

THE REGULATION OF DIVORCE

Questions about state intervention and private dispute resolution are not limited to custody or to mediation, but they can be raised more generally with respect to the state's role in regulating marriage and divorce. Marriage is a private institution in Japan, Africa, and many other parts of the world, albeit a private institution with many attendant social traditions (Eekelaar, 1991). In 1984, for example, over 90% of Japanese couples who divorced did so by informing a registration office of their decision (Yuzawa, 1990). In contrast, the state is a partner to marriage and divorce in Europe and the United States. In fact, civil regulation of marriage and divorce has always existed in the United States, and its history dates back for centuries in Europe.

European marriage once involved only a private contract between two family groups (Eekelaar, 1991). During the Middle Ages, however, the Roman Catholic Church apparently was instrumental in instituting the civil regulation of marriage and in outlawing divorce. The religious rationale for the Church's prohibition is unclear. The policy conflicts with ancient Jewish and Roman traditions, and divorce never has been forbidden by the Eastern Catholic Church (Eekelaar, 1991). Whatever the theological rationale, the Church strongly influenced civil regulations which outlawed divorce for several centuries prior to the Reformation. Civil divorce currently is prohibited only in Catholic Ireland (Eekelaar, 1991), although the Church continues to ban religious divorce for its members throughout the world.

Even after the Reformation, the civil control of divorce was strict. The laws in most European countries and in the United States held that divorce could be granted only if an offense occurred, that is, if there was "fault." Forms of "no fault" divorce actually were introduced in parts of Europe in the 19th century, but in England and the United States few actions other than adultery, cruelty, or desertion were deemed to be sufficient grounds for divorce. It is noteworthy that these laws often explicitly defined criteria that made it more difficult to prove that a husband was at fault than to prove that a wife was at fault (Eekelaar, 1991).

The regulation of divorce became less strict during the 1900s, despite the absence of major changes in legislation. Instead, the judiciary accommodated changing social attitudes and practices by using increasingly broad interpetations of the existing grounds for divorce (Plateris, 1974). As evidence of the change in judicial practice, the percentage of divorces granted on the specific grounds of adultery or desertion declined sharply in the United States between the 1860s and the 1960s, while the percentage granted on the more vague ground of cruelty increased significantly (Plateris, 1974).

No Fault Divorce

Legislative policy was altered dramatically in the 1970s and 1980s with the passage of "no fault" divorce laws. No fault divorce was first enacted in Great Britain in 1969, and in California in 1970; all 50 states have now adopted some form of no fault divorce (Freed & Walker, 1991). Relinquishing fault grounds was, in part, an attempt to streamline legal proceedings, to remove acrimony from them, and to avoid perjury, because many spouses lied under oath in order to obtain a divorce under fault grounds.

A no fault divorce may be granted when both spouses request it, and/or when the spouses have lived apart for a fixed waiting period. The time former spouses must live apart generally is 6 months or 1 year, although as of 1990, one state (Idaho) required 5 years of separation, and eight others required either 2 or 3 years of living apart (Freed & Walker, 1991). As of 1990, the no fault conditions of "irreconcilable differences" or "irretrievable breakdown" were the only grounds for divorce in 18 states, but the remaining states retained various fault grounds as an option (Freed & Walker, 1991). The majority of couples file no fault actions even when fault grounds are available, although the existence of fault rules may affect divorce bargaining (Freed & Walker, 1986).

The Deregulation of Divorce

No fault laws represent a substantial movement toward the deregulation of divorce. Adults living in the United States today not only are allowed to choose when and how to marry, but they also can freely decide whether to divorce. From a broad historical perspective, no fault divorce would seem to be a step in the direction of reinstating Western marriage and divorce as private institutions.

In fact, questions can be raised about the rationale for the government's regulation of divorce matters. The court's automatic supervision of custody decisions upon divorce under its *parens patriae* powers is not necessarily supported by psychological research. Psychological difficulties among children whose parents divorce are relatively few (see Chapter 9), while other family problems that threaten children's best interests (e.g., severe parental psychopathology, serious marital conflict) do not trigger state intervention in the family. The court's dispute resolution role in custody disputes also is questionable. Some interventions in divorce-related matters seem inconsistent with the court's repeated refusal to intervene in similar disputes between married parents. Courts have refused to enter into disputes between married parents about where their children should attend school, for example, but they routinely address the same issue in divorce (Cochran, 1987). Thus, in theory and in practice, there are a shrinking number of reasons for government intervention in divorce.

The movement toward the deregulation of divorce is yet another important impetus for mediation. Private settlement increasingly is seen as going hand in hand with private contracting in marriage and divorce. Husbands and wives increasingly are being given the right and the responsibility to make decisions both about whether to divorce and how to do so. In fact, the desire to decrease state intervention and increase family autonomy was one explicit rationale for recent changes in British divorce law (Bainham, 1990), and some British commentators have openly wondered if divorce should be completely deregulated (Eekelaar, 1991).

Of course, many natural incentives to stay married and disincentives to divorce remain, despite the dismantling of legal barriers to divorce. There are numerous adverse social, financial, and interpersonal consequences of divorce that make marriage a benefit and divorce a liability, minimal legal intervention notwithstanding. Rather than attempting to restrict divorce again, the trend in Western law is to attempt to alter some of these adverse consequences of divorce by strengthening the legal ties between parents and children, as is evident in new child support laws (Eekelaar, 1991; Emery, 1988).

CHILD CUSTODY

As noted earlier, the major childrearing decisions that must be made at the time of divorce are commonly framed in terms of custody and visitation. Child custody encompasses determinations about children's primary residence, as well as about which parent shall have primary parental authority. Visitation involves a secondary determination about how noncustodial parents will spend time with their children.

The terms custody and visitation have been criticized as being too negative, too general, and easily misinterpreted. Many find the terms distasteful, even pejorative. The idea of "visiting" with one's child is particularly unappealing to many parents, and the creation of many new postdivorce parenting arrangements has made the terms somewhat outdated. Another objection is that awarding custody to one parent and liberal rights of visitation to the other leaves too much ambiguity both about the children's schedule and about each parent's boundaries of authority in rearing their children.

In response to such criticisms, many mediators and lawyers instead use the terms physical custody or residence (where the children will live at what times) and legal custody or parental rights and responsibilities (how parental authority will be divided and how it will be shared). In fact, at least six state statutes have eliminated the terms custody and visitation, and instead reflect these new distinctions (McKnight, 1991).

Another trend in custody law is toward insisting upon greater specificity in childrearing determinations, so that parents know exactly where their children are to be at what times, and what types of decisions parents will make jointly or independently. In terms of the language introduced in Chapter 2, the trend is to define sharp boundaries in each parent's authority in rearing the children. The practice of being highly specific has been followed by many mediators and family lawyers for some time, and at least one state (Washington) has passed legislation requiring that parents submit a specific plan for postdivorce parenting (Ellis, 1990; Folberg, 1991). The relevance of changing terminology and parenting plans becomes clearer as custody rules are considered in greater detail.

A Brief History of Child Custody Rules

Custody rules were not always as vague as they are today. For the greater part of Western history, tradition and common law automatically gave fathers custody of their children. With its emphasis on property rights, this standard is often referred to as the *chattel rule*. Roman law gave men total control over their children (and their wives) as a part of their property rights, and men's authority over their families changed little through the Middle Ages (Derdeyn, 1976). By the 19th century, men's control over their families had diminished, but fathers' superior right to custody was still generally acknowledged. Legal cases from the period frequently reiterated the principle of father custody, often referring to the man's role as head of his family (Grossberg, 1985).

The *tender years presumption* emerged in the 19th century, and this new standard began a shift in custodial preference from fathers to mothers. According to this doctrine, children of "tender years" were assumed to be best cared for by their mothers. Mothers were asserted to be superior caregivers as a part of the natural order, an assumption that some historians trace to the specialization in men's and women's roles that occurred as a result of industrialization (Grossberg, 1985). During the 20th century, the age range believed to encompass children's tender years gradually expanded upward from infancy to include adolescence. By the 1960s, the presumption of father custody based on men's property rights had been completely replaced by a presumption of mother custody based on the tender years doctrine (Weiss, 1979b). The only limits on maternal preference were fault and maternal "unfitness." Women who were at fault for a divorce could be deprived of custody, as could women who were so severely impaired that mother custody was viewed as harming the children. Often questions of fitness turned on issues of conventional morality, particularly as related to sexual practices.

The current standard for determining child custody, the *best interests test*, indicates that custody decisions should be based solely upon what will be in a child's future best interests. The standard actually was established early in the 20th century as a part of the *parens patriae* role of juvenile courts (Grossberg, 1985). As noted, however, the tender years presumption strongly indicated that mother custody was in children's best interests. New ideas about men's and women's family and parenting roles, as well as questions of gender bias, caused the tender years presumption to be called into question during the 1970s and 1980s. These influences have resulted in the elimination of the tender years presumption from statutory law. The principle, however, certainly influences the exercise of judicial discretion implicitly, if not explicitly. In fact, a survey of California judges indicated that 85% still reported a preference for maternal custody even after the passage of gender-neutral custody legislation (Weitzman, 1985).

The Best Interests Standard and Its Problems

The erosion of the tender years presumption and fault grounds have made the best interests standard a vague principle. Most state statutes do contain some other guidelines for determining children's best interests (Freed & Walker, 1991), but they typically are very general. For example, the majority of states (44) have adopted the guidelines as outlined in the Uniform Marriage and Divorce Act (9(a) U.L.A. 91 (1976). This act states that in determining the child's best interests the court should consider the following:

1. The wishes of the child's parents as to custody.
2. The wishes of the child as to custody.
3. The interaction and interrelationship of the child with his parents, his siblings, and any person who may significantly affect the child's best interest.
4. The child's adjustment to his home, school, and community.
5. The mental and physical health of all individuals involved.

It is obvious that these vague guidelines offer little direction as to how judicial discretion should be exercised in determining children's future best interests. This is especially true when one recognizes that child custody is most likely to be contested when the parents' capabilities are not markedly different. If there were clear differences between the parents, the dispute would most likely be settled through negotiation, because the outcome of a court hearing would be clear to all involved.

In addition to the general problems that accompany indeterminate rules, the best interests standard is complicated by the facts that: (1) it has not been demonstrated that the future development of individual children can be reliably predicted even by experts; and (2) even if reliable prediction was possible, the potential debates about what alternative futures are "best" would be unending (Mnookin, 1975). That is, it is unlikely that even highly trained experts can predict children's best interests in close cases (Emery & Rogers, 1990). For example, is it best to be reared by a parent who promotes emotional security at the expense of achievement, or by a parent who encourages achievement at the cost of increased anxiety? Given these questions, it is not surprising that various substantive reforms have been offered as a means of remedying the problems created by the indeterminate best interests standard. The two most prominent standards are primary caretaker parent provisions and joint custody rules.

Primary Caretaker Parent

The *primary caretaker parent* standard is a straightforward rule. Whichever parent was the primary caretaker during the marriage is the preferred custodian after divorce. The rule has at least two major advantages. First, it is a clear, determinate principle. Deciding who was the primary caretaker during the marriage is not a difficult task, especially in comparison to determining what will be in a child's future best interests. Second, unlike the tender years presumption, primary caretaker parent provisions are gender neutral. A father who assumed primary responsibility for rearing a couple's children would be considered the primary caretaker. These are major advantages from the perspective of substantive law, and judicial interpretations in child custody cases increasingly reflect the usage of primary caretaker parent considerations (Folberg, 1991; Freed & Walker, 1991).

As with any determinative custody rule, however, primary caretaker parent provisions have created controversy. Thus, legislation on the standard is virtually nonexistent. Women's advocates often favor the provision, because it is gender neutral yet it protects women who assume responsibility for childrearing in their families (Fineman, 1988; Grillo, 1991). Advocates for men, in turn, often oppose the standard. They argue that it undermines men's relationships with their children and introduces inequity into divorce settlements. Father's rights advocates commonly point out that society displays a tremendous concern that men continue their financial obligations to their children following separation and divorce, but that there is a relative absence of concern for protecting continuity in father–child relationships (Roman & Haddad, 1978).

Another basic problem with the primary caretaker parent proposal is that it perpetuates the traditional concepts of custody and visitation (Scott, 1992). In theory, a parent who was responsible for 51% of childrearing would be the primary caretaker, and therefore entitled to sole custody following divorce. The provision would treat all nonprimary parents the same, whether they had done 0% or 49% of the parenting during the marriage. Thus, a parent who was responsible for almost half of the childrearing in marriage could end up with one-seventh (every other weekend) of the childrearing after divorce.

Joint Custody

The fact that childrearing is a shared task in marriage, albeit a task that typically is not shared exactly equally, has given rise to the joint custody movement. All traditional rules assume that only one parent must be awarded custody following separation and divorce. To put it more accurately, the assumption is that one parent must *lose* custody, because both partners had equal rights and responsibilities within marriage. As a way of acknowledging the role of both mothers and fathers in rearing children during marriage, it has been suggested that parents should jointly retain custody of their children upon divorce. Joint custody also has been argued to be in children's best interests.

Although the first joint custody statute in the United States was passed in North Carolina in 1957, most joint custody laws have been enacted in the last decade (Folberg, 1991). As of January 1, 1991, all but nine states had adopted statutes that explicitly allowed or encouraged joint custody (Folberg, 1991), and evidence indicates that joint custody awards are increasing (Freed & Walker, 1986).

Legal and Physical Custody

A number of controversies about joint custody have arisen, however. One debate concerns differences between joint legal and joint physical custody. *Joint legal custody* designates shared parental rights and responsibilities, but the children may spend a considerably greater portion of their time with one parent. In *joint physical custody*, not only is legal guardianship shared, but children also spend approximately the same amount of time with each parent.

Most parents with joint custody actually share only joint legal custody, and many such arrangements resemble traditional custody and visitation in terms of children's actual residence (e.g., one parent sees the children every other weekend) (Maccoby & Mnookin, 1992). Although some proponents hold that shared physical custody is the only true form of joint custody (see Folberg, 1984), this arrangement is the exception not the rule. Although joint legal custody is retained by approximately 75% of divorced parents in some progressive states (California, Washington), far fewer parents in these same states maintain joint physical custody (15–20% is the highest estimate) (Ellis, 1990; Maccoby & Mnookin, 1992). In less progressive states, the rates of joint legal and physical custody are much lower.

A second debate about joint custody concerns how strongly it should be encouraged. The full gamut of options has been proposed, including that (1) joint custody should not be allowed; (2) joint custody should be allowed only when parents agree to it; (3) joint custody must be allowed if parents agree to the option (some judges have opposed joint custody under any circumstances); (4) if parents cannot agree to joint custody, sole custody should be awarded to the parent who will most strongly encourage the children's relationship with the other parent; and (5) joint custody should always be the preferred option, one that can be ordered even over the objections of one of the parents (Folberg, 1991; Scott & Derdeyn, 1984).

A few states have adopted one of these positions, but there is much inconsistency across states. Most state statutes simply define the term "joint custody" and allow it as an option. The joint custody provisions for the 50 states as of 1990 are listed in Table 4.1.

Questions about Joint Custody

Strong joint custody statutes solve the problems caused by the indeterminate best interests standard, but clear-cut sole custody rules such as the primary caretaker parent provision would have the same effect. The question of whether joint custody leads to better psychological adjustment among children therefore must be considered. Joint custody has been found to have some benefits, and research indicates that the promotion of more positive relationships between all members of the divorced family is an important goal. However, family relationships do not differ as dramatically as had been hoped under joint and sole custody arrangements (see Chapter 9). The best available research on joint physical custody indicates that it may be either the best or the worst arrangement for children. When parental conflict is high, children are more likely to be caught between their parents under joint than sole custody. When parents cooperate, however, children fare better under joint than sole custody arrangements (Buchanan et al., 1991).

This finding leads to consideration of another question about joint custody: does it target the right solution at the wrong group of parents? Judicial custody determinations are made only when parents cannot agree, therefore awarding joint physical custody may be exactly the wrong thing to do because parental conflict is intense in these cases (Scott & Derdeyn, 1984). On the surface, an award of joint

Table 4.1. Joint Custody in the 50 States

State	Summary of Statutory Law and Case Law Trends
Alabama	No mention of joint custody in statutes; however, there is some acknowledgment of concept in case law.
Alaska	"Shared custody" is a statutory option; parents encouraged to develop own childcare plan outside of court.
Arizona	Joint custody is not preferred, but an option if parents agree and it is in the child's best interests; a "friendly parent" provision is one of several factors used to determine custody.
Arkansas	No mention of joint custody in statutes; case law allows joint custody but generally does not favor it.
California	Joint custody is presumed to be in child's best interests when parents agree; joint custody an option, but no preference for or against it upon request of only one parent; joint legal custody must distinguish mutual and sole decision making.
Colorado	Joint custody is an option; parental agreement to joint custody required except in "most exceptional cases"; spouse or child abuse generally precludes joint custody; a "friendly parent" provision is one of several factors used to determine custody.
Connecticut	Joint custody is presumed to be in child's best interests when parents agree to it.
Delaware	Joint custody is an option that is strongly encouraged.
Florida	"Shared parental responsibility" mandated, unless detrimental to the child; frequent and continuing contact and shared decision making encouraged; "friendly parent" provision one of several parenting considerations; spousal abuse may lead to sole parental responsibility.
Georgia	Joint legal custody is an option; courts must ratify any agreement between parents unless it is not the best interests of the child.
Hawaii	Joint custody is an option when either parent applies.
Idaho	Joint custody is presumed to be in the child's best interest unless preponderance of evidence is to the contrary.
Illinois	Joint custody is an option, but preference for maximizing involvement of both parents is not a presumption of joint custody; parenting plan required.

Table 4.1. *(continued)*

State	Summary of Statutory Law and Case Law Trends
Indiana	Joint legal custody is an option but may be made without joint physical custody; parental agreement important but not necessary.
Iowa	Joint custody and maximum continuing contact with both parents favored; "friendly parent" provision included with other criteria.
Kansas	Shared or joint custody is a preference, but case law may limit this; "friendly parent" provision included with other criteria.
Kentucky	Joint custody is an option but is not defined in statutes.
Louisiana	Joint custody is a presumption, unless parents agree to sole custody, one parent moves out of state, or it is not in child's best interests; parenting plan required; "friendly parent" provision.
Maine	"Shared parental rights and responsibilities" are mandatory when parents agree, an option otherwise; "friendly parent" provision.
Maryland	No mention of joint custody in statutes; discussed in case law.
Massachusetts	"Shared legal custody" is an option; no presumption for or against shared legal or physical custody.
Michigan	Joint custody is mandatory if parents agree, absent clear and convincing evidence otherwise; option when one parent requests it; "friendly parent" provision.
Minnesota	Joint legal custody is presumed to be in child's best interests if one or both parents request it.
Mississippi	Joint custody is presumed to be in child's best interests if parents agree, option otherwise; joint custody award obligates parents to share information and confer in decision making.
Missouri	Joint legal custody an option; parenting plan required; "friendly parent" provision; obligation to exchange information regarding the child.
Montana	Shared or joint custody is presumed to be in child's best interest if either or both parents request it, unless found otherwise; parenting plan required; "friendly parent" provision.

(cont.)

Table 4.1. *(continued)*

State	Summary of Statutory Law and Case Law Trends
Nebraska	No mention of joint custody in statutes; case law indicates joint custody is reserved for only rarest cases.
Nevada	Joint custody is presumed to be in child's best interests when parents agree; frequent association and continuing relationship with both parents encouraged.
New Hampshire	Joint legal custody is presumed to be in child's best interests when parents agree or one parent requests it; spousal abuse considered harmful to child.
New Jersey	Joint custody is an option.
New Mexico	Joint custody is presumed to be in child's best interest in initial custody determination; parenting plan required; "friendly parent" provision.
New York	No mention of joint custody in statute but authorized in case law.
North Carolina	Joint custody is an option.
North Dakota	No mention in statute; "alternating" custody allowed in case law.
Ohio	"Shared parenting" is mandatory when two parents request it, an option when one makes request; both subject to child's best interests; parenting plan required; "friendly parent" provision; exclusions for spousal or child abuse.
Oklahoma	Joint custody is an option; parenting plan required.
Oregon	Joint custody is mandatory when parents agree, *not* an option otherwise; court may not overrule parents' agreement; frequent and continuing contact encouraged when parents act in child's best interests; parents must exchange information about child's health.
Pennsylvania	"Shared custody" is an option; qualified encouragement of reasonable and continuing contact and shared childrearing.
Rhode Island	No mention of joint custody in statutes, but mentioned in case law.
South Carolina	No mention of joint custody in statutes, but case law suggests it is allowed only under exceptional circumstances.
South Dakota	Joint legal custody is an option.

Table 4.1. *(continued)*

State	Summary of Statutory Law and Case Law Trends
Pennsylvania	"Shared custody" is an option; qualified encouragement of reasonable and continuing contact and shared childrearing.
Rhode Island	No mention of joint custody in statutes, but mentioned in case law.
South Carolina	No mention of joint custody in statutes, but case law suggests it is allowed only under exceptional circumstances.
South Dakota	Joint legal custody is an option.
Tennessee	Joint custody or shared parenting is an option.
Texas	"Joint managing conservatorship" is mandatory when parents agree, an option otherwise, but prohibited when there is evidence of spousal or child abuse; frequent and continuing contact encouraged when parents have demonstrated ability; joint and separate decisions must be distinguished; "friendly parent" provision.
Utah	Joint legal custody is an option when both parents agree or when both parents appear capable of implementing it; "friendly parent" provision.
Vermont	"Shared parental rights and responsibilities" are presumed when the parents agree but prohibited otherwise; maximum continuing physical and emotional contact encouraged; "friendly parent" provision.
Virginia	Joint custody is an option.
Washington	"Mutual decision making authority" (vs. sole decision making authority) is mandatory when parents agree, an option otherwise; limitations for instances of spousal or child abuse; primary caretaker has greatest weight in determining residence, but "substantially equal residential periods" are discretionary; parenting plan is required.
West Virginia	No mention of joint custody in statutes, but acknowledged in case law.
Wisconsin	Joint legal custody is an option if parents agree, and possible if one parent requests it and there is an ability to cooperate; spousal and child abuse create presumption against joint custody; "friendly parent" provision.
Wyoming	No mention of joint custody in statutes, but allowed by case law.

Adapted from J. Folberg (Ed.) (1991). *Joint custody and shared parenting* (pp. 298-331). New York: Guilford. Copyright 1991 by Guilford Press. Adapted by permission.

custody may seem to be an equitable compromise, but it may be a compromise that is akin to dividing the child between two contentious parents.

The law has a broader function than dispute resolution, however. The law has an aspirational goal of influencing people who do *not* come into contact with a court. Thus, if statutes that encourage joint custody influence parents to be more cooperative following separation and divorce, they have policy value beyond offering guidance for judicial decision-making in contested custody cases. In fact, many state statutes contain "friendly parent" rules designed to encourage parents to elect joint custody or at least to cooperate in postdivorce childrearing. Under these provisions, if a sole custody award is made, preference is for the parent who will most strongly encourage contact between the children and the noncustodial parent (Folberg, 1991).

In summary, substantive joint custody rules make a useful distinction between legal and physical custody, but they fail to address some concerns about dispute resolution in contested cases. What is needed is a custody standard that is both determinative and pluralistic, and that promotes the realistic involvement of both parents in postdivorce childrearing.

The Approximation Rule

The *approximation rule* is a newly proposed custody standard that holds the promise of better meeting these goals. As proposed by Elizabeth Scott, the approximation rule indicates that postdivorce parenting arrangements should, as far as possible, approximate the parenting patterns that existed during the marriage (Scott, 1992). In many respects, the approximation rule is a hybrid of the primary caretaker parent and joint custody concepts. Like the primary caretaker parent provision, the approximation rule looks backward in time to determine the future, and both rules are far more determinate than the best interests test. Unlike the primary caretaker provision, however, the approximation rule does not perpetuate traditional conceptions of custody and visitation.

In this respect, the approximation rule is similar to joint custody. Many possible postdivorce parenting arrangements are envisioned by the rule, ranging from joint physical custody to every other weekend arrangements (Scott, 1992). Moreover, unlike joint physical custody, which implies frequent contact with both parents but is unclear otherwise, the approximation standard offers parents and professionals guidance in defining the parameters of their parenting arrangements.

The approximation rule thus is both pluralistic and determinative. Although untried, it would seem to hold much potential, if not as a legislative rule, then at least as an informal guideline in helping parents to negotiate their own custody agreements. The approximation rule fails to address the important need for even more specificity in postdivorce parenting arrangements, but that concern may be addressed by the following recent innovation.

Parenting Plans

Several states now require that parents submit specific plans for rearing their children after divorce. It is hoped that the required plan will encourage creative, individualized, and clear arrangements, as well as a cooperative coparental relationship.

Evidence from the state of Washington, which has implemented the most extensive parenting plan provisions, indicates that the majority of divorcing parents are able to specify details about both residence and various areas of coparental decision-making (Ellis, 1990). Most plans that were studied incorporated traditional custody arrangements, that is, primary residence was with the mother in 70% of the cases. Still, by requiring consideration of specific details, the new laws seem to have encouraged joint custody. Twenty percent of the Washington sample indicated that they elected for joint physical custody, while 69% of the parenting plans indicated that the parents agreed to joint legal custody. These percentages were considerably higher than what had been found in the years before the new law went into effect (Ellis, 1990).

Data are not yet available on whether the parenting plans in Washington or other states have resulted in improved parental relationships or whether they lead to lower or higher rates of relitigation (Ellis, 1990). The legal requirement to develop such a plan forces parents to be more specific, however—an important goal that was discussed in Chapter 2. Some common alternatives in the specifics of residence and decision-making are discussed in relation to mediation in Chapter 7.

Implications for Mediation

Innovations in the substance of custody law obviously are of great relevance to mediators. In fact, many recent changes reflect practices that began in mediation long before they were implemented in legislation. Mediators commonly have written agreements that contain more joint legal custody provisions and fewer physical custody plans, and that include many details about the specifics of postdivorce parenting (see Chapter 8).

Another substantive issue in child custody also is frequently addressed in mediation, although it has yet to be addressed in the law: Mediators often anticipate the need for changes in custody arrangements over time. Mediators frequently discuss this possibility with parents—an approach that anticipates future trouble spots but that also removes pressure from the immediate negotiations. Parents who can envision the possibility of changes in their children's future residence often are less entrenched in their current positions. For example, the possibility of a divorced father becoming more involved with childrearing as the children grow older may be attractive because it tracks changes in parenting involvement that frequently occur in married families.

SUBSTANTIVE LAW AND FINANCIAL SETTLEMENTS IN DIVORCE

There is one basic fact that must be recognized about postdivorce finances: a family's standard of living will decline no matter what settlement is reached. This is true simply because of economies of scale. Two households are more expensive to maintain than one. In fact, one estimate indicated that, for a family of four earning an average income, their standard of living would decrease by 11% as a result of divorce. The drop in living standards is even greater for poor families (Espenshade, 1979).

Empirically, it also is clear that divorced mothers and their custodial children bear the brunt of the economic decline that divorce inevitably produces (Duncan & Hoffman, 1985). Women's lower living standards following divorce are partially explained by the financial settlements that are reached and by poor compliance with those settlements. The major explanation for the gender difference, however, is the differential earning power of men and women. Postdivorce differences in men's and women's earnings mirror basic differences in the employment and compensation of men and women inside and outside of marriage (Emery, 1988).

Property division, alimony, and child support all are potential ways to reallocate finances between former spouses. These issues are important in their own right, and they also need to be addressed because financial disputes may be intertwined with custody disputes in a divorce (Maccoby & Mnookin, 1992; Scott, 1992).

Property Division

Property Division is the allocation of the assets brought to or acquired during the marriage by one or the other spouse. Except in eight states where property is divided equally upon divorce, judges determine property awards at their discretion according to what is *equitable* or fair (Freed & Walker, 1991). (California, Idaho, Indiana, Louisiana, New Mexico, Texas, Washington, and Wisconsin all had equal division statutes as of 1990.) In practice, equitable distribution of marital property often approaches equal distribution (Weitzman, 1985). Nevertheless, when property division is based primarily on a principle of what is fair, concerns are raised about indeterminate laws and the exercise of judicial discretion.

Marital versus Individual Property

Other than the uncertainties involved in deciding what is equitable, the major issue in property division is determining what constitutes marital property. Marital property is that which is owned by the two spouses jointly, as distinguished from that which is owned by each as an individual—individual property. Historically, common law held that a couple's property belonged to whomever held legal title to it, with the exception of the 10 "community property" states where marital assets have always been assumed to be owned jointly. (Arizona, Mississippi, and Nevada are community property states, as are all of the states that have equal property division, with the exception of Indiana.) Under common law provisions, courts awarded property according to its title, dividing only jointly held assets upon divorce. When only one spouse held title to a couple's most valuable assets such as a business, investments, or the family home, this clearly could result in inequitable property settlements.

Equitable distribution laws have changed this problem, as title is disregarded in distributing property, and "nonmonetary contributions to the marriage" are recognized and compensated. Still, the issue of deciding what is or is not marital property can be a thorny one. The major debates concern whether or not property owned before the marriage is excluded, whether or not inheritances or gifts are excluded, and whether or not career assets such as a pension plan, a professional degree, and business goodwill are excluded.

Some of these issues have been addressed by various state legislatures, but there is considerable confusion nevertheless. Of the 40 states with equitable distribution statutes, 18 also have laws indicating that all property owned by either partner should be considered in dividing property. The remaining 22 restrict the division of property to marital property (Freed & Walker, 1991). Inheritances and gifts are explicitly excluded from division in 21 states, they are clearly *not* excluded from division in another 13 states, and their status is ambiguous in the remainder (Freed & Walker, 1991).

Further complications arise when preexisting assets, gifts, or inheritances have been combined with marital property, for example, when an inheritance is placed in a mutual fund account together with marital assets. It may be impossible to distinguish the individual property from the marital property in such a circumstance. Thus, when assets are comingled, it is possible that everything will be considered to be marital property for the purposes of its division between the spouses.

The definition of marital property has expanded, and it may be becoming even broader. One major departure from the recent past is that an individual's pension plan generally is now assumed to be a part of marital property. This is an important change, because a pension plan often is a couple's second largest asset, exceeded only by the value of the family home. In some cases, a professional degree or business goodwill also is considered to be marital property, although the general trend across states seems to be that these items are excluded. Instead, higher alimony awards are a more common means of compensating spouses who supported their partner's education or establishment of a business (Freed & Walker, 1991).

Family Home

The disposition of the family home may be given special consideration in property division. A couple's home often is their most valuable marital asset, and it frequently must be sold in order to accomplish the equal or equitable division of property. In fact, one investigator found an order to sell the family home in one out of every three cases (Weitzman, 1985). Many feel that it is desirable to maintain this source of stability for children during divorce, however, even though only a few state laws contain provisions to encourage this.

For some couples, the value of a pension plan and the marital residence are similar enough to allow one spouse to assume ownership of the home, while the other becomes sole owner of the pension plan. Such a trade-off is complicated, however. Many pension plans cannot be converted into cash, it may be impossible to transfer the mortgage to the spouse living in the home, and emotional attachments to the house may make such a trade unattractive. Because of such complications, it is not uncommon for a dispute about custody to be intertwined with a dispute about the marital residence. One or both partners may assume that they will remain in the family home if they are awarded custody of the children.

Alimony

Alimony (or spousal support or maintenance) is a payment made from one spouse to another for the purposes of that spouse's support following divorce. In theory, this income transfer is made in order to maintain the standard of living that the recipient enjoyed during the marriage. As noted, however, economies of scale dictate that both spouses cannot maintain their former standard of living following divorce.

The concept of alimony seems anachronistic to some, especially given contemporary visions of gender equality in the workplace. The increase in the number of two-earner households, changing conceptions of men's and women's work and family roles, and the movement away from fault divorce all have served to undermine the rationale for one spouse supporting the other following divorce (Weitzman, 1985). Still, men's and women's roles in marriage often continue to reflect traditional breadwinner and caretaker specializations, and evidence makes it clear that women and children suffer financially relative to men following divorce (Duncan & Hoffman, 1985). It is perhaps because of these profound conflicts between social ideology and social reality that the rules for determining whether and how much alimony to award are among the most vague in divorce law (Eekelaar, 1991).

Despite changing social values and indeterminate laws, all states allow for alimony awards, except Texas which has never had alimony provisions. Eight states prohibit alimony payments to a spouse who is found to be at fault, and another 13 allow fault to be considered in determining whether to make an alimony award or in setting its amount (Freed & Walker, 1991). Thus, permanent and substantial alimony awards may be made upon divorce, depending upon a couple's circumstances. Women who are not at fault, whose husbands earn more income, who are older, who have been married for many years, and who have limited earnings (or earning potential) are likely to receive the largest and the longest alimony payments (Weitzman, 1985). Theoretically, alimony also can be paid to men, but this is a rare circumstance.

An Alimony Myth?

Although it is not surprising that men rarely receive alimony, what is surprising is that women rarely receive it either. Less than a fifth of divorced women in the United States report that they currently receive alimony, a fact that has caused at least one commentator to assert that there is an "alimony myth" (Weitzman, 1985). A similarly low percentage of divorced women receive alimony in Great Britain (Eekelaar, 1991).

One reason for this low percentage is that few divorced women meet the profile outlined above. Most divorces take place early in marriage when the couple is young, a husband's earnings are relatively low, and, in theory, a wife's earning potential is not much different from her husband's (Emery, 1988; Kitson, 1992). A second reason why the percentage of women receiving alimony at any one time is low is that some couples opt for "lump sum" alimony payments. The recipient receives a larger share of the property division in lieu of alimony. A third reason is that some unknown percentage of women are found to be at fault for breakdown of the marriage. Finally, the low percentage of divorced women who report that they are currently receiving alimony is partially a result of limitations in the duration of alimony awards.

Such short-term awards often are called *rehabilitative alimony*. This pejorative term refers to spousal support that is paid for a fixed time, in order for recipients to increase their earning power during the period of added financial support. They are being financially "rehabilitated." *Reimbursement alimony* is a related concept; a higher alimony award is paid for a fixed period of time. Reimbursement alimony is likely to be paid to spouses who have devoted time to enhancing their partners' careers. In general, such temporary alimony awards are more common among younger women with shorter marriages, greater earning potential, and husbands who earn less money (Weitzman, 1985).

Alimony Amounts

Other than the general criterion of maintaining the former spouse's standard of living, the specific rules for determining the size and length of alimony awards are amazingly vague. Ultimately, the decision to award alimony and, if so, how much to award falls to judicial discretion. And, as with other areas of indeterminate divorce law, judges often have informal rules for determining the size of alimony awards. One example is the "one-third" rule, which indicates that a homemaker wife should receive alimony equal to one-third of her breadwinner husband's income. Another common, informal rule is that the husband and wife should have equal after-tax income, when the income is based on all sources including child support payments and actual or imputed earnings. Other informal rules limit alimony payments to five or ten years, or to a period of time equal to the length of the marriage (Eekelaar, 1991; Weitzman, 1985).

Such calculations may not attend to income relative to family needs, however, so that the greater expenses needed to support children in one household are not taken into account. Moreover, unlike child support, alimony payments generally cannot be adjusted over time—a very important factor, especially for young families, because inflation can lower the value of fixed income.

In practice, alimony most commonly is determined by divorce bargaining between attorneys, and agreements can be influenced by a number of factors in addition to probable judicial awards. This means that divorcing spouses (or mediators) need to rely on the advice of local attorneys in determining likely outcomes for particular cases. More generally, the ambiguity of formal rules coupled with the existence of informal ones provides another example of how unarticulated social values are evident in the exercise of judicial discretion. An informal prescriptive morality exists, but it is found implicitly in legal practice, not explicitly in legislative guidelines. This is unfortunate because many benefits are to be gained when clear rules have been set down, as has been made obvious by changes in the way that child support is determined.

Child Support

While the justifications for financially supporting a former spouse clash with recent trends in societal values, the social and moral rationales for child support are unquestioned. Still, until recent years, the determination of the amount of child support to be paid upon divorce was as vague and controversial as is the current determination of alimony. Of at least equal importance, noncompliance with child support awards has been and continues to be a major problem.

Child Support Schedules

A great many of the conflicts involved in determining child support were resolved under the impetus of federal legislation passed in 1984 and amended in 1988, which contained incentives for all states to adopt presumptive standards that produce a specific dollar amount for child support awards (Landstreet & Takas, 1991). As of 1990, all but six states had passed specific statutory criteria for determining child support amounts (Freed & Walker, 1991). Many professionals note that the schedules are a major improvement over earlier, indeterminate criteria. Schedules provide clarity and simplicity, and they remove acrimony from the determination of child support (Landstreet & Takas, 1991).

Child support schedules differ from state to state both in the criteria they adopt and the size of typical awards, and this is the subject of some controversy. Still, the specific, presumptive schedules represent a substantial improvement over the recent past. In fact, many believe that the best support guidelines are the simplest ones. Wisconsin's schedule, for example, is a model of simplicity. According to this state's law, child support is determined by a percentage of the payer's income: 17% for one child, 25% for two children, 29% for three children, 31% for four children, and 34% for five or more children (Landstreet & Takas, 1991).

Although schedules greatly facilitate the determination of child support, complications arise even with clear standards. Among the most important controversies are whether the schedules should apply when (1) there are large disparities in the payers' before- and after-tax earnings (i.e., the payer has substantial expenses and tax deductions); (2) the payer has a substantial debt load in addition to child support obligations; (3) subsequent children are born to the payer; and (4) the parents have joint physical custody or split custody.

Perhaps the most important issue with respect to child support, however, is the need to modify support awards as time passes. The real dollar value of a fixed payment can be cut in half within several years. Over time, inflation, the payers' increased earnings, and the added expense of older children all diminish the value of a child support award, thus making quick and simple procedures for modifying awards necessary (Landstreet & Takas, 1991). On this point, it is worth noting that the simple procedures for determining child support in Wisconsin automatically adjust for rising incomes, which should reflect both inflation and increased earning power.

Compliance with Support Awards

Specific child support guidelines have greatly facilitated the determination of support award amounts, but compliance with child support awards remains a substantial problem. In 1981, 59% of all single mothers with children had been awarded child support, but only 47% of those awards were paid as ordered. In 28% of the cases, not a single payment was made (National Institute for Child Support Enforcement [NICSE], 1986).

The same federal legislation that encouraged the development of schedules was designed to improve compliance with child support orders, but its success in that regard has been much more mixed. The laws allowed states to keep a percentage of the child support payments they collected (and ordinarily would be used to reimburse the federal government for Aid to Families with Dependent Children (AFDC) payments), provided that collection rates met certain criteria. Thus, in theory more stringent enforcement of support would benefit the states, as they would keep a proportion of the child support collections, and it would also benefit the federal government, as total AFDC collections would increase by increasing child support compliance.

Among the mechanisms that are being used to increase compliance with support awards are garnishment of wages, interceptions of tax refunds, and civil or criminal contempt proceedings (NICSE, 1986). Evidence indicates that some of these measures have been effective, as collections have increased substantially in some states in the last several years. The collection of child support remains a substantial problem both for the state and for custodial parents, however (J. L. Peterson & Nord, 1990).

Taxes

In reviewing the implications of income transfers following separation and divorce, taxes must be carefully considered. This is particularly important because alimony and child support have very different tax implications.

One certainty applies to alimony despite vague rules for determining awards. Alimony payments are treated as a tax deduction for the payer and a tax liability for the recipient. Thus, in calculating the value of an alimony award, taxes need to be subtracted from the amount received. For example, a monthly alimony payment of $500 is really worth approximately $340 to the recipient, who must pay federal and state income taxes of approximately $160 (32%) on the $500 (depending upon their tax bracket). The earnings needed to pay a $500 alimony award are approximately $538, because the only taxes that are due are social security taxes (calculated at 7% in this example) (see Table 4.2).

This tax treatment of alimony is the opposite of the treatment of child support, which is tax free to the recipient but taxable to the payer. Thus, the after-tax value of a $500 child support payment is $500 to the recipient. In order to make a $500 tax-free payment, however, the payer of child support must earn approximately $820, $320 of which goes to federal and state income taxes and social security, as is illustrated in Table 4.2.

Because the spouse who pays alimony and child support often is in a higher tax bracket than the spouse who receives it, many divorced

Table 4.2. Alimony, Child Support, and Taxes

Income needed to pay $500 in monthly alimony:
$500 plus social security tax (no income taxes are due)
At 7% social security, amount = $538

Income needed to pay $500 in monthly child support:
$500 plus federal income plus state income plus social security taxes
At 28% federal, 4% state, and 7% social security, amount = $820

After-tax value of receipt of $500 in monthly alimony:
$500 minus federal income minus state income taxes
At 28% federal and 4% state, amount = $340

After tax value of receipt of $500 in monthly child support:
No taxes due, amount = $500

couples have disguised child support awards as alimony payments. That is, a single payment is made each month which, in fact, covers both alimony and child support, but which is treated only as alimony for tax purposes. This tax strategy can result in a net savings to the couple, because the combined payment is taxed at the recipient's lower rate. New laws have made it more difficult to follow this tax strategy, however.

Remarriage, Cohabitation, and Income Tranfers

Other than taxes, the only certainty about alimony is that it terminates when the recipient remarries. What is less certain is what effect the cohabitation of the recipient will have on alimony. Eleven states have statutes that address the cohabitation possibility in one form or another (Freed & Walker, 1991), but many divorcing parties and the lawyers (or mediators) wisely address the issue in a separation agreement before the situation arises. Neither remarriage nor cohabitation alters child support obligations, however, although the birth of subsequent children to the payer may alter the calculations.

Postdivorce Economics for Single Mothers

Property division, spousal support, and child support all improve the economic situation of children following divorce, but these financial settlements comprise only a small percentage of the income of single-mother families. On average, women earn 60% of their income in the year following divorce, while only about 10% comes from the combination of alimony and child support (Duncan & Hoffman, 1985). Of course, alimony and child support payments contribute a substantially greater percentage to income in numerous individual cases. Nevertheless, the data makes it clear that divorce settlements alone will not eliminate the economic hardships experienced by mothers and their custodial children. In order to maintain the predivorce living standards of children, a sum of money considerably greater than that associated with the added expense of raising children would have to be transferred from nonresidential fathers to residential mothers.

Other than making dramatic changes in property division, alimony, or child support, potential "solutions" to the financial hardships experienced by women and children following divorce include improved employment, public assistance, and remarriage. Women clearly attempt to raise their family income by increasing their employment following divorce. In one study, 51% of women reported working over 1,000 hours in the year prior to divorce, but 72% did so in the first year after divorce (Duncan & Hoffman, 1985). Even this substantial change probably underestimates the increase in women's working, because many women apparently work more prior to a divorce in anticipation of their later financial needs. The percentage of women who receive over $250 in public assistance also increases substantially from 5% before divorce to 19% afterward (Duncan & Hoffman, 1985).

Women's incomes still fall after divorce despite child support, alimony, increased hours at work, and public assistance. In the first year following divorce, the average income of women who do not remarry drops from $26,000 to less than $15,000 (in 1981 dollars). Men also experience a drop in income to 93% of the predivorce level during this first year. However, men's total incomes and especially their incomes relative to their needs do not suffer as much and rebound more quickly than do women's (Duncan & Hoffman, 1985). In fact, five years after divorce, men's income increases 23% over predivorce levels, and their income relative to their needs increases 29%. These figures are comparable to the rising incomes found among couples who remain married. With one exception, however, women's total income stubbornly remains about 30% below predivorce levels five years following divorce, and income relative to needs is about 10% below predivorce levels (Duncan & Hoffman, 1985).

The exception is women who remarry. Remarriage relieves the economic distress of divorced women more than any other single factor. Five years after divorce, the incomes of remarried women are 27% above predivorce levels, and income relative to needs is up 25%. Clearly, there are strong economic incentives for divorced women to remarry, and while encouraging remarriage may not be an intentional social policy, it is a de facto one. Remarriage may add rather than alleviate stress in family relationships, as was mentioned in Chapter 3, but it clearly resolves many financial problems.

SUMMARY

The substantive law guiding the settlement of divorce disputes is characterized most clearly by its lack of substance. The desire to accommodate pluralism and the increasing privatization of marriage and divorce have caused a retreat from the traditional prescriptive morality found in American family law. This has resulted in a vague, indeterminate set of standards which guide the ordering of a family's affairs upon divorce. This lack of clarity has created problems both for families and for the legal system.

Indeterminate laws are likely to exist only briefly from a historical perspective, and trends toward greater determinacy in divorce law already can be detected in new child support schedules, in equal property division rules, and in newly proposed custody standards such as the primary caretaker parent standard and the approximation rule. The greater specificity promised by these developments should ease burdens on families and on the courts. As substantive standards become more specific, the paramount importance of dispute resolution procedures in divorce law also should decrease.

In fact, many substantive innovations were born out of the efforts of professionals involved in resolving divorce disputes under indeterminate laws. Mediators are among those who have contributed to promoting substantive changes in the law governing postdivorce childrearing. For example, concepts such as parenting plans and joint custody were advocated by mediators long before they were addressed by state legislators. Thus, many of the innovations discussed in this chapter serve as an introduction to the practice of mediation. Others, such as the approximation rule, suggest new directions for future practice.

Despite the trend toward greater determinacy, divorce law remains vague on the whole. The indeterminate nature of the law provides a substantial rationale for encouraging couples to order their disputes privately in mediation and elsewhere. As is discussed in the next chapter, various additional considerations suggest why cooperative dispute resolution procedures such as mediation often are preferred over competitive ones such as attorney negotiations and litigation when it comes to resolving custody disputes.

CHAPTER 5

Custody Dispute Resolution Procedures in Theory and Practice

The basic philosophy of procedure in the American legal system is that formalized competition is the best method of protecting individual rights in legal disputes. This adversary approach is a cornerstone of the law in the United States. Disputing parties are assumed to be opponents whose competing interests run directly counter to one another. In theory, legal battles end with a winner and a loser, and various procedural guidelines have been developed in order to ensure a fair contest.

As an embodiment of this philosophy, each family member's opposing point of view may be formally represented in a custody dispute. Each parent's perspective is represented by an attorney who has the responsibility of advocating solely for that parent's individual interests. In fact, the idea of fighting for their individual "rights" may resonate with each parent's anger, as they may indeed view their circumstance as a "win–lose" proposition. The children also may be formally represented by *guardians ad litem*, lawyer or nonlawyer advocates who have a duty to represent the child's interests exclusive from those of their parents.

Various other professionals also may represent the child's perspective less directly in a custody dispute. Judges, custody evaluators, *guardians ad litem*, and mediators all have the formal obligation to work toward custody arrangements in the children's best interests. Each of these professionals also shares the child's perspective informally, as a result of their intermediary role in the dispute. Like the children, these professionals often find themselves in the middle of a conflict between two contentious parents. This middle position has caused many professionals to become concerned that adversary procedures may increase conflict between parents and thereby undermine, rather than serve, children's best interests (Emery & Wyer, 1987b; Landsman & Minow, 1978).

The concerns raised by professionals involved in custody dispute resolution form an important impetus for the custody mediation movement. In contrast to adversarial settlement, mediation is based on a cooperative philosophy of dispute resolution. The approach recognizes that separated and divorced partners have many opposing interests, but it acknowledges that they also have some mutual interests, especially with respect to their children. In short, there are "win-win" possibilities for resolving custody disputes, and cooperative dispute resolution is the optimal means for reaching such integrated outcomes. Contrary to what many parents and professionals seem to believe, however, a cooperative relationship is not a precondition for mediation. Cooperation is the philosophy of dispute resolution, but mediation sessions typically involve heated, difficult, and painful exchanges.

Thus, it is essential to distinguish dispute resolution in theory and in practice. In this chapter, the theory underlying both competitive and cooperative dispute resolution procedures is considered, and some practical aspects of resolving custody disputes through attorney negotiations and formal custody litigation also are discussed. The practice of custody mediation is reviewed in detail in Chapters 6 and 7. In considering competitive and cooperative alternatives for dispute resolution, it is clear that neither approach is monolithic in practice. Attorneys often strive to facilitate cooperation; mediation frequently involves anger and manipulative posturing. Despite variations in practice, however, theoretical analysis clearly differentiates dispute resolution alternatives.

GAME THEORY

Competitive tactics are neither specific to attorney negotiations, nor are they inherently "bad" in any abstract sense. Rather, according to the abstract, theoretical analysis of conflict from the perspective of game theory, competitive negotiations simply constitute the wisest bargaining strategy given an assumption of directly competing interests, as is made in the adversary system. Game theorists refer to the general approach to effective negotiating in a competitive framework as "distributive bargaining."

Competitive Approaches: Zero Sum Disputes and Distributive Bargaining

Disputes in which each party's interests are in direct opposition to one another can easily be represented as "zero sum" disputes. A zero sum dispute is a win or lose proposition. The more that one side wins, the more the other side loses. Financial conflicts in divorce can easily be conceptualized as zero sum disputes. What one side pays in spousal support, for example, the other side receives. The sum of the loss to one side and the gain to the other adds up to zero. In zero sum disputes, the primary issue to resolve is distribution, that is, how to divide whatever is being disputed (Raiffa, 1982).

When disputes involve zero sum outcomes, distributive bargaining is the most effective method of protecting one's own interests in negotiation (Raiffa, 1982). In distributive bargaining, each side begins by making an initial offer that is presented to the opposing party as an acceptable resolution to the dispute. In making their initial offer, each side is wise to adopt a position that favors their side. That is, the initial position should exaggerate their "reservation price" (Raiffa, 1982) or the minimally acceptable outcome for their side. In fact, it is most advantageous initially to take as extreme a position as is tenable. Extreme positions leave considerable room for bargaining toward the middle during subsequent negotiations (Raiffa, 1982).

Distributive bargaining is hardly unique to the legal system: It is evident in everyday financial negotiations. Negotiating over the selling price of a house is a familiar example of a zero sum game that typically involves distributive bargaining. When attempting to purchase a house that is being offered for sale for $160,000, a buyer who is willing to pay $150,000 for the home is unwise to offer that amount initially. An offer of $140,000 is a much better tactical beginning, because of strong norms to split the difference between two positions in distributive bargaining. An initial offer of $130,000 is even better from the buyer's perspective, because it increases the likelihood that the final price will be even more advantageous, perhaps $145,000. A dilemma, however, is that the buyer's initial position must not be too extreme, because the seller will not respond to it. In fact, the seller may refuse to negotiate in the future if the initial offer is too low.

Effective Tactics for Distributive Bargaining

Extreme positions are rewarded in distributive bargaining within uncertain limits. Someone who is selling a house sets an asking price that is as high as possible, as long as it will still attract offers. Someone who is buying a house makes an offer that is as low as possible, as long as it will attract a counteroffer. A parallel process applies to distributive bargaining in custody negotiations. Given an assumption of competing interests, each parent is wise to make a request regarding a custody settlement that exceeds what they are willing to accept, provided that the exaggeration will not cause the negotiations to break down completely.

Other tactics are effective in distributive bargaining. Two of the most important are intransigence and secretiveness (Menkel-Meadow, 1984; Raiffa, 1982). Accordingly, people trying to sell a house are doubly disadvantaged. They disclose their motivation to sell by putting the house on the market, and they reveal their initial position by setting an asking price. Because of their knowledge of the seller's initial position, buyers have the advantage of determining the middle ground of potential agreement with their purchase offers. Moreover, people who are less eager to buy a house hold an advantage over those who are more eager to buy, because they are less pressured by time to come to an agreement.

Thus, three wise tactics in distributive bargaining are to (1) let the other side make the first offer, (2) make as extreme an offer as is tenable, and (3) be patient in negotiating (Raiffa, 1982). In the custody context, this means that bargaining advantages accrue to the parent who is more comfortable with the present circumstances, more willing to take extreme positions, and less willing to discuss compromise arrangements, perhaps because they are less eager to settle (or to divorce).

Ritualized distributive bargaining clearly is preferred as a means of negotiating settlements for a wide range of disputes, but it is obvious that it can create problems in the child custody context. Exaggerated positions about desired custody arrangements, the refusal to discuss compromises, and time delays in reaching a settlement can be damaging to the parents' relationship, and such tactics ultimately may harm the children (Mnookin & Kornhauser, 1979). Many attorneys and parents are sensitive to this latter possibility, and they therefore attempt to minimize the tactical maneuvers of distributive bargaining in custody disputes.

Such sensitivity is important to recognize and encourage, but the present point has little to do with individual sensitivity. Rather, the point concerns the very nature of the negotiation process under an assumption of competition in a zero sum game. Distributive bargaining is not inhumane. It simply is the most effective means of maximizing individual gains when bargaining under competitive conditions (Raiffa, 1982). The alternative to distributive bargaining is exploitation. If only one side cooperates while the other competes, unbalanced outcomes are the result. In practicing in the adversary system, effective attorneys therefore wisely use the tactics of distributive bargaining whether they are negotiating child custody or any other matter.

Cooperative Approaches: Positive Sum Disputes and Integrative Bargaining

Cooperative dispute resolution procedures such as mediation are based on a different set of theoretical assumptions than competitive approaches. According to the cooperative perspective, disputants are viewed as potentially benefiting from cooperation even when they are emotional adversaries. Cooperative dispute resolution may be especially beneficial when disputants have an ongoing relationship, as in custody contests and certain other categories of disputes. This is because the method of dispute resolution can affect the continuing relationship. No dispute is a zero sum game when people will interact in the future.

In fact, an essential assumption underlying cooperative approaches to dispute resolution is that many conflicts are "positive sum" disputes, rather than zero sum conflicts. A positive sum dispute is one in which there does not need to be a winner and a loser, but instead there are win–win possibilities. More specifically, positive sum disputes lead to compromise solutions that, in terms of their joint benefit to the two disputants, exceed the joint benefit of one-sided solutions. The sum of what is received by each side is greater than zero, thus the term "positive sum."

Because of the possibility of win–win outcomes, disputants with positive sum conflicts share some common goals and interests. A problem, however, is that both sides may receive less individual benefit from the compromise solution than they would receive from a purely one-sided outcome. Thus, individual compromise sometimes is needed in order to achieve optimal joint outcomes in positive sum disputes. In all cases, cooperation in negotiation is required to achieve the optimal outcome. This cooperative approach to dispute settlement often is referred to as "integrative bargaining" (Raiffa, 1982).

The theoretical assumptions of positive sum conflicts and integrative bargaining are represented in the classic prisoner's dilemma game. The prisoner's dilemma is a well-established, general formulation of conflict developed by game theorists that involves a few simple assumptions about the potential outcomes of a dispute. It has led to the development of extensive, formal principles in many disciplines including psychology (Rubin, 1980), mathematics (Raiffa, 1982), and even evolution (Axlerod, 1984). The prisoner's dilemma is most easily introduced by an example.

An Example of the Prisoner's Dilemma

The prisoner's dilemma draws its name, not surprisingly, from a dilemma that prisoners may encounter. To illustrate the problem, assume that two men have committed an armed bank robbery. They are arrested and face certain conviction on a weapons charge, because each had an illegal gun in his possession. The prosecutor does not have enough evidence to link the suspects to the robbery, however. In order to get at least one conviction on the robbery, the prosecutor offers each prisoner the following deal. If he confesses to the robbery and testifies against his partner, the prosecutor will drop both the robbery and the weapons charge. The prisoner who confesses will go free, but the other will go to jail for 20 years.

The prosecutor obviously cannot accept confessions from both prisoners and let both go free, however. Therefore, if both partners confess, both will be convicted of the bank robbery, but the sentence for each will be reduced from 20 years to 12 years. In contrast, each prisoner will get only a 1-year sentence for the weapons charge if both remain silent, although the prosecutor is unlikely to review this possibility with the prisoners. Thus, each prisoner faces the choices outlined in Table 5.1.

In this example, it is obvious that it is in the prisoners' joint interest to cooperate with each other and for both to remain silent. In this case, the total number of years served by the prisoners combined is 2 years, as opposed to a 20-year joint total if only one confesses, and a 24-year combined total if both prisoners confess. The joint benefits of cooperation are clear. One dilemma faced by each prisoner, however, is whether or not he can trust his partner. It takes cooperation for the two prisoners to achieve their optimal joint outcome, and a wise prosecutor would do much to discourage communication and trust.

The prisoners face a much more basic problem than the prosecutor's maneuvering, however. The problem is that confession is the logical choice from the perspective of maximizing each of their individual interests, even though cooperation maximizes their joint interest. That is, regardless of whether one prisoner decides that the other will confess or remain silent, their economically rational choice is to confess.

In order to understand this important fact, consider each prisoner's individual perspective. If Prisoner A decides that Prisoner B will remain silent, Prisoner A's confession will result in no prison

Table 5.1. The Prisoner's Dilemma[a]

		Prisoner A	
		Stay Silent	Confess
	Stay Silent	A gets 1 year	A goes free
		B gets 1 year	B gets 20 years
Prisoner B			
	Confess	A gets 20 years	A gets 12 years
		B goes free	B gets 12 years

[a]An example of the prisoner's dilemma, a positive sum game. Table details payoffs to each prisoner based on their joint decisions to confess or stay silent. Note that the optimal joint benefit comes from cooperation, that is, when both prisoners remain silent.

sentence, while remaining silent will result in 1 year in jail for him. Confession therefore is the logical choice from the perspective of Prisoner A's individual interest. Similarly, if Prisoner A decides that Prisoner B will confess, confession again is the economically rational choice for Prisoner A. If Prisoner B confesses, then Prisoner A will get 12 years in prison if he also confesses, whereas he will get 20 years in jail if he remains silent. These outcomes can be confirmed by consulting Table 5.1. Whatever Prisoner A decides Prisoner B will do, it is in his individual interest to confess.

Because Prisoner B faces the identical dilemma, from the perspective of maximizing individual utility, both prisoners should confess. That is, they should compete with one another. When this happens, however, both the joint and the individual outcomes are worse than what would have been achieved if they cooperated. The joint outcome of competition (both confessing) is 24 years of prison time, whereas the joint outcome of cooperation (both remaining silent) is 2 years in prison. The individual outcome of competition is 12 years of prison time, whereas the individual outcome of cooperation is 1 year in jail.

Custody Disputes as a Prisoner's Dilemma

There are few better examples of positive sum conflicts than disputes over how children should be raised. Just as in the prisoner's dilemma, however, in this circumstance the problem is that cooperation entails both procedural and substantive sacrifices. Procedurally, cooperation requires at least some good faith communication between disputants, who often are angry and mistrustful. Substantively, cooperation often involves some compromise of individual interests for the joint good.

Thus, the task for mediators and others involved in cooperative dispute resolution is exactly the opposite of that of the prosecutor in the example of the prisoner's dilemma. Procedurally, mediators must work to facilitate communication and allay mistrust, while simultaneously containing and controlling the disputants' conflict. Substantively, mediators must attempt to uncover each side's "bottom line" or reservation price, in order to determine if their positions overlap. If they do, mediators can encourage compromises toward areas of agreement. More broadly, mediators must attempt to help separated or divorced parents recognize that they will have some form of an ongoing relationship. Because of this, cooperation is in their joint and individual interests, as well as in the best interests of their children.

Of course, the application of dispute resolution theory in practice is imperfect for both cooperative and competitive negotiations. Divorcing parents may hope or expect that they will have no future relationship; thus, despite the efforts of a mediator, they may continue in their conflict. Attorneys have an obligation to fight when their clients ask them to do so, but attorneys also have ongoing relationships with each other that temper their competitive negotiation tactics. In practice, moreover, the formalized procedures of the judicial system are used relatively rarely, because most custody disputes are settled through attorneys' out-of-court negotiations.

COMPETITIVE PRACTICE IN THE ADVERSARY SYSTEM: ATTORNEY NEGOTIATIONS

No national statistics are available on how custody disputes are settled. However, it is clear that most divorcing parents reach a custody agreement outside of court. In one recent study of a large California sample, only 1.5% of custody cases were decided by a judge. The remainder were settled through less formal procedures, including mediation, which was used to settle 11% of the cases. Other interventions such as custody evaluations led to settlement for a small percentage of cases, but the great majority were settled through out-of-court negotiations between attorneys (Maccoby & Mnookin, 1992).

California's mandatory mediation law clearly reduced the number of custody hearings in this study; thus it likely underestimates litigation in other jurisdictions. Moreover, half of the custody cases were classified as being contested, even though they eventually were settled out of court (Maccoby & Mnookin, 1992). In addition, evidence from other research indicates that as many as one-third of all divorced parents formally dispute custody at some point *after* divorce (Foster &

Freed, 1973-74). (Custody decisions can be changed throughout a child's years as a minor.) Thus, the small number of cases that end in a custody hearing at the time of divorce significantly underestimates the number of cases in which custody is disputed informally or eventually. Nevertheless, attorney negotiations are by far the most common means of resolving child custody disputes, as well as other forms of legal action (Ross, 1980).

As this fact has been recognized, attorney negotiations have increasingly become a focus of interest among legal scholars (Goldberg, Green, & Sander, 1985). There are few procedural rules that guide attorney negotiations, however, and some guidelines that have been proposed have been rejected by the American Bar Association (Goldberg et al., 1985). Rather, it is assumed that each clients' interests will be protected by the competition that is built into attorney negotiations. Like Darwin's theory of survival of the fittest, the adversarial nature of the legal system is designed to ensure that the best case wins.

The Attorney's Advocacy Role

Attorneys for each parent have the dual responsibilities of advising their clients about the substantive law and informing them about outcomes that would be likely should the case be litigated. In acting as advisors, lawyers also may discourage clients against pursuing a particular custody arrangement, counsel them against acting on their hostility toward their former spouse, or offer other forms of general advice (Mnookin & Kornhauser, 1979). The principal role of a legal advocate is to act on their clients' wishes, not to question their motivations. In one study, for example, only 19% of attorneys attempted to discourage their clients from seeking custody, even when they thought their client was not the better parent or when they believed their client was being vindictive (Weitzman & Dixon, 1979). In fact, Canon 7 of the American Bar Association's *Canon of Professional Ethics* indicates that lawyers must represent their clients "zealously within the bounds of the law" (American Bar Association, 1969). Thus, lawyers ultimately must serve as advocates who vigorously represent the expressed wishes of their individual clients, or they must resign the case (Scott & Emery, 1987).

Advocacy and Competitive Negotiations

The assumption of competition inherent in the adversary system means that, even if they want to cooperate, attorneys must assume that the other side is not cooperating, or they risk damaging their client's position. As noted, asking for too little initially increases the chances of giving away too much in the end (Raiffa, 1982). If they are zealously representing their clients, each attorney therefore should develop an opening position with respect to custody that exceeds what their client ultimately is willing to accept as a reasonable settlement. This means that differences between the two sides are exaggerated initially in order to leave room for making concessions during subsequent bargaining (Menkel-Meadow, 1984).

Each individual attorney also should determine acceptable fall-back positions in consultation with their clients, but these positions cannot be disclosed to the other side without undermining the initial proposal. In fact, many attorneys discourage communication between the former spouses, in order to protect against possible disclosures that would weaken their side's stance in the divorce bargaining. Other tactics that convey a sense of righteousness or inflexibility might also be used to convey the impression that one's initial position is one's final position. For example, time delays might be used by the side that is less anxious to settle, giving them the advantage that concessions may be made in order to speed up the negotiation process (Mendel- Meadow, 1984). Thus, "foot dragging" in negotiating agreements may not only have emotional motivations (see Chapter 2), but it also can have strategic underpinnings.

Variations in Style

Zealous representation in competitive negotiations can take many different forms, however. Many lawyers attempt to resolve custody disputes with as little divisiveness as possible, and research indicates that, in the general practice of law, most lawyers approach negotiations from a cooperative rather than a competitive stance (Williams, 1983). How can competitive negotiations be cooperative in style? Research indicates that cooperative attorney negotiators are effective when their approach is ritualized and polite. Descriptors such as "ethical," "reasonable," "courteous," and "facilitating" apply to lawyers who adopt a cooperative style of negotiation, even though they are also described as attempting to maximize the settlement for their own clients (Williams, 1983). Competitive attorney negotiators also are effective when they are described as wishing to maximize settlements for their clients, but these lawyers also are described as attempting to maximize their own fees and are characterized as "aggressive," "arrogant," and "rigid" (Williams, 1983).

Unlike what some claim, the general problem therefore is not that individual attorneys are "sharks" or "hired guns" in their practice. If adversary attorney negotiations create unnecessary conflict in custody disputes, the problem rests with the competitive system of dispute settlement, not with the individual lawyers. As game theory illustrates, truly cooperative negotiation requires the adoption of a different set of premises, not just a different approach to negotiation. It may be that changing the system, not the individual lawyers, is the best way to encourage cooperation in settling disputes between former partners whose future interests remain intertwined.

CUSTODY ADJUDICATION

Attorney negotiations are conducted in the shadow of the law (Mnookin & Kornhauser, 1979), that is, against the backdrop of likely court settlements. For this reason, attorneys must be knowledgeable about recent court settlements (and the tendencies of individual judges). They also must be prepared to go to court if they cannot reach a negotiated settlement that is in line with expectations.

According to one influential analysis, adjudication in the American system of justice has two fundamental features: (1) decisions are made by a neutral party who is not involved in the dispute, typically a judge; and (2) the disputants control the presentation of evidence (Thibault & Walker, 1978). Because of this latter condition, there is no incentive to be objective in presenting evidence, nor is objectivity the goal. Rather, the philosophy of adversary adjudication is to present only the evidence that is the most convincing and favorable to one's own side. For this reason, it has been argued that justice is a higher goal than truth in the American legal system (Thibault & Walker, 1978).

In preparing for a possible hearing in a custody dispute, each attorney therefore develops (and may eventually present) evidence that favors their side and is damaging to the other side. Virtually any negative information on the opposing side is potentially relevant to custody proceedings, because of the vague nature of the best interests standard and the historical influence of evidence related to fault in divorce and each partner's "fitness" as a parent (Catania, 1992; Mnookin, 1975). Thus, each side's evidence might include information on such sensitive topics as the other parent's "morality," sexual activities, religious practices, or lifestyle choices. Friends and relatives may be enlisted as witnesses who will attest to the superiority of one side and against the other, and mental health professionals also may be hired as witnesses by one or both sides. In fact, a trend in recent years has been to make custody adjudication increasingly complicated, as new actors have been introduced into the proceedings.

Children's Advocates

Several of these new actors in court procedures have the duty to represent and protect children. These representatives for the children serve various roles that are designed to promote the children's interests. The most important new roles are served by *guardians ad litem*, mental health professionals, and the children themselves.

Guardians ad Litem

Guardians ad litem are lawyer or nonlawyer advocates who are appointed specifically to represent the children's interests in custody disputes. Clearly, representing the children's perspective in legal proceedings over their custody is a sensible idea. In the past, the children's perspective had not been formally represented in hearings designed to serve their best interests, and the role of the *guardian ad litem* has been designed to fill that void.

There is considerable academic debate about the appropriate role that should be served by *guardians ad litem*, however (Scott & Emery, 1987). Some argue that the guardian should advocate for a child's wishes with respect to custody. Others suggest that they should serve as independent fact finders. Still others argue that guardians should mediate between the parents. Research with practicing *guardians ad litem* indicates that their efforts typically are directed toward resolving the parents' disputes, rather than advocating for some third position held by the children (Landsman & Minow, 1978). Perhaps because guardians serve an intermediary role that allows them to recognize the child's perspective, they see the problems created by the parents' conflict.

The role of a *guardian ad litem* can be an important one even when they fail to bring parents to agreement. Some of the activities of a guardian may duplicate judicial functions (Mlyneic, 1977–78), but their early involvement and greater informality have advantages over the judicial role. For example, guardians can warn parents and their attorneys against placing undo pressure on children who already are caught in the middle of a dispute between their parents (Scott & Emery, 1987).

Mental Health Professionals

Mental health professionals also have become increasingly involved in custody disputes by conducting evaluations of children and one or both parents. Professionals who conduct custody evaluations have the task of determining what family factors are most important to the children's emotional well-being, and evaluators perhaps may make a recommendation to the court about an eventual custody disposition. Some commentators suggest that mental health professionals should not offer specific recommendations to the court, however, because of imperfections in psychological evidence and because the obligation of making these decisions rests with the judge, not the evaluator (Emery & Rogers, 1990; Monahan, 1980; Weithorn, 1987).

Whether or not they make a formal recommendation, mental health professionals who conduct evaluations as a neutral "friend of the court" can have considerable leverage in a custody dispute. In fact, they often serve many of the same fact finder/mediator functions fulfilled by *guardians ad litem*. However, questions have been raised about the role of mental health experts who serve as witnesses for only one parent in a custody dispute. Such expert testimony invariably favors the side being represented and if it does not, the testimony is not likely to be introduced in court (Emery & Rogers, 1990). Moreover, one side's expert testimony can be expected to be countered by the testimony of the other parent's expert, and such a "battle of the experts" can introduce rather than remove confusion from the process (Monahan, 1980). In fact, because of these problems, the question has been raised as to whether it is ethical for mental health professionals to serve as experts for only one side in a custody dispute (Weithorn, 1987).

With respect to their assessment role, there is little evidence that mental health professionals can reliably and validly predict how alternative environments will affect individual children's future mental health. This is especially true when there is not a major difference in the childrearing provided by two parents, precisely the circumstance in which custody is most likely to be disputed (Emery & Rogers, 1990). As discussed in Chapter 4, moreover, the debate about what alternative futures may be "best" is a potentially endless one (Mnookin, 1975).

Despite the questions that can be raised about the reliability and validity of their assessments, the recommendations made by mental health professionals appear to have a very strong influence on judicial dispositions. The influence may be so strong that both evaluators and *guardians and litem* often serve not only as fact finders but also as de facto decision-makers. The same is true of mediators who make custody recommendations when parents fail to negotiate a settlement in mediation (see Chapter 6). In all three cases, the professional role is tantamount to that of an arbiter. Perhaps the less formal arbitration role of these new actors in custody disputes is a useful one, but whether or not they should serve such a crucial role is in need of further, explicit clarification in the law.

Children's Custody Preferences

Children themselves also have come to be more involved in adversary custody proceedings in recent years. There is some intuitive appeal in having children present testimony in proceedings about their future best interests. In fact, some have argued that children benefit from being given control over the custody decisions that may dramatically affect their lives (Melton & Lind, 1982).

Control has many psychological benefits, but the benefits are not ubiquitous. Research on learned helplessness, for example, indicates that internal attributions of control over *positive* events are related to better mental health, but internal attributions of control for *negative* events are associated with more mental health problems, particularly depression (C. Peterson & Seligman, 1984). Having to choose between one's parents is likely to be seen by many children as a negative event, thus having control over this particular decision may not improve their mental health.

The wishes of children with respect to custody must be carefully considered, of course, but children who have strong preferences are likely to make them known. It may be helpful for children to have advocates to help them express their wishes, but children who have a strong preference usually have a staunch ally in the family. The parent with whom they want to live is likely to be highly supportive and highly motivated to communicate the children's preference to anyone and everyone involved in custody decision-making.

When children's preferences are not clear, asking children to state a preference may be exactly the wrong approach. If being caught in the middle of their parents' conflict is a major source of their distress, then soliciting children's opinions as to who is their preferred custodian is hardly a solution to this dilemma. In such a circumstance, children are asked to make a decision that the numerous adults involved in a custody dispute could not make themselves. Rather than being given a right to control their own future, children may be given an unwanted and developmentally inappropriate responsibility when they are asked to state their custody preference. In married families, it is the responsibility of parents, not of children, to make such important decisions. Perhaps separated and divorced parents can and should accept the responsibility to make decisions concerning the future best interests of their own children, despite their own conflicts and their own pain.

Calls for Reform of Adversary Procedures

Court hearings where some or all of these various representatives for the children formally present their evidence are distasteful to many lawyers and to many judges (Catania, 1992; Landsman & Minow, 1978). Fortunately, formal custody hearings are relatively rare, as noted earlier. However, the threat of litigation can pervade the adversary bargaining that typically precedes an out-of-court settlement. The gathering of damaging evidence may be alluded to during the negotiations, for example, and many agreements are reached on, or at least near, the courthouse steps.

Dissatisfaction with custody hearings themselves remains widespread, despite the procedural innovations introduced by *guardians ad litem*, mental health professionals, and children's testimony. One reason for the continued dissatisfaction is that all of the procedural reforms have taken place within the context of the adversary system. Adversary procedures are accused of being unnecessarily divisive for parents who must maintain some type of future relationship (Catania, 1992). The system also is said to be overly invasive and paternalistic, intruding on family matters and removing the responsibility for determining children's best interests from the parents to the state (Mnookin, 1975). Finally, the settlement of custody disputes in the legal system is expensive, not only for parents, but also for the state, which must process large numbers of custody cases (Mnookin & Kornhauser, 1979).

Such dilemmas have been recognized by many practitioners and commentators. Some have even suggested that custody should be determined by the flip of a coin (Elster, 1987). According to this view, adversary custody disputes are so harmful that any determinative alternative that circumvents them, even a random one, is preferable to existing methods. Others have suggested that new procedures for resolving custody in the adversary system are not needed. Instead, what is needed is a new premise for dispute resolution. Mediation is the most prominent of these alternatives, one that is based on a theory of cooperative dispute resolution.

MATCHING OF DISPUTES AND DISPUTE RESOLUTION PROCEDURES IN THEORY

Although mediation may be preferred to the adversary settlement of custody disputes in many cases, it is not uncommon for naive or overzealous comparisons to be made between alternative forms of dispute resolution. In particular, many debates about cooperative versus competitive approaches to dispute resolution take the form of arguments about which approach is best in a global sense. It increasingly has been recognized, however, that there is no single "best" approach. Rather, the selection of the better method depends upon the nature of the dispute, the relationship between the disputants, the balance of power between them, and the allocation of decisional and/or procedural control (Goldberg et al., 1985).

Nature of the Dispute

As game theory illustrates, the question of whether the dispute is a zero sum or a positive sum issue is of basic importance to the choice between competitive versus cooperative methods of dispute resolution. Cooperation is necessary to achieve optimal joint outcomes in positive sum disputes, but cooperation can be exploited in zero sum disputes. Thus, competitive negotiations are preferred in this latter circumstance. A problem, however, is that many real life disputes are difficult to classify into these two categories. Every zero sum dispute can be framed as a positive sum conflict, for example, if transaction costs are considered to be a part of the outcome. That is, if the cost of conflict resolution (e.g. lawyer's fees) is factored into the outcome, then all zero sum disputes become positive sum disputes. Both buyer and seller would benefit from eliminating the transaction cost of a real estate agent's commission, for example, as implied when houses are listed "for sale by owner."

On the other hand, optimal joint outcomes are easily identified when they are fixed in a prisoner's dilemma game, but they are not so readily apparent in many real life disputes. Mediators and parents do not know with certainty that a particular custody arrangement is the best one for the children, for example. Clearly, their task would be much simpler if this could be known. Thus, much of the success of cooperative dispute resolution depends on the ability of all involved to invent and recognize win–win possibilities.

Ongoing Relationship

Whether the disputants will have an ongoing relationship is another issue of great importance to the choice between competitive versus cooperative dispute resolution. Both theory and practice indicate that competitive approaches are preferred when there will be no future relationship between the disputants, while cooperative approaches are preferred when there will be an ongoing relationship. These conclusions have been elegantly demonstrated in simulations run by game theorists, who have shown that selfishness can be served by cooperation given a positive sum conflict and the opportunity for ongoing interaction (Axelrod, 1984). It is equally clear, however, that the individual's interests are served by competition, not cooperation, when future interaction will be absent (Axelrod, 1984).

The theoretical and experimental findings with respect to an ongoing relationship are mirrored in the major practical applications of cooperative dispute resolution procedures. Mediation and other forms of cooperative dispute resolution are much more likely to be used for conflicts in which the disputants do have an ongoing relationship. These include family, neighborhood, labor-management, environmental, and international disputes (Goldberg et al., 1985).

Power Imbalances

The balance of power between the disputants is a third issue that is important to the choice between cooperative and competitive dispute resolution. Many commentators have suggested that cooperative dispute resolution is only appropriate when the disputants' power is relatively balanced, whereas formalized competitive settlement procedures are better suited for balancing power when it is unequal. In fact, the ultimate procedural goal of the American legal system is to balance power between the weak and the strong. This theoretical goal certainly is not always fulfilled in practice (Menkel-Meadow, 1984), but it clearly is more adequately achieved in formal adjudication than in informal mediation.

Safeguards against Imbalances

In the custody context, it has been argued with particular vehemence that there are substantial power imbalances between men and women, and that an adversary approach to custody disputes therefore is necessary (Fineman, 1988; Grillo, 1991). Some of the specific issues in this debate are discussed in Chapter 8, where gender differences in my own research are discussed, and in Chapter 10, where mediation is considered from a broad, social perspective. Irrespective of the specifics of gender issues, however, it is clear that cooperative dispute resolution is more vulnerable to exploitation by one side. For this reason, mediators have developed various procedural safeguards to guard against power imbalances.

The first safeguard involves screening cases. A history of family violence is one important consideration in screening cases that may be inappropriate for mediation (see Chapter 6). A second means of addressing power imbalances in mediation is through the use of various tactics. The mediator's ability to control conflict and his or her skill at uncovering hidden issues can contribute substantially to balancing power in the process, for example. Perhaps the most important mediator tactic is the simplest one, however. Mediators retain the right to end mediation themselves. Dramatically unbalanced power or dramatically unfair negotiations are legitimate and essential reasons for mediators to end the process.

A third means of addressing power imbalances perhaps is the most important procedural safeguard. Mediators should strongly urge their clients to retain an attorney who will offer them an independent, adversary review of their agreement before it is signed. By so doing, the same procedural safeguards and substantive advice are available to parents who reach custody settlements through mediation as are available to parents who reach settlement through attorney negotiations.

Procedural and Decisional Control

Control is another very important difference between mediation and adversary settlement (Thibault & Walker, 1978). In mediation, parents retain complete control over the decisions that are reached and much control over the procedures used to reach them. Mediators guide the process, and they often suggest possible settlement options. Moreover, mediators may have subtle (or not so subtle) influences on the partners' decisions. Nevertheless, parents alone decide the arrangements they will make for rearing their children in mediation. Mediation ends if they cannot or will not agree.

Former partners control both procedures and decisions less directly when they are reached through attorney negotiations. Unlike mediators, attorneys have a clearly defined role in advising their clients about more and less favorable settlement options, particularly about how proposed settlements compare with likely judicial decisions. In fact, perhaps the most influential legal theory of attorney negotiations suggests that their outcomes are strongly influenced by judicial determinations, because they take place in the "shadow of the law" (Mnookin & Kornhauser, 1978). Thus, although the decisions are always left up to the client, relative to mediation, attorney negotiations seem to lower the parents' perceptions of having decisional control.

In addition, it is obvious that decisional control is completely given up by separated and divorced partners who enter litigation. When they go to court, parents hand over the responsibility for making major decisions about rearing their children to a third party, the judge. Much procedural control also is lost by parents who litigate, at least relative to the less formal procedures of mediation and out-of-court attorney negotiation.

Research on procedural justice demonstrates that decisional and procedural control are extremely important to party satisfaction with dispute settlement. Even when they lose a dispute, parties are more satisfied with this unwanted outcome when they feel that they have had greater procedural control (Lind & Tyler, 1988). In my research on mediated and litigated custody disputes, parents were found to be more satisfied with the outcome when they felt that they had the more decisional control over it. This was true for men and for women, and even for parents who felt that they had lost what they wanted. In fact, decisional control was found to be a significantly *more* powerful predictor of satisfaction for those who lost rather than won their disputes (Kitzmann & Emery, 1993). Finally, consistent with theoretical analyses, parents who mediated felt that they had more control over the decisions that were reached than did parents who litigated their custody disputes (Kitzman & Emery, 1993).

SUMMARY

The anger that many partners legitimately feel as a result of separation and divorce often propels them to want to fight for their "rights" rather than to cooperate in determining postdivorce parenting plans. Adversary settlement therefore is appealing emotionally, and it clearly is the most effective means of protecting each party's individual interests when there is a zero sum dispute and no likelihood of future interaction. Theoretical analyses indicate that competitive procedures result in suboptimal outcomes when positive sum settlements are possible, however, as well as when the disputants will interact in the future. Because win–win possibilities are clearly in the best interests of the child, and because mothers and fathers must maintain some sort of a relationship following divorce, there are substantial reasons for exploring postdivorce childrearing options in a cooperative forum. One problem with attempts at cooperation, however, is that one side may attempt to exploit the other. Thus, it is necessary to build in procedural safeguards to protect each side from dramatically unbalanced outcomes in mediation. Of these, perhaps the most important is attorney review of mediated agreement.

CHAPTER 6

Negotiating Agreements I
Determining Policies and Conducting the First Session

B ecause mediation is based on a different set of assumptions about dispute resolution in divorce, part of the task of negotiating a custody agreement is completed before the disputing parties step into the mediator's office. The very existence of mediation programs conveys the essential message that cooperative coparenting is an important goal for former spouses who remain parents. Mediation also offers separated and divorced parents a forum for communicating about their children. The simple but essential act of bringing parents to the bargaining table is an additional step toward negotiating a custody agreement. Finally, mediation often encourages attorneys to become less adversarial in their out-of-court negotiations. Thus, mediation facilitates the task of negotiating a custody agreement by influencing the bargaining of divorce lawyers.

Although such structural benefits of mediation are essential to recognize, the individual mediator's skill clearly affects whether or not parents are able to negotiate a custody agreement. Mediation sessions often are affectively charged, and the former partners' interactions can be full of hidden meanings. Even the most talented mediator cannot always contain the partners' understandable anger. They are losing a marriage, a lifestyle, a standard of living, and perhaps their children. Surely, these losses entitle former spouses to feel some anger. Still, mediators must manage the partners' expression of their animosity, or the mediation process will fail. Of course, mediators also must work toward reaching a substantive agreement in a short period of time. Clearly, the task of managing intense emotions while negotiating a custody agreement demands much skill.

Some skills are a matter of individual style, personality, or preference, but commonalities can be abstracted in the practice of mediation. This chapter and the following one outline some of the common themes that I have developed from my work as a practicing mediator. Similar strategies used by other mediators also are discussed in these chapters. Much of the material found here is an elaboration of a treatment manual describing the approach used in research on short-term, comediation in a court setting (Emery, Shaw, & Jackson, 1987). Details are also interjected from my experience mediating alone in private practice over longer periods of time. The setting can affect the dynamics of mediation in ways that often are important. Private clients typically are more educated, affluent, and motivated to mediate than are parents seen in a court program. The powerful authority of the court is missing in the private practice setting, however. Despite these differences, the basic outline of conducting mediation remains the same in public and private practice.

The emphasis in the present chapter is on setting the stage for mediation and on conducting the first, critical mediation session. The policies and procedures adopted by a mediator or mediation program are essential both to the negotiations themselves and to the acceptance of mediation by the legal community. Thus, the stage for mediation must be set with great care. One major task of the first mediation session is to define the specifics of the partners' custody dispute in some detail. A second task is to redefine the dispute as a problem of communication between the parents, not just as an abstract legal debate.

SETTING THE STAGE FOR MEDIATION

Divorce or custody mediation was virtually nonexistent in the United States before the middle of the 1970s. Although the number of programs exploded during the 1980s (Myers, Gallas, Hanson, & Keilitz, 1988), mediation is still a relatively new concept in many communities. Because of this, public education often is the first, crucial step in setting the stage for a mediation program. The public at large typically must be given general information about children's adjustment to divorce, child custody, and divorce mediation. The professional community also often needs to be given such general information. All members of the professional community must be informed about the specific policies of a local divorce mediation service.

Cooperation with Attorneys and Judges in Developing Policies

Although it is important for mediators to reach mental health professionals with educational efforts, it is essential for mediators to be in contact with members of the local bar. Contrary to what many mediators believe, the majority of attorneys are receptive to the idea of mediation, especially when it is limited to custody disputes. In fact, attorneys often become advocates for well-run custody mediation programs.

Lawyers are likely to raise many questions about the specific policies and procedures adopted by a new mediation program or practice, however. Basic questions include who will be referred to mediation, what disputes will be negotiated there, how agreements will be drafted, and whether mediation will remain confidential (Emery & Wyer, 1987b). Mediators who are establishing a new service or altering an existing one can learn much from having to answer these and other questions raised by members of the bar. Moreover, the service that a mediator offers can be improved substantially as a result of the attorneys' involvement and feedback.

Judges who preside over divorce and custody proceedings also need to be consulted about new mediation services. One reason for soliciting judicial input is that some mediation policies directly affect courtroom proceedings. These policies simply cannot be implemented without judical cooperation. For example, a mediator may want to maintain confidentiality when mediation ends without an agreement. A judge potentially can order a mediator to testify, however, even over the objections of the mediator and perhaps the parents, as discussed later in this chapter.

Another reason for seeking the advice of judges is that the support of the bench can be a boon to a mediation service. Judicial support is critical to garnering the wider acceptance of a new mediation program among the general public and especially among the members of the bar. (Trial lawyers are not eager to disagree with the judges who hear their cases.) Fortunately, judges often are strong advocates of mediation from the outset. As noted earlier in the book, judges often see that children are caught in the middle of their parents' conflicts during custody disputes. Mediation also is attractive to judges because it promises to reduce backlogged court dockets. Thus, for a variety of reasons judicial support often is the linchpin to successfully setting the stage for a new mediation service.

Specific Questions about Alternative Policies

Because custody mediation is a recent social invention, a number of alternative policies and procedures continue to be debated by mediators, attorneys, and judges. Standards of practice have been drafted for lawyer and nonlawyer mediators, but many disagreements about preferred practices for mediation remain unresolved at this time. Thus, the specific issues related to mediation policies and procedures can be more readily framed as questions rather than answers. Until uniform guidelines are developed, these questions have no "right" answers. In consultation with the bench and the bar, individual mediators and mediation programs must develop answers—clear policies and procedures—that fit the needs and preferences of their locality. Some key questions and alternative answers are outlined in the following subsections.

What Issues Will Be Mediated?

Other than the grounds for divorce itself, there are four legal issues that must be addressed in a divorce agreement: property division, spousal support, child support, and custody/visitation (see Chapter 4). These four issues can be reduced to two main topics: money and children. *Custody mediation* is limited to negotiating children's issues, specifically residence and decision-making (physical and legal custody). Child support sometimes is included in custody mediation, but determining child support has become a much more routine matter since the implementation of support schedules (see Chapter 4). *Comprehensive mediation* includes disputes about the children, but it also incorporates the financial issues of spousal support, property division, and child support. Comprehensive mediation also may be used with childless couples or couples who have grown children.

Many of the arguments for limiting mediation to custody disputes have been alluded to in earlier chapters. The essential point made by this side of the debate is that adversary settlement is destructive to children whose best interests are supposed to be paramount in custody disputes. Parents are free to choose how they will save or spend their money (excepting child support), but the protection of children is a broader concern. In short, there are more rationales for changing the adversary system for resolving custody rather than financial disputes in divorce. A second argument in favor of custody mediation is that most mediators are mental health professionals who have expertise relevant to custody, but no special skills related to financial matters in divorce. Attorneys, in contrast, typically have expertise in financial matters, but they are not trained in the psychological aspects of divorce and child custody.

Support for comprehensive mediation is based on the observation that disputes about money and the children often are intertwined. Because of this, it can be difficult, sometimes impossible, to address custody separately. The simplicity of resolving disputes in a single setting also is seen as a benefit of comprehensive mediation.

Currently, custody mediation is practiced far more commonly than comprehensive mediation, particularly in public settings (Emery & Wyer, 1987b; Myers et al., 1988). Custody mediation also seems to be preferred by members of the bar. Attorneys often concede that mental health professionals are more skilled in the psychology of divorce custody, but they emphasize the lawyer's expertise about financial disputes in divorce. Comprehensive mediation has been rated very positively by clients (Kelly, 1989), and many lawyer and nonlawyer mediators offer comprehensive mediation as a part of their private practices. Nevertheless, it is likely that almost all public mediation will continue to be limited to custody disputes (Emery & Wyer, 1987b).

Should Mediation Be Voluntary, Discretionary, or Mandatory?

Mediators have little or no direct control over whether mediation is voluntary, discretionary, or mandatory. Mediation programs that have no connection with a court obviously must work with clients who seek the service on a voluntary basis. Public or private programs that receive court referrals also may be voluntary, but discretionary referrals may be ordered by a judge on a case-by-case or jurisdiction-by-jurisdiction basis. Finally, an attempt at public or private mediation may be made mandatory by state law or local court rule.

While the power to make mandatory or discretionary referrals is controlled by judges and/or state legislatures, mediators must be aware of and educate others about the meaning of these alterative procedures. It is particularly important to be careful in educating the public and informing individual clients about mandatory mediation. Attendance at one or more mediation session is the only thing that is or can be mandated. No one can mandate that parents reach an agreement in mediation. Access to the courts cannot be denied because of mandatory mediation or any other form of alternative dispute resolution.

What Cases Will Be Excluded from Mediation?

Even when an attempt at mediation is mandatory, some cases clearly are inappropriate for this form of dispute resolution. There are no uniform criteria for making exclusions, however. Arguments for excluding cases typically revolve around either the participants' inability to represent themselves in mediation or concerns about dramatically unequal bargaining power. Severe mental illness, mental retardation, or substance abuse often are viewed as potentially impairing the individual's ability to represent themselves adequately in mediation. While these are important considerations, it typically is uncontroversial if cases are excluded for these reasons. The potential for unequal bargaining power often is the source of vehement controversy, however. This is particularly true with respect to questions of family violence.

Child or spouse abuse both require careful consideration as screening criteria. A history of child abuse obviously is of great importance in determining custody arrangements. The intimidation of the victim by the perpetrator in mediation similarly is a major concern when spouses have been abused by their partners. Difficulties in defining and substantiating abuse greatly complicate the development of screening criteria, however, as does the possibility of false allegations of abuse.

Some mediation programs routinely exclude cases if there is a substantiated history of family violence. Because of the possibility of false accusations, an allegation alone may not be a desirable exclusion criterion, however. Mandatory mediation programs often address concerns about abuse and unequal bargaining power by allowing partners to come for separate mediation sessions. Some programs even allow a "support person" to attend the individual meeting. If a parent does not wish to continue with mediation after attending this educational session, then the first meeting is the last one.

Although there are differing opinions about how cases should be screened for mediation, there is widespread agreement about two procedures. First, mediators should retain the right to end mediation themselves if they determine that bargaining inequities are too great. Second, it should be made absolutely clear that pending charges of either child or spouse abuse are *not* negotiated in mediation. When formal charges are pending, mediation can be suspended until an independent legal determination has been made. Mediation may or may not proceed at a later date, depending upon the outcome of the legal hearing.

Should Mediators Evaluate the Content of Agreements?

Mediators are responsible for directing the process of dispute resolution, but a guiding principle is that the parties, not the mediators, are responsible for determining the content of agreements. In the previous paragraph, however, it was strongly indicated that mediators should retain the option of ending mediation when it is grossly inequitable. These two policies of neutrality and balancing inequities are at odds with one another. A mediator cannot decide whether or not to withdraw from a case without evaluating an agreement. Thus, mediators either must accept any agreement that is negotiated by the parties, or they must recognize that neutrality has limitations in mediation.

The latter choice is the prudent one. This is true both because of the potential for substantial inequities in mediation, and because it is impossible for anyone to be completely free from biases. Thus, neutrality is a worthy goal of mediation, though a difficult one to achieve. Mediators must examine and attempt to be explicit about their own biases. The most prominent contemporary issue is the promotion of joint legal or physical custody, options that have been embraced more readily by mediators than by trial lawyers (Emery & Wyer, 1987a; Fineman, 1988; Waldman, 1993).

Exorting mediators to recognize their biases is not the same as urging them to give up these preferences. As argued in Chapter 4 and elsewhere, mediators have been innovative in embracing ideas such as joint legal custody and detailed parenting plans. Nevertheless, if neutrality is a goal of mediation, then the content of mediated agreements must conform generally to local legal norms (Waldman, 1993). Otherwise, mediators are advocates for substantive as well as procedural innovation. Ironically, the trial bar indirectly can help mediators to recognize how their preferences compare with local legal norms. A mediator may be unaware of his or her own biases, but trial lawyers will soon discover them. Much as they shop for judges, clever attorneys shop for mediators who are likely to favor a given client's position. An equally clever mediator can discover hints about his or her own biases by noting the extent to which attorneys encourage mediation for particular types of cases.

Will Mediation Be Confidential?

When mediation ends without an agreement, a controversial question is whether or not the mediator should maintain confidentiality. Confidentiality embraces both the events that occurred during mediation and any expert opinions the mediator may have formed during the process.

Many believe that mediation is no longer mediation unless confidentiality is guaranteed. When they know the mediator can make a recommendation in court, parents may be inhibited in discussing alternative custody arrangements. Some parents may become more concerned with winning the mediator's support than with reaching an agreement in this circumstance. Mediation also can become de facto arbitration when the mediator can make a recommendation in court. The mediator's opinion may be apparent to the parents, or a coercive mediator may reveal an opinion intentionally in order to push the parents toward agreement. Such tactics can be effective in producing agreements, because the mediator's testimony can powerfully influence judicial decision-making (Chapter 4).

Coercive tactics seem to be at odds with the goals of mediation that have been elaborated in this book. Nevertheless, some mediators and judges believe that mediation explicitly should *not* be confidential. The threat of mediator testimony does encourage settlement, and early settlement can be a positive outcome. Moreover, mediators become very familiar with parents and their circumstances during the process of attempting to negotiate a settlement. Thus, they may be in an advantgeous position to make a sound recommendation.

My preference for confidentiality has been noted elsewhere in this book. An issue that clouds the question of confidentiality, however, is whether or not it can be guaranteed. A judge potentially can order a mediator to testify based on the principle of the child's best interests. Even an explicit agreement that is signed by the parents (see Figure 6.2) may not guarantee confidentiality. The court has a duty to serve children, not parents, and it therefore may determine that the agreement is invalid. The only guarantee of confidentiality is when legislatures establish that communications in mediation are privileged, as has occurred in several states. In states without such laws, the question of whether confidentiality should be offered is one that can be answered more readily than the question of whether confidentiality can be guaranteed.

What Is the Role of Attorney Review?

As noted in Chapter 5, attorney review of mediated agreements is a wise safeguard against power imbalances. In fact, this procedure can help mediators to balance the competing goals of maintaining neutrality and ensuring equity in mediation. A lesser burden falls upon the mediator to protect against inequities when each partner has an independent advocate.

A number of questions still must be answered about attorney review, however. Should the attorneys who review the agreement be cooperative or adversarial in conducting the review? Can the agreement be reviewed for both parents by only one attorney? How strongly should a mediator urge an unrepresented client to seek counsel? Several state bar associations have determined that it is dual representation when only one attorney reviews a mediated agreement for two parents, but answers to the other questions are less certain. My preference is to put the recommendation to seek counsel in writing (see Figure 6.2) and to seek a more critical, adversarial review of mediated agreements.

How Is Mediation Different from Therapy?

Some aspects of the question of how mediation differs from therapy are answered easily; others are not. Like some forms of family therapy, mediation is a short-term and problem-focused intervention that is designed to resolve a family conflict. Unlike therapy, however, the overriding goal of mediation is to negotiate a fair, acceptable agreement (Kelly, 1983). Improving family relationships or promoting mental health are not direct goals of mediation, although it is hoped that these will be indirect consequences of the procedure.

Although mediation must be limited according to the goal of negotiating an agreement, part of the benefit of alternative dispute resolution is that emotional issues can be addressed to some degree. Not surprisingly, therefore, different mediators focus more or less on psychological concerns. Some short-term approaches strongly limit the exploration of emotional factors (Saposnek, 1983); others expect mediation to proceed through several stages, some of which emphasize emotional issues (Gold, 1992); even group mediation has been attempted with some success (Johnston & Campbell, 1988). Perhaps the most practical way to limit the exploration of the emotional issues is to establish firm time limits on the process at the outset of mediation, as discussed later in this chapter.

A related issue is whether the mediator should move from mediation into therapy or from therapy into mediation. The simplest and best rule is to avoid such transitions. For reasons that should be obvious, this is particularly true for individual therapy. Such transitions also are tricky for couples or family therapy. After conducting more open-ended couples therapy, it is difficult to impose the structure demanded by mediation. This problem is compounded by the likelihood that one partner does not want the relationship to end, and therefore may feel the therapist/mediator has failed them or shifted allegiances.

Moving from mediation into divorce or family therapy is somewhat less problematic than the reverse transition. Many parents return to mediation periodically for help in renegotiating agreements or resolving other conflicts, and this reflects well both on the individual mediator and on mediation in general. Still, I prefer to construe these additional meetings as mediation, not therapy. As a result, the number of sessions typically is limited, and the focus remains on specific issues. The rationale for this position is the same as the one outlined in the preceding paragraph. Once a mediator becomes a therapist, it is difficult to become a mediator again. Because the couple may need a mediator repeatedly, it is wisest to preserve this role.

Training

Another key issue to consider in setting the stage for mediation is who the mediator(s) will be and how they will be trained. In 1988, the majority of mediators practicing in public sector programs held degrees in social work (Myers et al., 1988). The number of social workers, psychologists, psychiatrists, and attorneys who currently offer private mediation as an extension of their general practices is uncertain. There is little doubt, however, that the practice has grown among both legal and mental health professionals (Milne & Folberg, 1988).

The training of mediators is a topic of continuing uncertainty. Formal degree programs are offered by a handful of universities, and courses in alternative dispute resolution are becoming more common in law school curriculums. Still, most mediation training currently occurs in private workshops or in training sessions offered by the leading mediation organizations, the Association of Family and Conciliation Courts and the Academy of Family Mediators. Only a handful of states have developed specific regulations for the certification of mediators (Myers et al., 1988). Commonly, training requirements specify attendance for a fixed number of hours at a specialized mediation training session. Some supervised experience conducting mediation also may be mandated. Guidelines also typically require an advanced degree in the law, mental health, or social work for the certification of mediators. Thus, in its current incarnation, mediation seems to be developing as a subspeciality within several different disciplines, rather than as a profession in its own right.

Co-mediation

Co-mediation with an experienced—or equally inexperienced—mediator of the opposite sex is one creative and intensive method of training. Videotaping mediation sessions presents a problem as a training tool, because of concerns about ensuring the confidentiality of mediation sessions, including the possibility that a videotape could be the object of a subpoena in a subsequent court hearing. Thus, the peer or expert supervision inherent in co-mediation is an attractive feature. Custody mediation can be harrowing to conduct, and it is reassuring to have another mediator in the room when learning the complex skills it requires.

Co-mediation has additional benefits, the most important of which may be balancing the genders of the mediators and the clients. In the midst of a divorce, men often feel that their circumstances only can be understood by other men, and women frequently believe that they can only trust other women. Concerns about mediator–client alliances are directly or indirectly a part of all mediation sessions, and an implicit alliance along gender lines is avoided or at least balanced in co-mediation.

Co-mediation also can be of help in balancing perceived alliances in other ways. Mediators face the constant challenge not only of remaining objectively neutral, but also of remaining subjectively neutral in the eyes of both parents. This difficult task can be made easier when there is a second mediator in the room to whom a partner can turn when feeling slighted by the other mediator.

In addition to its value in balancing perceived alliances—and in preventing real alliances from developing—co-mediation has other advantages. While one mediator directs the content of the session, the other is free to observe the process. The mediators can reverse roles when appropriate; the mediator who has been more passive can comment on the process or redirect the content to an overlooked topic. Another advantage of co-mediation is that it allows the mediators to assume "good cop/bad cop" postures at times. For example, one mediator can be confrontive in interpreting problems that arise in mediation, while the second mediator deals with the resistance the confrontation creates by addressing the same issue from a more empathic stance. It should be noted that most of the interpretations offered in my approach to mediation are interpersonal, not intrapsychic, in nature. A common example is the suggestion that a couples' continued fighting over seemingly trivial matters is, in fact, a sign of their continued involvement with one another, not of their emotional distance (see Chapter 2).

The potential benefits of co-mediation are numerous, and some mediators have extended them further by not only pairing males and females but also pairing attorneys and mental health professionals (Gold, 1988; Kelly, 1989). The majority of mediators work alone, however. The obvious benefits of mediating alone include fewer logistical problems, less professional time and expense, and the absence of the need to coordinate intervention plans with a co-mediator. The co-mediation option clearly is worth considering despite its expense, however, particularly for relatively inexperienced mediators.

Time Limits

The use of time limits is a simple but critical consideration in setting the stage for mediation. The custody mediation described in Chapter 8 was short-term and time-limited, lasting no longer than six 2-hour sessions. There were several reasons for having the time limitation. One rationale was to develop a time-limited program that was practical for courts; a second was to have a set reason for ending mediation when it was unproductive; a third rationale was to take advantage of the subtle pressures to reach an agreement that are created by a ticking clock.

This last benefit of time-limited mediation probably is the most important one. The likelihood of reaching an agreement increases as the time allotted for mediation decreases. This effect of time pressure is familiar to attorneys who reach settlements "on the courtroom steps," as well as to mental health professionals who note that the final minutes of the therapy hour often are the most productive. Whether they work in a public or a private setting, mediators therefore are urged to set a time limit on the negotiations. In my experience, 12 hours is a reasonable time limit when custody, visitation, and related parenting issues are the only topics being mediated. Some mediators have suggested time limits as short as 3 to 6 hours, however (Saposnek, 1983).

Even when limits are set, the amount of time allotted for mediation always can be extended for a variety of reasons. All of the 1- or 2-hour mediation sessions may not take place on consecutive weeks, moreover, because of the parents' need to gather more information, consult their attorneys, make major life decisions (e.g., about changes in residence), carefully think through the implications of an agreement, or experiment with various childrearing arrangements for a period of time. Despite such possibilities, it is essential that time limits be set at the beginning if the stage for mediation is to be set appropriately. Time limits both are more difficult to impose and carry less meaning if they are introduced once an open-ended process has begun. If an exception is to be made, it is easier to loosen up on an existing rule than to impose a formerly nonexistent one.

Ending Mediation without an Agreement

A policy for ending mediation without an agreement also must be established from the beginning of the process. The most common rule is that both partners and the mediator each retain the right to end mediation at any time without penalty. The decison to terminate can be made after the first session or at any time subsequently. Even when mediation is mandatory, the only requirement is attendance at one session, as was noted earlier. Although this open-ended invitation to terminate mediation may appear to undermine the process, my experience as a practitioner suggests that it has the opposite effect. When the voluntary nature of mediation is conveyed, the respect for parental autonomy and the absence of coercion seem to engage parents more deeply in the process.

Setting the stage for mediation involves a number of essential considerations. The issues outlined in this section are important concerns. In fact, most of the policies and procedures outlined here bear on central legal and ethical issues in resolving divorce disputes. Mediators can find guidance in the standards of practice that have been drafted (Bishop, 1988). Many uncertainties remain about the appropriate conduct of mediators, however, and the only way to resolve these unknowns is through careful evaluation of the alternatives. How the stage is set for mediation also can have a profound effect on the dynamics of the process, as discussed in the following overview of the first mediation session.

THE FIRST MEDIATION SESSION

Unlike later meetings, the first 2 hours of mediation are highly structured in my approach to the process. The initial 2-hour session has five distinct parts: an introduction to mediation, child focus, problem definition, initial individual caucuses, and problem redefinition (see Figure 6.1). The structure is intended to allow the mediators to present some important didactic information; to reassure parents that a safe, organized framework for discussing emotionally charged issues will be followed; and to guide parents through some important emotional and substantive issues. If its goals are achieved, the disputing parents have solved few problems at the end of the first session, but they have been educated about the process of mediation and are becoming emotionally prepared to use it.

Introduction to the Mediation Process

Although the first 15 minutes of mediation are largely didactic, the session begins with a recognition of the emotions involved in coming to the bargaining table. Parents are complimented for their willingness to attempt mediation, and their feelings of pain and anger about their past and present relationship are acknowledged, legitimized, and normalized. The focus quickly becomes educational, however, as the

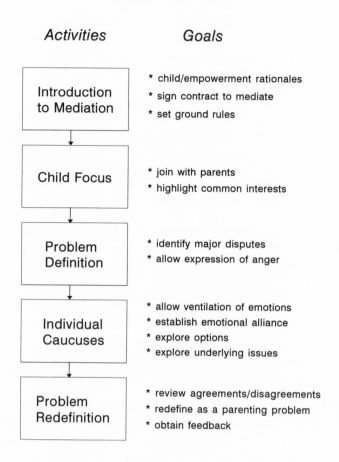

Activities   *Goals*

Introduction to Mediation
* child/empowerment rationales
* sign contract to mediate
* set ground rules

Child Focus
* join with parents
* highlight common interests

Problem Definition
* identify major disputes
* allow expression of anger

Individual Caucuses
* allow ventilation of emotions
* establish emotional alliance
* explore options
* explore underlying issues

Problem Redefinition
* review agreements/disagreements
* redefine as a parenting problem
* obtain feedback

Figure 6.1. Five parts and major goals of the first mediation session.

mediator contrasts mediation and custody hearings, suggesting that parents have the opportunity to control their own future in mediation, whereas a decision will be made for them in court. An accurate characterization of the situation for parents in a court mediation program is a statement such as, "Some decision is going to be made about your dispute. It's up to you whether you want to make the decision yourselves or ask the judge to decide for you." The mediator's statement confronts parents with the reality that a decision about custody *will* be made, and it often creates sufficient psychological reactance to motivate parents to want to make their own decisions.

A similar statement can be made to parents who are seen privately. Clearly, parents also exercise more control over their children's future when they decide issues face to face in mediation than when they negotiate them through their attorneys. In fact, a number of parents seek out private mediation, because they wish to make these decisions themselves.

Empowerment

Whatever the setting, empowering parents to determine their own children's future best interests is one of the primary rationales for mediation (see Chapters 4 and 5). It therefore is accurate to acknowledge the importance of parental control from the outset of the process. Empowerment is more than an abstract philosophy, however. It often becomes a motivating force for reaching an agreement. From the very beginning of the first session, parents are given the authority—and the responsibility—to make decisions about their children's upbringing. Divorcing partners often get caught up in a blame game. Divorce is a difficult responsibility to shoulder, and many former spouses attempt to lighten their loads by shifting most of the burden onto their mates. Mediators, however, pay little attention to the past or to who is to blame for a couple's failures. Instead, they put the responsibility for making decisions about the children's future back onto the shoulders of the two parents—together.

The Children's Interests

Although self-determination is held to be important, the principal rationale given for pursuing mediation is its potential to benefit the children. The likelihood of the children being hurt by parental acrimony often is raised, but the emphasis is on the need for parental cooperation regarding the children, irrespective of the specifics of a custody agreement. Discussion of the harm produced by conflict and the benefits of cooperation typically does not need to involve authoritative pronouncements on the part of the mediators. Most parents clearly realize that their conflicts are destructive. Despite their own sometimes overwhelming pain, many parents also sense the need for cooperation in coparenting in the future. Still, a statement such as, "I am here for the same reason you are; I'm interested in your children's emotional well-being," can remind parents of their mutual interest in their children. It also can help the mediator to ally with the parents in attempting to meet the shared goal of promoting their children's welfare.

Parents can be empowered further even as concerns about their children are raised. Divorce cannot be changed, but relationships between parents and between parents and children can be improved even after a divorce. Thus, the mediator's emphasis on coparenting and parent–child relationships contains the important message that parents can continue to promote their children's positive mental health even after a divorce. Contrary to what parents may have read or been told by family and friends, divorce does not doom their children's development. The parents still can exercise control.

Thus, the two major themes of custody mediation are established from the outset of the first session. First, the parents themselves know what is best for their own children, and they have the power to make these decisions themselves. Second, the parents' present and future actions can influence how their children will adjust to their new family circumstances.

The Mediation Contract

After the rationales for mediation are briefly explained, the topic shifts to the procedures for mediation. The process is briefly explained, and if the parents have no questions, they are asked to sign a mediation contract (see Figure 6.2). The parents review a written document that states that they are in mediation voluntarily, can end the process at any time, and are encouraged to consult an attorney independently. Most importantly, the contract states that, should mediation fail to result in a written agreement, neither parent will subpoena the mediators to appear at any hearing. (Readers should know that such contracts can be challenged. See Folberg, 1988; McIsaac, 1985; *Protecting Confidentiality in Mediation*, 1984.)

Originally, the contract to mediate was designed primarily as a protection for the mediator. In practice, however, it seems to have served the more important function of committing parents to pursue mediation in good faith. The contract to mediate benefits the parents as well as the mediators. In discussing the contract with parents, it therefore is worth pointing out that the terms ensure them that the mediators are not conducting a custody evaluation, passing judgment on the parents, or making decisions for them. Rather, the role of the mediators is limited to facilitating the process of communication in the hope that the parents can arrive at their own resolutions to their disputes.

Ground Rules

Once the contract to mediate is signed, several ground rules for the present and future sessions are outlined to the parents. Parents are

We agree to participate in a program of mediation with Robert E. Emery, Ph.D. as a means of attempting to resolve our differences concerning _____. We understand that either one of us may withdraw from mediation at any point in time, and that this withdrawal will not be used as evidence in any subsequent court proceedings. Further, by our signatures below, we each agree to waive our individual rights to call Robert E. Emery, Ph.D., as a witness at any future custody, visitation, or support hearing. We waive this right in order to maximize the potential of reaching a mediated agreement by ensuring the confidentiality of the mediation proceedings.

We understand that it is strongly recommended that we each consult an attorney in regard to our individual rights in the process and outcome of mediation.

Signed   _____

Date   _____

Figure 6.2. Contract to mediate.

told that the mediator is in charge of the sessions and that respect for that authority is expected. The parents are warned that they may be interrupted, told to stop talking, or perhaps asked to leave the room. The parents are also told that in mediation they will be asked to focus on the issues at hand rather than the emotions behind them. In addition, the mediator notes that the parents should expect to focus on the present and future rather than on the past during the course of mediation. The difficulty of following some of these rules is acknowledged, but it is made clear that the ground rules will be enforced nevertheless.

In establishing ground rules, the basic message is that the mediator is in control. This is conveyed, in part, to underscore the mediator's authority. It also is intended to reassure the parents that mediation will be a safe place for them to discuss emotionally charged issues (Coogler, 1978; Folberg & Taylor, 1984). It is extremely difficult for many separated parents to exchange ideas without becoming extremely upset, and the mediator must be both authoritative and empathic. For these reasons parents also are told that they are free to take breaks if mediation becomes overly emotional. In fact, they are reassured that failure to reach an agreement is an acceptable outcome of mediation. When parents are told that mediation is not for everyone, however, the comment often produces the paradoxical effect of enhancing the parents' desire to make it work for them.

Flexible Structure

Privately, the mediator recognizes and expects that the ground rules will not be followed fully. The process of mediation is not that simple emotionally or practically. More importantly, the rules are not intended to be rigid. Instead, they are intended to lay the framework for the mediator to redirect conversation or to short-circuit arguments later in the process. Once a rule has been established, it either can be enforced or an exception to the rule can be made if it appears to be important to do so. Without the preexisting rule, parents may feel that they are being treated unfairly when they are interrupted by the mediator, asked to focus on issues rather than emotions, or encouraged to look toward the future instead of the past. As with setting time limits, the rule carries greater weight if it is established at the outset rather than imposed in response to a particular problem in mediation.

The establishment of ground rules also illustrates the more general use of a flexible structure in mediation and in postdivorce parenting. It is also important that guidelines for mediation be explicitly established, but it is equally important for clients to learn that the rules can become more flexible once a workable pattern of communication begins to form. A parallel process of first establishing a firm structure, then gradually loosening it, is also later suggested to be a useful way of viewing the negotiated custody agreement. Once the parents develop a foundation of cooperation by closely following the mediated settlement, they may become more flexible in following the spirit rather than the letter of their separation agreement. Just as the ground rules provide a structure to fall back on when problems arise in subsequent mediation sessions, the details of the mediation agreement serve the same purpose for the parents when problems arise in its execution.

The introduction to mediation is completed by outlining a few more procedures. It is mentioned that it usually takes 6 to 10 hours for parents to reach an agreement in mediation, and that no more than 12 hours of mediation will be held in any case. Some comment about phone calls in between sessions also may be made at this time. Telephone calls are far more frequent between mediation sessions than between sessions of psychotherapy, and these contacts place demands both on the mediator's time and neutrality. As one way of addressing this issue, it is my practice to limit telephone consultations by charging for them. Although this procedure is unfamiliar to mental health professsionals, it is standard practice for attorneys.

Finally, the goals for the first session are outlined for the parents. The couple is told that the mediator will work primarily with them together, but also will meet with each person separately in the first and perhaps future appointments. The parents are reminded that the mediator wants to gain information about the parents' situation to determine if mediation is appropriate for them. The parents also are encouraged to use the first session to find out more about mediation and the mediator, and to make decisions about whether or not they want to continue. Parent are told that they are free to terminate mediation either because the process seems inappropriate, or because the "fit" with the mediator does not feel right. Parents seem to particularly appreciate this last suggestion. It encourages them to be good consumers in shopping for professional services.

Child Focus

The introductory section of the first mediation session usually takes about 10 minutes to complete. During this time, parents seem to become more relaxed and less angry, sometimes even a little bored. In an attempt to create an atmosphere that is conducive to negotiation, the mediator's verbal and nonverbal behavior can be deliberate, quiet, and calm. This tactical slowdown may be particularly effective when parents seem especially nervous or agitated at the beginning of mediation. Many parents come into the session prepared to "argue their case," but they are forced to wait through the mediator's presentations before doing so. Although parents may be ready to voice their disagreements after the introduction to mediation, they are not allowed to do so quite yet. The first thing that the parents are asked to talk about freely is not their disagreements, but an area of agreement: the things they like about their children (Mumma, 1984).

The transition to the child focus begins with a statement such as, "As we discussed, a major reason for going through the stress of mediation is for your children's welfare. I would like to know a little more about what your children are like before we talk about the disagreements you are having about them." This opening surprises many parents who are preparing to air their grievances at last. In fact, the comment often leads to an animated conversation between the parents. If it is managed well, this discussion often is fun for the parents and the mediator. Parents may dig pictures out of wallets, and they can tell tales of their children's antics. The conversation seemingly reminds the parents of their common interests and history in raising their children. If this is the reaction that the question prompts, the mediator can direct the conversation to focus on the children's strengths, and commend the parents for their individual and joint success in rearing their children. In so doing, parents who may feel like failures can be reminded of their successes in raising their children.

On the process level, the mediation session becomes more open and unstructured while discussing the relatively safe issue of the children's strengths. As the discussion proceeds, the mediator can pull back from being directive, and can share a genuine interest in the children's well-being. Negative comments by either parent can be ignored or blocked until the parents engage in at least some mutual, positive dialogue regarding their children. After a few minutes, the discussion typically is brought to a close with a statement about using mediation to find a way for each parent to continue to be an effective support for the children.

On some occasions, emotions are so high that it is impossible to get parents to engage in even a brief, amicable discussion regarding their children. If divorced partners are angry enough, they can turn the discussion of any issue into a debate about who should get the credit for success or blame for failure. When attempts to find common ground about the children's strengths repeatedly fail, the child focus is ended prematurely. In this circumstance, the mediator can raise questions about whether the fighting is typical of the parents' relationship. Brief questions can be asked about the effects of such parental disputes on the children. Although in this case the tenor of the child focus is negative and unpleasant, the underlying messages are the same as when a supportive conversation takes place. The parents each are concerned with their children's welfare. Their behavior has and will continue to influence their children's emotional health. Their job is to find a way that they can assure that their parental influence will be a positive one, both individually and jointly.

Problem Definition

It is not until well into the first interview that parents finally do get to "argue their case" in this approach to mediation. About 20 minutes after the session begins, parents are asked to present their perceptions of their differences about the children. They also are asked to briefly share some ideas about the solutions they prefer to pursue. Parents are prompted to provide the information about their disputes in a highly structured manner, however. Each parent is given about 5 minutes to offer "his or her side of the story," uninterrupted by the other parent. The parent who is asked to listen may be given a pencil and pad for writing notes as an aid in maintaining silence.

As each parent speaks, the issues raised are summarized and clarified by the mediator, who uses direct probes, reflection, and empathic statements. In summarizing the issues presented, the mediator has several goals. The most important is simply to ensure an accurate understanding of the topics of dispute. The areas of disagreement that are outlined at this point typically become the major topics of discussion in future mediation sessions. Thus, the information conveyed is extremely important to gather and comprehend. This also is the time for the mediator to obtain more information about the parents' current arrangements for spending time with the children, child support, work schedules, and other practical matters that will bear on the content of later negotiations.

Another important goal of the mediator's summary is to begin to redefine the issues at hand. Part of this redefinition involves semantics, as language that is intensely symbolic is replaced with more neutral terms. Words such as "time-sharing," "decision-making," and "parenting arrangements" are substituted for terms such as "custody," "visitation," and "separation agreement" (see Chapter 4). Another part of the redefinition is more substantive in nature. This involves reframing the problem at hand. In subtle ways, the mediator hints that part of the problem appears to be the parents' inability to agree about how best to parent their children. The abstract legal dispute really is not so abstract.

The reframing of the custody dispute as a parenting problem is equivalent to the structural family therapy notion of redefining children's psychological problems as problems of parenting (S. Minuchin, 1974). It is suggested that the issue is not just a matter of custody. Certainly custody arrangements need to be determined, but the parents need to find ways to work together irrespective of the time-sharing plans they eventually agree upon. Such reframing is subtle at this point in the first session, and parental objections are not disputed. More emphatic redefinition of the dispute occurs toward the end of the first session, as is elaborated upon in more detail later in this chapter.

Anger and Arguments

The discussion of differences about their childrearing plans often ignites each parent's anger. When the prohibition against responding to the other parent is lifted, it therefore is not unusual for the discussion to become embroiled. The parents' conflict is instructive to the mediator in many ways. The parents' style of arguing with one another gives insight into their past and current relationship. Both parents may be intensely caught up in the dispute. One partner may be "hysterical," while the other is cool and reserved. The discussion may be passive or intellectualized, but punctuated with sarcastic comments. Conflict may be avoided altogether.

The intensity and topics of dispute also serve as signals about the key issues that need to be addressed in mediation. The conflict may be affectively charged and ubiquitous, suggesting broad issues in the parents' relationship. In contrast, the conflict may focus on a particular topic. Parents may have a generally cordial relationship, but they become heated about an issue that is a source of intense disagreement. In some cases, disputes about issues seemingly unrelated to custody are revealed during an angry discussion. For example, an argument about custody arrangements may quickly turn into an even more vehement dispute about one partner's callous rejection of the marriage and the other's inability to face reality.

Controlling Conflict

Although mediators must learn to control conflict and have confidence in their ability to do so, it is equally necessary to develop considerable tolerance for arguments. On the one hand, if parents feel a mediator cannot control the expression of the intense emotions that often erupt at this point in the process, the mediator's credibility may be lost and the parents' optimism may be dashed. On the other hand, if the parents feel that the mediator has not understood their feelings or allowed them an opportunity to express them, the rapport established earlier may be destroyed. When and how to stop parents from fighting therefore is a matter requiring careful judgment.

Strategies for controlling conflict range from detached listening to very firm directives to stop talking. A common initial technique is to simply observe the parents, allow them to fight, and when they finally turn to the mediator in frustration, query whether this is a typical encounter. Humor is another technique that can be effective in derailing angry interchanges, but it must be used with considerable care. Parents may feel that they are not being taken seriously, and their anger may be redirected toward a mediator who is perceived as insensitive.

Allowing Some Conflict

When conducting mediation for the first time, various co-mediators and I experimented at length with a number of methods for avoiding the fighting at this early point in the first session. We were anxious about the intensity of the conflicts, and concerned about demonstrating our ability to control angry arguments very early in the process. Over time, however, we became convinced that the confrontation at this early point in mediation actually facilitated later problem-solving.

Why this might be so is not perfectly clear. It may be that the fighting allows parents to think more clearly once their emotions have been discharged. It may be that the arguments reveal critically important information to the mediators. Or it may be that parents need to experience one more failure in their attempts to negotiate before they are fully willing to accept the structure imposed upon them by the mediation process. In any case, parents often turn to the mediator for help after such a fight, and the mediator is wise to take advantage of the parents' appeal to outside authority for assistance in managing their discussions and resolving their disputes.

Just as some partners fail to have a cordial discussion during the child focus, others do not argue during the problem definition section of the first mediation session. In these cases, parents are allowed to proceed with their even-handed discussion. It is expected, however, that most couples eventually will have angry exchanges in mediation. In fact, parents who are very calm and controlled at the beginning of mediation sometimes turn out to be either so strategic—or so firmly locked into their bargaining positions—that they refuse to compromise in later discussions. Contrary to what might be expected, mediation often seems to be more successful with those parents who initially appear to be more acrimonious than with partners who, on the surface, seem to be cooperative.

The problem definition stage is brought to a close when the arguments between the parents are brought under control, or when the partners simply reach a stalemate in their discussions. The parents' areas of agreement and disagreement are briefly summarized, and the mediator promises to address each of the issues at a later point in time. Before moving on with that task, however, the parents are interviewed individually as they have been told to expect.

Initial Individual Caucuses

In co-mediation, each parent is interviewed alone by both mediators in the initial caucus. All subsequent caucuses follow this same format. It would be a more efficient use of time to have each mediator caucus separately with each parent, but concerns about forming alliances between one parent and one mediator outweigh the desire for efficiency. If a 2-hour interview has been scheduled, caucusing with each parent alone takes place about 45 minutes into the first mediation session. If a 1-hour session is held, the caucusing is postponed until the second interview, and the parents are told in advance about the upcoming individual meetings.

When the parents are together with the mediator just before the caucus, they are truthfully told that the purpose of the caucus is to gather more information about their personal views of the disputes at hand. When the caucus begins with each parent alone, he or she is encouraged to share information that may be of assistance to the mediator in conducting the process successfully. Each partner especially is encouraged to disclose information that may have been difficult to discuss in front of the other parent, but will be of help to the mediator in guiding the negotiations. Parents also are told that information obtained in caucus will be held in confidence during the conjoint meetings, unless a parent has specifically given permission for the mediator to raise a point.

The individual caucus serves several purposes in addition to information gathering. Perhaps the most important is that it provides the parents with an opportunity for emotional ventilation. Feelings of hurt, pain, and anger often are aroused by the discussion of disagreements that immediately precedes the caucus. Although parents are allowed some opportunity for expressing their emotions, the intensity of the discussion is kept in check while both parents are in the same room. During the caucus, however, a full expression of emotions is encouraged. Thus, each parent is allowed to vent his or her feelings in a safe setting shortly after their emotions have been strongly aroused.

The caucus also provides the mediator with an opportunity to establish rapport with each parent as an individual. The mediator can feel and express empathy for each parent's emotions, but still remain neutral with regard to the issues. That is, it is possible to establish an emotional alliance with each parent, while avoiding a strategic alliance with either one. If both parents feel that they are heard, respected, and understood, they can gain some trust in the mediation process. They thereby build a small degree of trust in each other.

Underlying Issues

A bridge between the emotional and substantive purposes of the caucus is to use this time to begin to discover "real" or underlying issues in the parents' disputes. For example, what appears to be a difference about overnight visitation may prove to be a disagreement about "overnight guests" when the children also are in the home. When such an underlying issue is discovered by the mediator, it may be addressed directly, or it maybe approached more obliquely in later negotiations. The choice of tactics depends on how sensitive the issue appears to be, and whether it can be resolved indirectly or must be agreed upon explicitly.

Reconciliation Possibilities

An important underlying issue that affects many predissolution negotiations (and some postdivorce negotiations) is the possibility of a marital reconciliation. This topic typically is brought up directly in the initial caucus so that the mediator may better understand each parent's agenda. In a number of cases, both partners are uncertain whether or not they want to pursue a divorce even though they have initiated mediation. The possibility of marital therapy can be raised in such circumstances. What begins as mediation may, in fact, become marital therapy. Divorce therapy is another alternative that some parents choose to pursue instead of mediation. Unlike marital therapy, divorce therapy does not make reconciliation its primary goal. Like couples therapy and unlike mediation, the goal of divorce therapy is for the partners to express their own emotions and to better understand the feelings of their partner.

If only one partner expresses a desire to reconcile during a caucus, he or she is reminded that mediation is not intended to be marriage counseling. Whether or not the parents eventually reconcile (and a number of partners apparently do), the hope of mediation is that the parents will benefit from developing some working arrangements for their children in the meantime. In fact, this is exactly what the mediator can tell a partner who maintains a fervent desire to reconcile despite the spouse's opposition.

Of course, the mediator must maintain continued sensitivity to one partner's hope of saving the marriage during subsequent negotiations. The issue of reconciliation may not be discussed directly in conjoint sessions, but the partner's hopes are often apparent in his or her behavior. In fact, a partner who wants the marriage to continue sometimes makes inequitable concessions in an attempt to win back the former spouse. Clearly, this is a possibility that mediators must guard against.

Support for a spouse who does not want the marriage to end typically is best offered in individual caucuses. As noted earlier, the leaver is likely to be more eager to negotiate a separation agreement. Thus, the spouse who is still attached to the marriage may come to resent and attempt to undermine mediation. These feelings and tactics can be acknowledged far more tactfully in caucus than in joint sessions. As mediation continues, individual caucuses also may be needed to help the left partner cope with the increasing awareness that reconciliation fantasies are, in fact, just fantasies. A referral for individual therapy often is appropriate at this time.

Overlapping Options

The fact that many seemingly straightforward legal issues in reality are symbolic reflections of underlying emotional concerns is one reason why mediation can be a useful forum for negotiation. Of course, there are important substantive issues to address in mediation, and these areas of dispute are the major topic of the initial caucus. The details of the parents' differences on the specific childrearing (and perhaps financial) issues are explored further in the initial caucus, and each parent's ideas in regard to potential solutions also are explored in some detail.

The mediator asks about each parent's own hopes for a settlement, and it also is essential to obtain information about their attorney's advice. Strategic behavior on the part of attorneys may be uncovered in this way. In many cases, however, it becomes clear that the lawyer is much more realistic about likely outcomes than is the parent. In fact, a mediator may encourage a parent who is being especially intransigent and unrealistic to consult his or her lawyer about what would happen if the case proceeded to court. In so doing, the mental health mediator avoids the unauthorized practice of the law, and the lawyer mediator avoids dual representation. At the same time, the parent is likely to be confronted with a bit of reality delivered from a credible source —their own attorney.

It is not unusual for a mediator to discover an overlap in the two parents' positions while exploring potential solutions with each parent independently in the caucuses. An acceptable compromise solution becomes immediately apparent. Discovering such overlap is, in fact, one of the main reasons for conducting the caucuses. If they have engaged in positional bargaining to this point, each parent often is unaware of the overlap before the beginning of mediation (see Chapter 5). Knowledge of overlapping positions obviously is of critical importance, but the mediator must use it cautiously. Confidentiality has been promised, and the range of overlap may still leave considerable room for negotiation.

It is also common, of course, for the mediator to discover no overlap in the parents' positions during the initial caucus. Still, there are always some points of agreement that can be uncovered based on the joint and individual discussions that have taken place to this point in the first mediation session. With great care taken to protect the confidentiality of the individual caucuses, the parents' areas of agreement and disagreement are reviewed during the problem redefinition section of the first mediation session.

Problem Redefinition

The first mediation session ends with a review and redefinition of the substantive differences that have been raised up to that point. The review is based primarily on information obtained during the problem definition discussion. Thus, in a 1-hour initial session, the problem redefinition can occur without the caucuses. In reviewing the disputes, differences between the parents are explicitly acknowledged as being substantial and important. Areas of agreement are highlighted. The goal of this emphasis is to note the parents' common interests and to convey at least some optimism about reaching a resolution.

After the areas of agreement and disagreement are reviewed, it is suggested that the parents' inability to negotiate their differences is the problem of paramount importance. The parents' inability to resolve their problems is noted to be the most basic issue that must be addressed and hopefully changed. This redefinition or reframing of the dispute may take the form of a general suggestion that the parents need to find a way of communicating that allows them to resolve their disagreements. Depending on what has occurred earlier, however, the redefinition may be more direct, specific, and painful to hear. For example, it may be forcefully stated that it appears to the mediator that each parent is attempting to hurt the other through the children.

Whether the feedback is gentle and general or confrontational and specific, the discussion of the parents' differences can be balanced with a return to the optimistic portrayal of their ability to control their own future. There are always many areas of agreement, even when custody is disputed with rancor. Neither the parents nor the mediators can afford to lose sight of this fact. The parents may have irreconcilable differences in their relationship, but they nevertheless have resolved many differences about parenting in the past. They have the opportunity to do so again in the present and in the future. As is always the case, part of the job of being a good parent is making some personal needs and emotions secondary to those of your children.

As the first session is coming to a close, the mediator can ask the parents for feedback about the accuracy of the summary of agreements and disagreements, as well as thoughts about the problem redefinition. Differences in perception can be briefly clarified or simply acknowledged at this time. The mediator can then ask the parents if they wish to continue with mediation. If they are at all hestitant, the parents can be encouraged to mull the decision over for a few days. A second appointment is scheduled, but the parents are told that they are free to cancel it for any reason or for no reason whatsoever. In considering their decision, parents are reminded that the first session was unusual. Future sessions will emphasize problem-solving far more than information-gathering.

Depending upon the family's circumstances, the mediator also may direct a brief negotiation at this point in the first session. The negotiation often takes the form of a discussion about some temporary agreement that can be implemented between the first meeting and the next scheduled session. A visit for the coming weekend might be arranged, for example, or a united response in regard to appropriate discipline might be negotiated by the parents. This brief interchange almost always results in an agreement, because the parents are only asked to follow it until the next appointment. In so doing, the parents are given a taste of successful negotiation. Hopefully, this will foreshadow what the parents will encounter in subsequent meetings.

The first session is brought to a close by again noting the parents' laudable efforts in coming to mediation, reiterating their obvious concern for their children, and offering a directive. It is recommended that they refrain from talking with each other about their disagreements outside of mediation while the process is ongoing. This prescription is designed to protect the progress that has been made thus far. If the parents do not talk outside of mediation, they are following the mediators' advice. If the parents talk outside of mediation but get into an argument, they observe the problems that result from *failing* to follow the mediators' advice. Finally, if the parents talk outside of mediation and have a fruitful interchange, so much the better.

SUMMARY

A number of policies and procedures must be carefully evaluated and implemented before mediation begins. This is essential both because these decisions involve important legal and ethical issues, and because they can substantially shape the process of mediation itself. The following are among the most important questions for mediators to transform into policy according to individualized circumstances:

1. What disputes will be mediated?
2. How will referrals take place?
3. What cases will be screened out of mediation?

4. What role will attorneys fulfill in reviewing agreements?
5. Will mediation remain confidential when it does not result in an agreement?

Mediators are wise to consult members of the local bar and especially of the bench in developing answers to these questions. In any case, it is essential to inform the legal community about final policies and procedures. In setting the stage for mediation, additional crucial decisions include mediator training, whether to attempt co-mediation, and establishing time limits on the process of mediation.

The first mediation session is crucial to the success of the process. A highly structured procedure for conducting the first session was outlined in this chapter. The major sections of the first session include (1) an introduction to mediation that has the goal of setting ground rules for the meetings; (2) child focus, a time when parents are asked to share information about their children's strengths; (3) problem definition, when disputes are outlined and arguments between parents often erupt; (4) individual caucuses with each parent, which offer the mediator the opportunity to explore the range of possible solutions and to uncover underlying issues in the parents' relationship; and (5) problem redefinition, during which time the mediator reframes the custody dispute as a problem in the parents' ongoing relationship. These procedural and psychological tasks help to set the stage for substantive and focused problem-solving in subsequent mediation sessions.

CHAPTER 7

Negotiating Agreements II

Focusing on Issues, Brainstorming Options, and Drafting Parenting Plans

T he first mediation session gives parents a chance to voice many of their concerns, become more aware of issues that underlie their disputes, and gain confidence in the mediation process. The first meeting also helps to prepare parents emotionally for the problem-solving that will occur in subsequent mediation sessions. Hopefully, the parents begin to feel empowered, to recognize the importance of disentangling the children from parental conflicts, and to look a bit more toward the future rather than the past. Having acquired some knowledge about the specifics of the dispute, the individuals involved, and the nature of their relationship, the mediator also is ready to begin more detailed negotiations after the highly structured first session.

The second and all subsequent mediation sessions are much less structured than the initial session. The responsibility for the discussions rests increasingly with the parents and less with the mediator as the negotiations proceed. Although the meetings are less highly structured, common process themes and substantive topics do characterize the middle and later phases of mediation. The process themes discussed in this chapter include separating issues from emotions, brainstorming alternatives, identifying interests through evaluating options, and experimenting with parenting plans. The substantive focus is on the topics that eventually form the content of the separation agreement. These include legal custody (decision-making), physical custody (residence), parenting rules, methods for coparental communication, financial matters (at least those related to the children), and procedures for resolving disputes and/or renegotiating the agreement in the future.

As mediation nears an end, the focus shifts to the details of drafting, reviewing, and implementing the written agreement. In addition to this important activity, common process concerns often arise as an agreement is about to be reached. For example, a minor dispute may escalate into a major conflict that threatens the entire agreement as mediation is about to come to a close.

The process and substance of negotiating custody agreements are discussed in this chapter. The topics are illustrated with vignettes from case histories, and specific mediator strategies and alternative substantive settlements are presented in some detail. The goal is to convey the range of differing experiences in mediation as well as some common themes across individuals.

PROCESS ISSUES IN THE MIDDLE MEDIATION SESSIONS

A number of prominent mediators have elaborated on themes that characterize their approaches to negotiation in mediation (Bienenfeld, 1983; Coogler, 1978; Haynes, 1981; Irving, 1980; Johnston & Campbell, 1988; Kressel, 1985; Lemmon, 1985; Moore, 1986; Saposnek, 1983). Although each technique is unique in style or focus, a remarkable similarity is found across these diverse systems of mediation. The common themes perhaps have been characterized most clearly, and certainly most popularly, by Fisher and Ury (1981) in their influential book, *Getting to Yes*.

Fisher and Ury (1981) offer a four-phase model of "principled negotiation." In their terms, the tactics of principled negotiation involve (1) separating the people from the problem; (2) focusing on issues, not positions; (3) inventing options for mutual gain; and (4) using objective criteria to evaluate options. In brief, these four phases refer to the mediator's attempt to help the disputants to view their disputes more objectively; to focus on their broader goals rather than their fixed negotiating positions; to be creative in considering possible alternative avenues of resolving the dispute; and to evaluate alternatives based on objective and clearly defined criteria.

While unaware of Fisher and Ury's (1981) approach, I initially conceptualized the process of negotiation in mediation in terms of the general problem-solving model (D'Zurrilla & Goldfried, 1971). The problem-solving model includes the steps of (1) identifying the problem, (2) brainstorming alternatives, (3) evaluating possible solutions, (4) selecting and implementing one alternative, (5) evaluating the outcome, and, finally, (6) returning to the beginning of the iterative process if the selected outcome proves to be unsatisfactory. After practicing as a mediator for a number of years and reading the work of other mediators (much of which did not exist when I began mediating in 1981), it became clear that the problem-solving model shares a great number of similarities with other methods of mediation, particularly Fisher and Ury's (1981). Thus, while the present overview of the process of mediation relies primarily upon my preferred terminology and intervention strategies, these similarities should be noted (see Figure 7.1).

Focusing on Issues instead of Emotions

The first step in the problem-solving model is to identify the problem objectively—a goal similar to Fischer and Ury's (1981) objective of separating people from their problems. Both approaches attempt to keep personal feelings from intruding on negotiations. Both also assume that problems can be resolved more readily if they are viewed more dispassionately.

In my approach to mediation, much of the first session is designed to facilitate this important goal of focusing on issues rather than emotions. Emotions are recognized and legitimized, but issues are highlighted as the focus of mediation. Indeed, issues rather than emotions are urged to be the focus of the parents' future relationship as partners in the business of parenting their children. In subsequent sessions, the mediator frequently can ignore the emotions that surface by redirecting the discussions back to substantive topics. This may be accompanied by an empathic statement and a reminder about the limited goals of mediation. Such redirection is accepted more readily when a parent feels understood by the mediator. Thus, the emotional alliance established in the first session can be critical to subsequent negotiations.

Despite the focus on issues, it often is necessary to unearth underlying emotions, offer interpretations, or encourage the expression of feelings in later mediation sessions. The goal of these interventions is not therapeutic, however. Rather, as with the first session, the goal is to prevent strong emotions from clouding substantive discussions by allowing the parents' feelings to be ventilated in a controlled manner. In so doing, it is essential that the discussion of emotional topics is limited both in frequency and length. Some people will refuse to focus on the issues at hand if the mediator fails to enforce ground rules. Others may give up on the process if it begins to seem more like therapy than mediation.

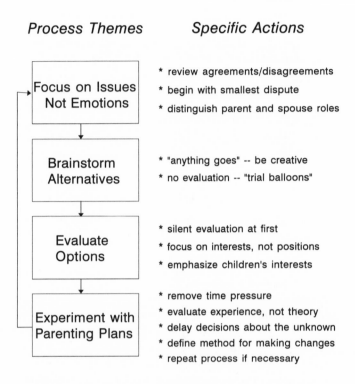

Process Themes   *Specific Actions*

Focus on Issues Not Emotions
* review agreements/disagreements
* begin with smallest dispute
* distinguish parent and spouse roles

Brainstorm Alternatives
* "anything goes" -- be creative
* no evaluation -- "trial balloons"

Evaluate Options
* silent evaluation at first
* focus on interests, not positions
* emphasize children's interests

Experiment with Parenting Plans
* remove time pressure
* evaluate experience, not theory
* delay decisions about the unknown
* define method for making changes
* repeat process if necessary

Figure 7.1. Common themes in the process of mediation.

Reviewing Areas of Agreement and Disagreement

Several strategies can be used to help parents to keep their focus on solving problems. One uniform feature of the middle sessions is to begin each meeting with a review of the major substantive topics that were discussed in the last meeting. Areas where a tentative agreement has been reached are summarized at the beginning of the session, and disagreements are outlined as part of the agenda for the present or future mediation sessions. The issues may be reviewed verbally, although they often are summarized on a spreadsheet or listed on a large flip chart that is standing in the room.

In addition to facilitating record keeping, a particular benefit of a written document, especially a flip chart, is that it frequently becomes the focus of attention during mediation sessions. The parents and the mediator may literally face a flip chart together at times during the negotiations. This often seems to serve as a metaphor for mediation. Rather than each parent always opposing the other, the list can become a shared obstacle that brings the parents and the mediator together in an attempt to overcome it.

Address Smaller Problems First

In working through the list of problems, my preference is to guide the process so as to work progressively from smaller, more readily solved problems to larger, more intractable ones. Indeed, the pattern of working from smaller to bigger problems is set in the first mediation session. As noted in Chapter 6, the negotiation that takes place at the end of the first session intentionally is framed as needing only a temporary resolution. Thus, many parents already have resolved a small dispute before they begin to address some of their bigger ones in subsequent meetings.

The style of working from smaller to bigger problems is advocated by many other mediators (e.g., Haynes, 1981), but other tactics are possible to use. "Logrolling" is one alternative. In logrolling, several disputes are considered simultaneously in order to trade off compromises across issues (Moore, 1986). Elements of logrolling are found in my approach, as the entire agreement is reevaluated as a package before it is signed. Nevertheless, the step-by-step method of moving from smaller to larger problems is preferred during these early phases of mediation. The approach almost always results in at least some minimal success, and these small victories can provide motivation and optimism about reaching a complete agreement. Even if an agreement is not reached about all of the issues, moreover, the strategy of resolving smaller issues first has the benefit of narrowing the scope of the disputes. It usually is possible for a couple to carry part of their agreement away from mediation, even if negotiations eventually reach an impasse.

Distinguish between Parental and Spousal Roles

An educational aspect of focusing on issues not emotions involves continually helping the partners to distinguish their roles as spouses from their roles as parents. In a two-parent family, spousal roles and parental roles become intertwined over time. When a couple separates or divorces, these roles must be disentangled. Even though the spousal role ends, the parental role continues. Many partners have difficulty, however, in preventing the hurt or anger that they legitimately feel toward one another as spouses from disrupting their effectiveness as parents (see Chapters 2 and 3).

A particularly important issue in helping partners to separate parental and spousal roles is to deal with one or both partners' continuing attachment to the former spouse. The problem with most parents who are seen in mediation is *not* that they care too little about each other. Rather, the problem is that they care too much and express in their feelings in inappropriate ways. That is, more couples seen in mediation are enmeshed rather than disengaged (see Chapter 2).

As has been noted frequently, the children are one of the few things that tie former spouses together, and one or both partners in an enmeshed relationship may use a dispute about the children as a deliberate or unintentional means of maintaining contact with the other. The anger expressed by one or both parents can serve as a protective mask for old emotions that may be harbored secretly, and the children provide a reason for contact that is legitimate in the parents' eyes. A fight over the children also provides a ready excuse to new lovers or new spouses who may otherwise question the need for contact between the former partners.

An angry fight about the children may not seem much like a romantic contact, but the anger expressed is informative to the former spouses. Intense emotional reactions often are interpreted as meaning that the other still cares, even when the affect expressed is anger instead of warmth (Emery, 1992; see also Chapter 2). This irrational rationality of emotions is expressed in the truism, "love and hate are not far apart," and is illustrated by one of the first mediation cases that I conducted.

> T.J. and Millie had been divorced for nearly 4 years when T.J. petitioned the family court for a custody hearing. T.J.'s petition was unusual. Rather than making a specific request for a change in custody or visitation, it simply requested that a hearing be held. The parents' court record indicated a long history of disputes. In the 5 years since the separation, their three teenage children, two boys and a girl, had lived with the two parents in almost every conceivable combination. The three children had lived primarily with their mother for a time, but all three also had lived primarily with their father. The two boys had been with their father, while the daughter was with her mother. The mother had kept the two youngest for another period, while the father had the oldest. The different arrangements went on and on, and none had lasted longer than several months. During all of this confusion about custody, both parents had gotten remarried, which added some support, but mostly further complications, to an arrangement that already was chaotic.
>
> Millie and T.J. came together for their first mediation session, which was held inside a courthouse. The courthouse was an imposing building in the heart of the community. The conference room where the media-

tion sessions were held also was impressive. The room contained a long conference table surrounded by about 20 chairs. The formal setting gave considerable authority to the mediators during what were often difficult and heated negotiations.

T.J. and Millie seemed decidedly unimpressed with the setting, however, at least as evidenced by their arguments. From the time that T.J. announced that something had to change about their custody arrangements—he was not sure what—he and Millie argued loudly and ceaselessly. They hurled accusations back and forth at one another, and waved pencils in each other's faces. (The pencils were carefully placed on the conference table along with pads of paper, so that parents could jot down ideas during their "rational" problem-solving.)

The inexperienced co-mediators could make little sense of these interminable arguments. It was obvious that the parents were working against each other in rearing their children, and it was equally clear that the children were suffering as a result. Discipline was nonexistent. If one parent tried to crack down, their efforts were soon subverted when the teenager complained to the other parent. This parent would agree that the mother or father was unfair, and he or she promised that things would have been different if the child was living with them. In fact, several changes in custody were made at a child's initiative, apparently as a way of avoiding discipline.

The mediators could see the problems caused for the children by the parents' constant bickering and subversion, and they tried numerous strategies for controlling the conflict. No technique, whether subtle and mild or strong and direct, had a discernable effect on Millie and T.J.'s fighting, however. When allowed free reign, the parents did not stop fighting out of frustration. When told firmly to be quiet, each partner would do so for a few minutes. Soon the debates began again. The arguments lasted for most of the first 2-hour session, and they dominated the second 2-hour meeting. No progress was being made, and the mediators were discouraged.

The loud, apparently angry fighting continued through the first half of the third mediation session. Then, in desperation, one of the mediators remarked that T.J. and Millie seemed to be enjoying themselves. The arguing stopped almost immediately, and the pencils stopped waving. T.J. and Millie slowly broke into smiles. They agreed that they were having fun. Their fighting in mediation reminded them of life when they were married. They liked it. It was energizing. More importantly, it proved to each of them that the other was still "hooked." After all, Millie observed, if T.J. did not care, why would he get *so* angry? T.J. grinned as Millie said this. The change in the atmosphere in the room was remarkable, and wholly unexpected by the mediators.

Following this breakthrough, Millie and T.J. spent the remainder of the third and most of the fourth mediation session discussing their past and present feelings about their marriage, their divorce, and their children. During these emotionally intense and strikingly honest discussions, it became obvious to them and to the mediators that they still cared deeply for one another. Since they had acknowledged these warm feelings directly, they no longer needed to test each other indirectly through their fighting. They no longer needed to fight about their children in order to get the angry response that meant that the other was still "hooked." Sadly, T.J. and Millie also admitted to each other that a reconciliation was impossible despite their warm feelings. They had to let go and get on with their lives.

Having addressed, if not fully resolved, their continuing feelings toward one another, Millie and T.J. were able to agree that they had to do a better job of parenting their children. The parents freely admitted that their children had manipulated them with comments about the other parent. They both acknowledged that their inconsistent parenting and chronic conflict were causing problems for their children at home, in school, and with their peers. They needed to reestablish their joint authority as the children's parents.

As parents working together for the first time since the divorce, T.J. and Millie decided to involve their children in mediation in an unusual way. They brought their three teenagers with them when they came back for the final mediation session. The children sat on one side of the long conference table, and the parents sat together on the opposite side. The mediators sat off in a corner. Rather than asking their children where they wanted to live, the two parents told the children what the living arrangements would be. They also outlined a set of rules for both homes that would be enforced from that day forward. When the parents had finished their lecture, the oldest mumbled, "I guess anything is possible." But the children looked relieved, as well as skeptical, about their parents' resumption of their role as parents.

Millie and T.J.'s two-sided attachment was atypical because partners may reconcile when they both feel invested in their relationship at the same time. If they had not both been remarried, perhaps T.J. and Millie would have reconciled. Although their circumstances were unusual in this way, Millie and T.J. revealed a pattern of interaction that I have observed repeatedly in heated custody disputes. Notwithstanding the many real differences that parents have about childrearing, intense anger often reflects the continued emotional investment that at least one partner maintains in the relationship.

One-Sided Attachments

An obvious question about one-sided attachments is how they can be maintained. After a few, perhaps many, attempts at provoking a reaction without success, the invested partner should simply stop trying. In many separations and divorces, this is what happens to the partners' relationship. However, other factors may make attachments linger. Invested partners may be so devastated by the separation or so fearful of being alone that they continue searching for signs of caring and hopes of reconciliation much longer than they would in other relationships. In other cases, the invested partner may suffer from a personality disorder and the attachment is a sign of individual psychopathology (Johnston & Campbell, 1988). Another occurrence that can prolong attachments is when the invested individual provokes a strong, angry reaction from the partner, but the reaction is misinterpreted as a sign of emotional investment. There are many very rational reasons for parents in a custody dispute to be angry at each other (Somary & Emery, 1991).

Perhaps the most common reason for chronic fighting, however, is the development of a pursuer–pursued relationship as former spouses attempt to redefine boundaries of intimacy. When the partner who is more attached (the pursuer) fails to provoke the desired reaction, he or she may step back and attempt to disengage completely from the relationship. When this happens, the partner who is less attached may turn from the pursued into pursuer. This partner may be less invested in an intimate relationship, but he or she is likely to be more invested in maintaining a friendship with the former spouse. Thus, this partner now attempts to engage the other in a friendly way, at least until he or she is successful at doing so. In a two-step that can last for years, the partners again reverse roles when the partner who is more attached misconstrues the other's attempts at friendship as a sign of intimate interest (see Chapter 2).

The Benefits of Businesslike Relationships

The mediator's goal is clear when former partners have difficulty defining a clear boundary of intimacy, as was the case for Millie and T.J. The strategy for intervening with enmeshed couples is to begin to change their mode of interaction from an intimate one to a more businesslike acquaintanceship (Ricci, 1982). The ideal of divorced parents eventually developing a more friendly relationship may grow out of a businesslike arrangement, but the process of separating parental and spousal roles takes time. The short-term objective is for the parents to develop a more formal partnership in parenting their children. The extent to which this partnership will become a friendship is an issue that will be determined by time, by the former spouses, and by their life circumstances. It will not be decided by the mediator, who must have more limited goals.

How does the mediator address the underlying issues of lingering attachments, hopes for reconciliation, and unclear boundaries of intimacy? Mental health professional mediators often find it tempting to explore and resolve these emotional issues directly. This is what happened accidently in the case of Millie and T.J. Their mediation sessions were unusual, however. In fact, such a direct exploration of emotions is exactly the wrong approach for most parents who come to mediation. It is essential for mediators to recognize the emotional dynamics involved in a custody dispute, and it is important for mediators to convey this understanding to parents. Nevertheless, it is far more productive for mediators to focus on issues rather than emotions.

In fact, focusing on issues not emotions is not only a necessary step in problem-solving, but it is also an indirect therapeutic intervention. Separated and divorced parents need to learn to define a clear boundary of intimacy. From the first session, the mediator establishes formal, structured rules for their relationship. Separated and divorced parents must accept emotional distance from one another. A business-like relationship is encouraged during mediation sessions. Separated and divorced parents must learn to separate their parental and spousal roles. This goal is defined and reinforced by mediators. In short, the manner in which parents learn to relate to one another during mediation is a model for their future relationship.

Brainstorming Alternatives

Brainstorming is a key component to my approach to mediation, as it is in the general problem-solving model and, to a lesser extent, in Fisher and Ury's (1981) approach to principled negotiation. In brainstorming, parents are encouraged to temporarily suspend judgment. They are explicitly asked to generate creative, even outlandish, solutions to their disputes. They are told to do so without evaluating the desirability or the suitability of the various alternatives, however. Simply put, anything goes during brainstorming.

Creativity

Brainstorming can be effective in stimulating creativity in solving problems in mediation and elsewhere. In one case, for example, a mother and father had a custody arrangement that was working very well from both of their perspectives and from the perspective of their 7-year-old daughter as well. The parents had agreed that the mother would have legal and physical custody, and the daughter would spend every other weekend and one evening during the school week with her father. The arrangement was working smoothly, a generous amount of child support was being paid with regularity, and the second grader was doing well personally, with friends, and in school. (With the continual focus on the most difficult cases in mediation and in clinical practice, it is easy to forget that the great majority of children and families do make such positive adjustments to separation and divorce.)

A problem had arisen for this successful postdivorce family, however. After two years of working in a clerical job, the mother had decided that she needed more education. Her plan was to move back to her hometown and get a professional degree at a university there. The move was very well thought out. It would allow the mother to be near her family, who had offered to provide her with financial, emotional, and childrearing support while she went back to school. The father also came from the same hometown, and the mother was very willing to promote her daughter's relationship with the paternal grandparents. Unfortunately, the hometown was a few hundred miles away from where the mother and father were now living.

Despite the fact that the plan was reasonable, the father was opposed to the move. He had been fulfilling his part of the separation agreement for two years, and he could not change his employment without considerable planning. In fact, the father had anticipated the possibility of a move in advance. He had included a clause about relocation in the divorce agreement, which the mother had signed. According to the terms of the agreement, relocation would lead to the revocation of custody by the mother. The legal validity of the clause was uncertain, thus making the issue all the more contentious. The parents' cooperative postdivorce relationship was deteriorating as a result of their legitimate but incompatible desires, which seemed to boil down to two alternatives: move or not move.

The brainstorming technique helped these parents to consider a much wider range of alternatives. The mother could move with the daughter but return to her present location in four years. She could move without her daughter for the same period of time, but resume custody when she returned. The grandparents could move to where their daughter was now living. The father could pay extra support for childcare and tuition, so the mother could go back to school in her present location. The daughter could go to boarding school. Everyone could move to a neutral site in a third locality. Many more silly and not-so-silly alternatives were generated in an atmosphere that was eased somewhat by the novel suggestions, but remained tense nevertheless. Playing the brainstorming game for real is very different than playing it for fun.

After a few sessions and some careful thought outside of mediation, these parents were able to arrive at an integrated solution despite the tensions that had arisen. The mother would remain in her present location for an additional year. During this time, she would take the basic courses that she needed to complete before beginning her full-time education. In order to make the schooling possible, the father would provide money for tuition. He also would take care of his daughter for a second weeknight while the mother attended evening classes. The father agreed not to oppose the mother's move with the daughter at the end of the year's time, however. In the meantime, he would have another year with his daughter, and he could begin job hunting in the vicinity of his former hometown. He had a year, not a few weeks, to find a new job. Privately, the father noted that he also had the hope that his former wife would change her mind about moving after another year. Perhaps she would even meet someone new.

It is difficult to imagine how such an integrated outcome could have been achieved outside of mediation. If the parents had discussed options on their own, they probably would not have been as creative, or their discussions might have become embroiled. The enforceability of the relocation clause in the separation agreement certainly would have been a major focus of litigation, and the decisions made in court likely would have been limited to the two outcomes that the parents had conceived initially: move or not move. With mediation the parents were able to brainstorm an option that was imperfect, but far more creative and acceptable than anything they had considered previously.

Trial Balloons

Brainstorming can open the door to creativity by encouraging people to develop novel ideas. This benefit of brainstorming holds in any problem-solving circumstance, but there are benefits that are unique to mediation. By encouraging parents not to consider the consequences of the options they generate, and to share even wild ideas with each other, the brainstorming technique provides parents with a safe opportunity for "floating a trial balloon." That is, the rules of brainstorming encourage parents to reveal possible solutions they may have been weighing, but have been hesitant to discuss openly. For example, I have had a number of parents suggest reconciliation as a possible solution to the dilemma of a custody dispute in the safe haven created by the "anything goes" rule of brainstorming. Despite the pain of likely rejection, the rule gives each partner an out, a chance to save face. The proposal to reconcile can be quickly retracted or simply ignored if it prompts little response from a partner. This is exactly what happens in most cases. Still, the rules of brainstorming are helpful in allowing partners to at least raise the possibility.

Brainstorming also can allow parents to float other sorts of difficult trial balloons. One such circumstance is when a mother does not want to assume the major role in postdivorce childrearing. Society hopes that fathers will be involved with their children after divorce, but such involvement is expected of mothers. Because of social expectations, it can be exceedingly difficult for women to admit to themselves that they do not want primary residence, let alone to suggest it their former spouses. Brainstorming allows partners to mention alternatives that they have considered secretly, but never voiced. Once the topic is broached for the first time, it can be discussed seriously and in more detail later when the options are evaluated.

Identifying Interests through Evaluating Alternatives

The third step in the problem-solving model is to evaluate the various alternatives that have been identified through brainstorming. One of the rules of brainstorming is to suspend outright evaluation, but partners cannot help but to evaluate the alternatives privately as they are raised. One benefit of the silent evaluation is that each partner has the time to consider their evaluation at some length. As they mull over an option, the partners may come up with more acceptable variations on a given solution, or they may find that an option that at first seemed unacceptable becomes more appealing as it is considered over time. For example, when it is first proposed, a plan for joint physical custody may seem totally unacceptable to a parent who wants sole custody. As he or she weighs the option, however, the same parent may see the benefits of the children having more frequent contact with both parents, as well as the personal benefit of having more free time. Thus, what seemed like a win–lose situation at first sometimes is transformed into a win–win solution as it is considered over time.

Focus on Interests Instead of Positions

Fisher and Ury (1981) discuss a specific technique that can be of considerable help to parents as they evaluate the alternatives that they have generated. In considering their options, the partners should consider their underlying interests, not just their fixed bargaining positions. A *position* is one party's proposed solution to a problem, and it usually contains strategic elements such as overstatement. In contrast, an *interest* is the underlying goal that the position is designed to fulfill. Insisting on a fixed dollar amount of spousal support is an example of a position. A desire to have sufficient financial assistance to assure that a change in residence will not be necessary in the immediate future is an example of an interest (see Chapter 5).

Focusing on interests instead of positions is an element of negotiation that is not found in the problem-solving model, but is prominent in several approaches to negotiation (Moore, 1986). Positions can cloud negotiations because they limit the range of potentially acceptable solutions that can be considered. In fact, bargaining positions often intentionally mask the underlying interests that they are designed to fulfill. Thus, when evaluating alternatives, it is of value for mediators and parents to look beyond fixed positions to examine the interests that they are designed to protect.

The children are one continuing joint interest shared by all separated or divorced parents. The child focus that forms a prominent part of the first session thus remains a theme throughout the process of mediation. If the mediator allies with anyone, it is with the children (Saposnek, 1983), and this alliance is used to push the mediation process forward when it gets bogged down. Parents may be reminded to consider the child's interest when discussing a complex, 50/50 joint physical custody arrangement; they may be asked to speculate on their children's feelings when discussing whether visitation should be scheduled or unscheduled; or, when they seem ready to give up, they may be reminded that they, the parents, can be the ones to decide what is in their children's future best interests.

Parents also can be usefully reminded to focus on underlying interests when discussing more circumscribed problems. When the focus is shifted from positions to interests, areas of agreement may be seen more readily and creative solutions often become more apparent as well. One couple I saw, for example, easily reached an agreement about the mother having sole custody. The details of most holidays also were negotiated with relatively little difficulty. The parents became embroiled, however, in fighting over whether their son should spend every Thanksgiving holiday with his father, or whether he should spend alternate Thanksgivings with each of his two parents. After fighting back and forth for some time, the parents were encouraged to reveal their interests. That is, they were asked to share the reasons behind their bargaining positions. At this point, the father stated that he wanted to establish Thanksgiving as a ritual where he and his son would visit with the boy's paternal grandparents who resided several hundred miles away. In fact, he had spoken with his mother about this possibility on the telephone several times. He had assured her that he would not agree to any plan unless it contained some such arrangement. Surprised at hearing this, the mother noted that she had opposed the option because she did not want her son to spend every Thanksgiving alone in his father's apartment. When she heard the plans, she readily agreed to letting her son be with his father every Thanksgiving. This holiday was far less important to her than Christmas, and she actually was pleased with the prospect of her son maintaining contact with his grandparents.

Criteria for Evaluation

Another helpful technique in evaluating options is to discuss the criteria for evaluating them in advance. Some mediators explicitly recommend that disputants adopt a standard of fairness before beginning to review the alternatives that have been generated (e.g., Haynes, 1981; Moore, 1986). Others urge negotiators to use objective criteria in evaluating outcomes (Fisher & Ury, 1981). These strategies are especially important to follow when negotiating financial aspects of a divorce settlement. Negotiations proceed much more smoothly once a couple agrees that their standard of fairness will be a 50/50 division of assets, for example. They also can agree to value expensive assets such as their home based on one or more objective appraisals, rather than haggling with each other over the worth of each asset.

Standards for evaluating child custody alternatives are not as clear. Promoting the children's best interests is the overriding goal, but determining children's interests is not an objective process. Mediators can provide information to parents about research findings on children and divorce (see Chapter 9) as well as information based on their own experiences. Despite this education, the responsibility for evaluating the alternative parenting plans ultimately rests with the parents in mediation. They can be reminded frequently to keep the children's best interests in mind, but it is up to them to determine those interests.

This shift in responsibility often requires mediators from a mental health background to adopt a new cognitive set. Mental health professionals assume more authority and responsibility for decision making in assessment and therapy than is typically assumed in mediation. Thus, mental health professionals must learn to give up some degree of control when they become mediators. It often is tempting to intervene more broadly or to act as the expert, but it must be remembered that the paramount goal of mediation is to encourage and respect the parents' autonomy.

Experimenting with Parenting Plans

Experimenting with one alternative, reevaluating it, and if necessary working back through all of the stages of problem solving is the final step in my approach to mediation. This iterative procedure is, in fact, basic to the problem-solving model. Experimentation can be an essential aspect of mediation, although it is discussed infrequently in the mediation literature. Implementing alternatives on an experimental basis relieves parents of the pressure of immediately arriving at the single, perfect solution to their disputes. It also gives them the opportunity to evaluate and perhaps change their parenting plan in the most objective way possible: based on how the plan actually works for their family.

A concern about experimenting with various alternative arrangements is that children benefit from achieving stability in their postdivorce family life. In fact, I have argued that both parents and children benefit when custody arrangements are stable over time (Emery, 1988; Emery et al., 1984; see Chapters 3 and 9, this volume). In practice, however, many parents apparently experiment with alternative arrangements informally (Maccoby & Mnookin, 1992), and a more formal trial period may actually add structure to this practice. Confused and embroiled couples may jockey constantly for position with their children. Often the maneuvering occurs within the confines of the same household. An agreement, even a temporary one, can allow such parents to separate physically, and perhaps it can help them to begin to separate emotionally. Even if the arrangement changes, this approach has the benefit of helping distressed parents to come to *some* agreement in the meantime. When such a temporary agreement is constructed, however, the parents must be cautioned about setting a precedent. They should be encouraged (as always) to discuss the arrangement with their respective attorneys.

The strategy of experimentation is far less difficult in some other circumstances. I have worked with a number of parents who have disputed about whether to send their children to a certain school, for example. In this situation, it often is easier for parents to agree to a temporary plan that calls for a formal review during the school year. Not only is such a plan more palatable for parents in coming to a decision, but it also is very similar to the informal compromises that married parents make on a routine basis. Considering how parents would make decisions if they were still married always offers a good point of perspective for evaluating the disputes between divorced parents.

Even longer time intervals may be scheduled for reviewing agreements about specific issues such as schooling or about global ones such as a child's primary residence. For example, some mediation agreements call for a review to take place in several years. The choice between public and private education may be deferred until elementary school is completed, or time-sharing arrangements may be scheduled for renegotiation at a particular stage of development, such as when an infant becomes a preschooler or an 8-year-old child moves into adolescence. Once again, the time schedule in these formal reviews frequently parallels the normal reevaluations that married parents conduct informally and routinely throughout their children's development.

Children, Stepparents, and Grandparents in Mediation

Mediators differ in terms of whom they include in the process of negotiation, particularly on the roles to be played by children, stepparents, and perhaps grandparents. As discussed in Chapter 4, the role children should play in custody decisions is a controversial question, whether one is considering mediation, litigation, or out-of-court negotiation between the parents' attorneys. Initially, I believed that children should play an important part in the mediation process, given that promoting children's best interests was a major rationale for attempting mediation. For this same reason, however, experience has led to a complete reversal of that position.

Instead of being given the *right* to have input into custody determinations, it seems that children who are asked about their custody preferences are given the *responsibility* to decide something that their parents cannot agree upon themselves (see Chapter 4). The implicit and explicit message conveyed in mediation, however, is that the parents share both the right and the responsibility to make decisions about their children's welfare. For this reason, I now rarely obtain children's independent input in mediation.

The same rationale applies to stepparents and grandparents. These parties are routinely excluded from mediation, not because they are unimportant, but because the responsibility for making custody decisions rests with the biological parents, not with these other adults. As important as stepparents and grandparents may be in childrearing following separation and divorce, the biological parents must assume responsibility for determining and defining the basis of these roles.

As with every rule in mediation, a few exceptions are made to excluding children, stepparents, and grandparents from the mediation process. Some teenage children have clear preferences with respect to primary residence, are able to articulate them, and can offer sound rationales for their choices. In such cases, mediation may be used to help the children to voice their opinions to their parents, particularly to the parent with whom the child does not wish to reside. The goal of the process in this case is to help the teenager to be clear and convincing, and to minimize the feelings of guilt and rejection that may be felt by the adolescent and the parent respectively.

Stepparents or grandparents also may be included in the mediation process under unusual circumstances. When these relatives are very involved in rearing the children or when they clearly are part of the reason why an agreement cannot be reached, the mediator may ask them to attend a session or two. Generally, these meetings do not include both biological parents, as one parent is likely to feel outnumbered in the presence of extended family from the other side. Rather, a session may be held that is attended by only one biological parent and his or her relatives. The goals of such meetings are to give the stepparent or grandparent some voice in the process, but simultaneously to support the biological parent's responsibility (or authority) to make decisions about their children's lives.

SUBSTANTIVE PARENTING ISSUES AND LEGAL ALTERNATIVES

Focusing on issues instead of emotions, brainstorming alternatives, identifying interests through evaluating alternatives, and experimenting with parenting plans all are important procedural strategies in mediation. Custody mediation does not occur in a substantive vacuum, however. Mediators must establish a high degree of expertise in their understanding of the legal, economic, social, and psychological aspects of divorce. This is true despite the fact that mediators wisely encourage their clients to seek independent advice on many matters from lawyers, accountants, and mental health professionals. Mediators need some expertise if only to know when to refer a client elsewhere. Ideally, a mediator should have sufficient expertise to know when outside advice is suspect and a second opinion should be sought.

In the context of custody mediation, the primary expertise required is knowledge about the various time-sharing and decision-making arrangements that parents may adopt, as well as an understanding of the common social, psychological, and legal concerns that may be associated with the alternatives. Legal issues are discussed at length in Chapters 4, 5, and 10, while psychological concerns are reviewed in detail in Chapters 2, 3, and 9. In what follows, some of the major issues are considered much more briefly from the practical perspective of how they arise and may be addressed in custody mediation.

Global Parenting Concerns

When parents separate, communication about children commonly breaks down, in part because there is no forum for discussing these issues. In order to provide such a forum, "parenting" typically is one topic listed on the agenda at the beginning of the second mediation session, and it is often the first issue to be discussed. Parenting concerns are relatively easy to address. The problems often are clear and are shared by the two parents, and the partners typically do not begin mediation with rigidly fixed bargaining positions about postdivorce parenting.

Two general categories of parenting concerns frequently arise in mediation. The first includes parenting issues that all separated or divorced parents encounter, such as developing or altering their means of communicating about coparenting. Many parents struggle with this problem, which can be solved by planned telephone calls, a brief conversation when the children are exchanged, or written notes. Another common topic discussed with most parents is the consistency of the rules that are set for the children between the two different households. The children's needs for stability and predictability are important to consider, but so is each parent's desire to be autonomous in his or her own home. Discussion of such common parenting problems provides the mediator with an opportunity to learn more about the parents and to provide them with some useful information and strategies.

Protecting Children from Parental Conflicts

A second set of parenting interventions is not universal, but unfortunately common. These involve working with the parents to develop strategies for keeping their children from getting caught in the middle of their parental conflicts. Some parents seen in mediation seem to be engaging in a tug of war, each trying to pull the children over to their side. The parents frequently fight in front of the children, either when they are exchanged or over the telephone. One parent may tell the children about all of the failings of the other, and that parent may reciprocate in kind. Inconsistent discipline can result from a failure to communicate, but it also may be a deliberate attempt to subvert the other parent's authority. Children may be quizzed about what happens in the other parent's home or told to carry inappropriate messages back and forth between households.

In circumstances like these, spousal anger obviously is intruding on effective parenting, and the mediator's alliance with the children must be made clear to the parents. As a tool in this regard, mediators can use their own reactions to the parents' arguments as both a barometer and a mirror. If the mediator is made uncomfortable by the intensity of the parents' anger or their attempts to pull the mediator into an alliance, these actions surely are distressing for the children. After gauging their own reactions, mediators can reflect these concerns back to the parents. In so doing, it is essential to acknowledge the legitimacy of the parents' anger, even as they are encouraged gently or forcefully to keep the children out of the middle of it.

Although it is important to recognize the adverse consequences of the parents' conflict, the mediator is not responsible for resolving all of the partners' issues or emotions. Rather, the overriding goal of interpretation and confrontation is to help parents to gain sufficient insight into their conflicts to allow them to move forward with the negotiations. In some cases, referrals to mental health professionals for individual or divorce therapy are appropriate or necessary for the mediator to make. Except in cases of abuse, however, the mediator's major therapeutic goal rests with the hope that the renegotiation of the relationship that is implicit in the terms of the mediated agreement will be of long-term benefit to both the parents and their children.

Residence or Time-Sharing

The review of parenting concerns and differences early in the second mediation session often lays the groundwork for subsequent discussions of residence and decision-making. The framing of legal custody as "decision-making" and physical custody as "residence" can help parents to recognize that these are *their* disagreements. They are not debating some legal abstraction that they can neither comprehend nor control. They are arguing about how they, the parents, will rear their children.

The issue of residence typically is discussed before decision-making is considered. If they already have separated, parents must have negotiated some informal residential arrangement before coming to mediation, and it is essential that the mediator pay careful attention to its details. Even if it is regarded as temporary, the initial time-sharing pattern frequently helps to determine the arrangement that becomes a part of the formal custody agreement.

I also have worked with many parents who enter into mediation prior to a marital separation. In some cases when the partners are still living together, one parent clearly hopes that mediation will become marital therapy. In this circumstance, it is essential for the mental health mediator to distinguish between couples therapy, divorce therapy, and mediation at the outset, and to reach an understanding with both parents about which process is to be pursued. Other parents who are still living together are emotionally disengaged, and they use mediation to consider alternative arrangements with care. Finally, in a number of circumstances, one parent is eager, perhaps desperate, to separate, and he or she is willing to accept almost any settlement. A number of tactical advantages accrue to the partner who is more willing to continue the marriage for whatever reasons. In order to achieve a balance, the mediator may have to slow down the process for one parent and speed it up for the other.

Hidden Agendas

Disputes about time-sharing can be extremely difficult, in part because a number of different interests or concerns may underlie them. One hidden agenda occurs when a partner opposes the end of the marriage by opposing any reasonable parenting arrangement, as has been discussed throughout this book. Underlying concerns about the other parent's living circumstances or parenting also may form the basis of a dispute about physical custody or visitation. Because both of these issues have been discussed previously, they are not considered further here.

Lack of Clarity

An issue that does need some further discussion is when the dispute about residence stems from arrangements that are poorly defined or not defined at all. When the children's schedule is open-ended, logistical problems of all types are likely to arise, and both the parents and the children can have their expectations dashed as a result. In general, my strong bias therefore is to push parents who have flexible residence arrangements to specify them in great detail (see Chapter 3).

There are two basic rationales for encouraging specificity. The most important is that children benefit from structure and predictability in their lives following their parents' separation. If the children are expecting a visit from their nonresidential parent on the weekend, it is important that they not spend time waiting for the visit to take place, only to be disappointed when it does not occur. Even when visits are frequent, very flexible time-sharing can be problematic for children, as it can disrupt their own schedules with their friends and school activities, as well as adding uncertainty to their relationships with their parents.

A second rationale for being specific about residential arrangements is to make boundaries clear in the coparenting relationship. Parents' expectations about their children's schedules typically do not match one another, and setting specific details at least clarifies their expectations. There also is less need for parents to communicate with one another if the details about residence are specified in advance. The opportunities for conflict are reduced if the need for communication is limited.

Alternative Time-Sharing Arrangements

There is a surprisingly large number of disputes about time-sharing that reflect hidden agendas about saving the marriage, concerns over parenting, or problems due to lack of clarity. Of course, many parents do have real disagreements about how to share time with their children. When parents have a clear dispute about residence, brainstorming and focusing on interests can be helpful techniques for creating new solutions. The concept of the children's best interests also can be used to frame these discussions. The objective of a residential agreement is not to "divide the child" in order to satisfy the parents. Rather, the goal is to devise an arrangement that benefits the child. An agreement is far easier to reach when both parents truly recognize their need to work together for the benefit of the children. Parents may come to see each other as potential sources of support, not parenting competitors, if they are able to put the children's interests first.

While parental self-determination is a guiding rule, the mediator often can help parents by offering some substantive suggestions. During brainstorming the mediator has an opportunity to insert ideas. In the midst of brainstorming, the mediator may make outlandish suggestions in order to encourage creativity or perhaps to confront parents about the absurdity of some of their disagreements. When the parents fail to discover an alternative on their own, the mediator also may contribute more practical options during the brainstorming phase. Mediators must not impose their preferences on parents, but active suggestions can increase the range of options being considered. The mediator's suggestions also may help both parents to save face in the negotiations, because the suggestions come from a neutral source. A list of common time-sharing alternatives is summarized in Table 7.1.

In my experience, many parents eventually negotiate a postdivorce residential arrangement that approximates their predivorce parenting arrangements (see Chapter 4). Their standard of fairness often seems to approximate earlier family relationships. It may be helpful for parents to consider this principle as they negotiate their arrangements. The principle also reminds mediators that their goal is to reestablish family stability on the parents' terms, not to create some idealized postdivorce parenting arrangement.

Education and Advice

Parents have the responsibility to make final decisions, but if neither of them plays devil's advocate, it can be helpful for the mediator to do so. It is far better for the mediator to anticipate a problem that does not arise than to fail to anticipate one that does. Thus, while mediators are not expected to provide answers, they can ask questions that are educational.

One example of standard educational advice is the suggestion that complicated time-sharing arrangements may offer more benefits, but they also are more difficult. Such arrangements call for more coparenting cooperation than do simpler parenting plans. Joint physical custody therefore is likely to create future problems for many parents seen in mediation, particularly those seen in court mediation programs. Parents who are contesting custody probably are poor candidates for joint physical custody, which should not be advocated as a compromise between contentious parents (Scott & Derdeyn, 1984). While joint custody should not be pushed on reluctant parents, it should not be discouraged for parents who are interested. Rather the pros and cons of the alternative can be discussed with parents, so that they can make a decision that is better informed.

Changes in Residence

Some of the most difficult negotiations about residence occur when one parent wants to move to a geographical area a considerable distance away from the other. In this case, creativity in regard to summer vacations, school holidays, the sharing of travel expenses, and telephone contact often is of help in bringing the parents to an agreement. One parent still may feel more like a loser, however, even when numerous practical compromises are suggested.

For some parents, these feelings are alleviated by discussions of their sense of loss, the importance of parental influence even from a

Table 7.1. Common Residence Arrangements

Weekly schedules: one primary residence

(1) Weekdays and three weekends a month with one parent; first weekend of every month with the second parent. (The weekend may be as long as Thursday evening to Monday morning, or as short as Saturday morning to Sunday evening.)

(2) Weekdays and every other weekend with one parent; every other weekend with the second parent. (This may also include a weekday visit with the second parent, for example, every Wednesday from 5 to 7, or from 5 to 8 on Thursdays prior to an "off" weekend.)

Weekly schedules: joint physical custody

(1) Weekdays with one parent; weekends with the second parent. (The weekend can be defined to include one, two, or three overnights.)

(2) Weekdays with one parent, weekends (or every other weekend) with the second parent during the school year. The schedule is reversed during summer vacation. (Some variation on this arrangement is common when parents are separated by a large geographical distance.)

(3) Saturday at 5 p.m. to Wednesday morning with one parent; Wednesday after school until Saturday with second parent. (Or similar schedules that remain the same on a week-to-week basis.)

(4) Every other week with each parent. (Two-week rotations also are common. Sunday afternoon or evening generally is the best time to make exchanges.)

Vacation and holiday schedules: important days to consider

School vacations at Thanksgiving, Christmas, and in the spring; summer school vacations; religious holidays; children's birthdays; each parent's birthday; Mother's Day/Father's Day; Halloween; Fourth of July; traditional family holidays or events.

Alternating holidays: A schedule is set, and the children alternate between residences from year to year. For example, Year 1: Thanksgiving and spring school vacation with mother, Christmas vacation with father. Year 2: Thanksgiving and spring vacation with father, Christmas vacation with mother.

Dividing holidays: Holidays can be divided in various ways, but the schedule remains the same every year. For example, Thanksgiving vacation with one parent, Christmas vacation shared (with an exchange on Christmas afternoon), spring vacation with the second parent.

Fixed holidays: Some holidays, particularly more minor ones, can be fixed because they are of more importance to one parent than the other. For example, one, two, or more weeks of summer vacation with each parent can be arranged by April 1 of each year; Mother's Day, Father's Day, and each parent's birthday can be spent with the appropriate parent.

geographical distance, the possibilities of changes in the children's primary residence in the future, and the children's best interests. For other parents, their chances of winning in court are so small that they agree to a compromise even though it is less than optimal from their perspective. For at least a few parents, however, the only solution is for a third party to assume the responsibility of making a decision about relocation. Mediation does not always result in an agreement, and getting agreements is not the overriding goal of the process. Rather, the goal is to provide parents with the opportunity to discuss their options, and such discussions can be helpful even when they do not directly result in a compromise solution.

Parental Responsibilities or Decision-Making

In addition to residence, parents also must agree about legal custody, the allocation of parental responsibilities, or, more simply, decision making. The term "custody" carries tremendous symbolic importance in the eyes of many parents. Sole legal custody may be a valued symbol of one parent's assumption of primary responsibility for rearing children or of the legal custodian's right to raise their children autonomously. Similarly, joint legal custody may be a public statement of the parents' commitment to raise their children cooperatively, or it may symbolize one parent's continued psychological connection with their children despite reduced physical contact.

Symbolism is important. It may account for much of the increase in joint legal custody in various states (see Chapter 4), and the symbolism of joint legal custody may be of particular importance in the context of mediation. I have worked with a number of parents who refused to accept an agreement that gave the other parent sole legal custody and primary residence, but they readily accepted the same residential arrangement if joint legal custody was maintained. In fact, far more joint legal than joint physical custody agreements have been negotiated in my studies of mediation and adversary settlement (Emery, Matthews, & Wyer, 1991), a finding also noted by others (see Chapter 8). Joint legal custody may have somewhat different legal ramifications than sole legal custody, but the terms generally are ill-defined in the law. In any case, it is doubtful that these subtleties motivate many parents' preferences for one or the other term. Rather, symbolism is what most often appears to be at stake.

Practical Decision-Making

For these reasons, the discussion of legal custody in mediation begins by acknowledging its symbolism, but also by noting that the term is not the most important issue to resolve. Parents may wish to consult their attorneys about the legal implications of terminology, but it is suggested that decision-making is the real issue at hand. A five-minute didactic overview can both diffuse tensions about terminology and empower parents. Many parents have difficulty understanding the implications of the term custody, but parental decision-making is a familiar concern.

In my approach, the practicalities of defining decision-making are straightforward. Irrespective of the custody label, it is suggested that the parents may want to share major decisions about their children's upbringing, but that they each will want the freedom to make day-to-day decisions without being second-guessed by the other parent. The major decisions to be shared typically are highly circumscribed. They may be limited to education (choice of schools), religious training, and elective medical, dental, and psychological care. These major decisions are contrasted with day-to-day decisions regarding which each parent must respect the other's autonomy. It is suggested that the children will benefit if the parents can be relatively consistent about rules such as bedtime, but each parent has final authority to make and enforce rules in his or her own household.

Underlying Issues

Disagreements are common during the discussion of decision-making. Sometimes the dispute is caused by an underlying interest that has been unstated or unanticipated. When parents are of different religious backgrounds, for example, one partner's insistence on sole custody (or the other's insistence on joint custody) may be designed to ensure that the children are raised according to the preferred religion. Some parents have similarly strong views about the choice of public or private schools. Although such differences may not be readily resolved, the chances of settling them are improved when all parties understand the nature of the "real" dispute.

In fact, acknowledging the existence of the underlying issue is a major step toward resolving it. In a surprising number of cases, the parents only think they disagree about childrearing. When given the opportunity to talk, they discover that they do not have a dispute. In other cases, parents are anticipating a dispute that may or may not arise in the future. In this circumstance, the conflict often can be resolved temporarily by negotiating an agreement not about the actual decision, but about how the disagreement will be resolved in the future. For example, the parents may agree to return to mediation when a child reaches a certain age in order to renegotiate arrangements at that time. Married parents continually discuss and renegotiate decisions about their children's upbringing, and mediation can be a forum where divorced parents are given the same opportunity.

Disputes about major decisions such as religion or schooling are not the only disagreements that arise when decision-making is discussed. More minor parenting concerns also may come to the surface at this point. These concerns may encompass specific issues such as a child's diet in each parent's household (e.g., vegetarian, restricted sweets), or they may involve more general issues about the coordination of rules between the homes. If such disputes do not involve some broader power or intimacy struggle (which they frequently do), one common path to resolving them is to discuss feelings of loss of control over the children with one or both parents. Each parent's direct influence over their children's lives is reduced as a result of divorce. Like the loss of parental control that occurs as children grow older, parents need to recognize and give themselves time to come to grips with this inevitability. They have no other choice.

Coparenting Communications

Another important topic to discuss about decision-making is when and how the parents will communicate about routine matters that concern their children. Weekly telephone calls can be arranged, for example. The parents can use this time to share information about medicines the child is taking; to discuss discipline, misbehavior, or the upcoming schedule of events; or perhaps even to share a few happy stories. For parents who have a more difficult relationship, written communications may be less stressful, while a routine lunch meeting may be preferred by parents who have a more cooperative relationship.

It is important to note, and perhaps discuss with parents, that the designation of a method of communication not only gives them an opportunity to coordinate their parenting. It also increases their independence from one another by defining clear boundaries about when communication is and is not appropriate (see Chapter 3). Except in emergencies, parents can be encouraged to communicate according to their prearranged schedule, but to avoid direct contact with one another otherwise.

There is little left to the meaning of the term "custody" once parents agree about how they will make major and minor decisions about childrearing. What remains is the symbolism of the legal terminology. In the current climate of postdivorce parenting, many parents agree to a designation of joint legal custody, which I prefer. Some parents still opt for a sole legal custody agreement, but a growing group of parents choose yet another option. They do not designate legal custody. These parents view their own agreement about parenting their children as superseding legal terminology.

Financial Matters Related to the Children

Mediators must have some awareness of the parents' financial circumstances and disputes even when mediation is limited to custody issues. Financial arrangements with respect to the children are a particular concern, because they may play a strategic role in a custody dispute. For example, the mediator must learn about the couple's plans about property settlements, especially their arrangements for the family home if there is one. Many parents agree explicitly or implicitly that the children should remain in the same house, at least for a period of time. In such a circumstance, a custody dispute obviously concerns much more than custody.

Because the children's best interests are not independent from their financial circumstances, custody mediators who take their responsibilities to children seriously also must be concerned about finances for this reason. Mediators must be careful not to intrude into issues that parents (and their lawyers) have defined as separate from mediation. Still, it is helpful to educate parents about some possible financial concerns related to their children. Some of this education may be basic, as parents may be unaware of the existence of child support schedules, for example. Other suggestions can be aimed at helping parents anticipate future trouble spots. Childcare costs, medical insurance, and unreimbursed medical, dental, and psychological expenses are among the specific issues that I frequently urge parents to discuss between themselves and with their attorneys. The cost of college education is another financial matter that separated or divorced parents can be encouraged to anticipate. Some options for parents to consider for saving for this major expense include opening a custodial account to which they both begin to contribute immediately, agreeing to continue child support through the college years, or agreeing in advance to make fixed payments or proportional contributions to their children's college education.

WRITING AGREEMENTS

There are a number of different ways in which the details of a developing agreement can be tracked during the process of mediation, and there also are a number of different procedures for writing the final agreement. Agreements can become complicated and memories can be distorted, so it is essential to maintain an ongoing record of the tentative decisions that are made. The mediator can use case notes to do this informally earlier in the process, always taking care to review the details with the parents at the beginning and end of each meeting. As the agreement takes shape, however, a more public record is preferable because it both takes less time and is less likely to cause controversy.

Public records can take several forms. One possibility is to write the various details on a large flip chart and to post old sheets on the wall at the beginning of a new session. Another option is to have one of the parents track the details of the agreement, and bring in copies of their notes to each session. Similarly, the mediator can write up the details of the developing agreement, and share copies with the parents. A draft of an agreement that is written up by either of the party's lawyers also may be used to summarize the issues that have been tentatively agreed on up to a given point in mediation.

All agreements made in mediation are open for renegotiation until the entire package of issues has been agreed upon. At this point, the session notes can be rewritten for clarity into a draft of the agreement. The draft can be written by the mediator, one of the parents, one of the lawyers, or by the parents and mediator together in the mediation session. Custody mediation agreements typically contain a number of points about parenting, as well as specific plans about time-sharing, decision-making, and legal custody (see Table 7.2). They also often include a clause about how future disputes will be resolved, such as an agreement to attempt mediation before initiating legal action in the future. Informal terminology and plain English are preferred to a legalistic document, especially in the draft agreement. After a draft is completed, the parents are encouraged to object to it, to change their minds, and especially to have their attorneys review it. A follow-up session is then scheduled at a later date to allow both parents time to contact their attorneys and think through the details of the agreement.

Some parents prefer to write up informal or temporary agreements rather than full-scale legal documents, and they wish to end mediation at this point. Provided that they fully understand the advice to contact counsel, their desires are accepted. Most parents have the document reviewed by attorneys, however, and a few changes inevitably result from this process. Sometimes the objections are minor, perhaps even silly. Often they include important additions that were overlooked in mediation. The attorneys may renegotiate the final details themselves in some circumstances, or they may encourage the parents to resolve them back in mediation. In a few cases, the agreement completely breaks down during the course of the attorney review.

Table 7.2. Sample Custody Agreement

Weekly time-sharing schedule

(1) Katie and Andrew will live with their mother during the school week.

(2) Katie and Andrew will live with their father on alternate weekends from Friday at 5 p.m. through Sunday at 7 p.m.

(3) Katie and Andrew will spend every Wednesday evening with their father from 5 p.m. to 7:30 p.m.

Holiday time-sharing schedule

(1) Beginning with Thanksgiving 1994, Katie and Andrew will be with their mother from 5 p.m. the Wednesday immediately before Thanksgiving Day through the following Sunday at 7 p.m.

(2) Beginning with Christmas 1994, Katie and Andrew will be with their father from 5 p.m. on their last day of school before Christmas vacation through 2 p.m. on December 25. The children will be with their mother from 2 p.m. on Christmas Day until 7 p.m. on the Sunday before school resumes.

(3) Beginning with Easter 1995, Katie and Andrew will be with their father for the entire Easter weekend from 5 p.m. on Friday through 7 p.m. on Easter Sunday.

(4) The above schedule for Thanksgiving, Christmas, and Easter will alternate yearly between the two parents.

(5) The parents agree to arrange times that will allow each parent to spend at least 3 hours with Katie and Andrew on the children's respective birthdays.

(6) Katie and Andrew will spend Mother's Day and mother's birthday (February 27) with their mother, and Father's Day and father's birthday (November 13) with their father.

(7) During the summer school vacation, Katie and Andrew will spend 2 weeks vacation with their father and 2 weeks vacation with their mother. Specific dates will be determined by April 1 of each year.

(8) Holiday schedules will replace the weekly schedules.

Parenting and decision making

(1) The parents agree to work together in raising Katie and Andrew in the children's best interests. The parents will work to establish similar rules in their households, to encourage the children's relationships with both parents, and to avoid making negative comments about one another to the children.

(2) The parents agree to jointly share decisions about the children's religious training, education, and elective medical, dental, and psychological care.

(3) The parents agree to speak on the telephone each Sunday evening between 8 and 9 p.m. to exchange information about the children.

(4) The parents will retain joint legal custody of Katie and Andrew.

Table 7.2. *(continued)*

Amending this agreement

(1) If either parent plans to move more than 25 miles from their present address, notice will be given to the other parent at least 3 months prior to the move to allow time to renegotiate this agreement if necessary

(2) If the parents are unable to resolve any differences about the details of this agreement or about rearing Katie and Andrew, they agree to attempt to reach an agreement with a therapist or mediator before initiating any legal action.

The possibility of these varied outcomes makes it essential to schedule a follow-up mediation appointment in advance. This subsequent meeting provides an opportunity for the parents to negotiate a few further points and give the mediator feedback on what has transpired. It may offer the parents one last chance to negotiate cooperatively, or the final meeting may be a time to review the accepted document and to anticipate trouble spots in the future.

The final document can vary greatly in detail, form, and appearance. Some final mediation agreements are brief, use informal language, and are written by the parents themselves. Others are long, legal documents rewritten by the attorneys and containing many standard legal phrases. There are many variations in between these extremes. In my view, the best agreements contain many details about parenting plans as well as whatever legal safeguards the parents find reassuring. Good agreements also retain much or all of the parents' own wording with respect to rearing their children.

ENDING MEDIATION

Ending mediation can be difficult. The writing of the agreement is a symbolic acknowledgment that the relationship has ended. More practically, it means that the sessions are ending, and many parents privately enjoy their contact during mediation. The signing of a final agreement also can be frightening, because it makes changes more difficult to renegotiate in the future. For these reasons, some people quarrel about insignificant issues as mediation is coming to an end. The goal of this quibbling often seems to be to prolong contact with the former spouse or to avoid coming to a final decision. By this point in time, an interpretation about the meaning of ending mediation is accepted by most parents, particularly if it is made in caucus, not in front of the former partner.

Even for parents who retain little emotional investment in the marriage, ending mediation can be difficult. Parents frequently express gratitude for having been given the option of mediation. However, their mixed emotions often include being tired, relieved, and typically quite sad. The partners have not reconciled; that was not their goal. What they have done is to separate in a way that hopefully was less difficult than the alternatives. Still, the grief over their multiple losses is painful to the partners. Mediation is not simply a way to negotiate an agreement. It is a way of saying good-bye.

SUMMARY

The process of custody mediation becomes less structured beginning with the second session and continuing through the drafting of the final agreement. Nevertheless, certain procedural and substantive themes characterize its middle and late phases. The problem-solving model offers one way of conceptualizing the process of negotiation. The major steps in the model include (1) identifying problems by focusing on issues rather than emotions; (2) brainstorming alternatives, while suspending evaluation so that creative solutions can be invented or voiced for the first time; (3) evaluating options in terms of children's needs and parents' underlying interests; and (4) allowing for experimentation, a stance that reduces pressure by allowing parents to alter agreements in the near or more distant future.

The substantive topics addressed in the middle and late phases of custody mediation include the usual legal issues, as well as additional, specific concerns about postdivorce parenting. In order to minimize the symbolism of legal terminology, it is helpful to frame physical custody in terms of residence and legal custody in terms of decision-making. These terms also emphasize the fact that custody disputes are coparenting disputes, and they suggest topics that need to be addressed in detail for successful postdivorce parenting. Other topics not contained in the law also can be important to discuss in mediation. An example is establishing a means for the parents to communicate about routine childrearing matters. Finally, mediation also might be used to address a variety of issues that may underlie a dispute about child custody.

The final product of mediation is a written agreement that eventually may be drafted into a legal document. There are several ways in which both the draft and the final agreement may be written. In all cases, attorney review of the agreement is an important safeguard. Still, parents can be encouraged to preserve some of their own language in the document. More importantly, they can be encouraged to maintain not only their legal agreement but also the moral commitment to parenting that they made to one another in mediation.

CHAPTER 8

Research on Custody Mediation

There are compelling rationales for attempting the custody mediation alternative, and practical experience suggests that the process is successful not only in negotiating agreements, but also in helping former partners to begin to renegotiate their relationships. Ultimately, however, it is an empirical question whether or not mediation fulfills its ambitious goals of facilitating dispute resolution, improving satisfaction with the process, and easing parents' and children's adjustment to postdivorce family life. Research on mediation is incomplete, as is to be expected given the recency of its development. Nevertheless, many benefits of mediation have been documented, although research also suggests some cautions and limitations.

In comparing the mediation and adversary settlement of custody disputes, it is useful to distinguish three areas of outcome. One set of outcomes relates to the administration of justice. This includes such issues as what percentage of partners reach an agreement in mediation, how the content of mediated agreements compares with settlements reached through the adversary system, and the extent to which parents comply with the settlements over time. A second set of outcomes concerns party satisfaction with the process and outcome of mediation and adversary settlement. Satisfaction includes ratings of traditional psychological concerns, such as feeling that the professionals were concerned about you, as well as satisfaction with concerns that are traditionally the focus of the legal system, such as feeling that your rights were protected. Finally, a third set of important outcomes compares mediation and litigation in terms of parents' and children's psychological well-being. The impact of the two alternatives on ongoing family relationships is an equally important outcome, one that is closely associated with individual psychological health.

Research on child custody mediation is reviewed in this chapter, while the much more extensive body of evidence on divorce and family adjustment is summarized in Chapter 9. The emphasis in the present chapter is on my own investigations in the Charlottesville Mediation Project, a field experiment in which the outcomes of the mediation and the litigation of child custody disputes were compared systematically. The findings of other investigators are discussed to supplement or expand upon the results of this series of studies, but the present chapter is not intended to be a comprehensive overview of all studies on mediation.

AN OVERVIEW OF METHODS OF THE CHARLOTTESVILLE MEDIATION PROJECT

Various findings from the Charlottesville Mediation Project have been reported elsewhere. The major reports include a general rationale for the study (Emery & Wyer, 1987b), a comparison of outcomes for an initial sample of parents (Emery & Wyer, 1987a), a replication study (Emery, Matthews, & Wyer, 1991), a 1-year follow-up of parents who participated in both earlier studies (Emery, Matthews, & Kitzmann, 1994), and a report on children's psychological outcomes 1 year after dispute resolution (Kitzmann & Emery, in press). The present chapter is an integration of the major findings and conclusions of this research. Interested readers can find more details on methodology, data analysis, and specific results in these other reports.

Experimental Design

Some aspects of the methods of the Charlottesville Mediation Project are important to highlight here because these details underscore some of the unique strengths and limitations of the study. The use of random assignment with real families with very real custody disputes was perhaps the greatest strength of the investigation. Families who were disputing child custody were approached at random and asked either to attempt to mediate their custody dispute or to participate in a study of the court (the litigation control group). Of those families who were approached, 71% agreed to attempt mediation and 84% agreed to participate in the court study, a total of 71 families in all (35 in mediation, 36 in litigation). Those who agreed to join the study were virtually identical to those who declined participation in terms of demographic characteristics and prior court records (Emery et al., 1991).

Because of the experimental design, any differences found between the two groups can be confidently said to be caused by the contrast between the mediation and adversary settlement procedures in the study. The findings demonstrate causality, not merely correlation. Confidence in the study's internal validity is increased further by a replication study that obtained broadly similar results to an initial investigation (Emery et al., 1991). Other notable features of the study include a 1-year longitudinal follow-up assessment and the collection of objective data from ongoing court records. Finally, the use of a structured mediation intervention (Emery et al., 1987; see Chapters 6 and 7, this volume) makes it possible for others to replicate the research.

Sample Limitations

The limitations of the Charlottesville Mediation Project are important to recognize in interpreting the results of the study. The most important limitations stem from the nature of the sample—only families who had petitioned the court for a custody hearing were included in the investigation. Thus, the study focused on a small subset of all separated and divorced families (Maccoby & Mnookin, 1992), specifically parents who have very acrimonious relationships. It also is important to note that the parents in the sample generally were young, and the majority of their children were of preschool age or younger. The majority of both men and women in the sample also had low incomes. In addition, it is essential to reiterate that spousal support and property division were not addressed for either the mediation or the litigation groups, because the court only had jurisdiction over custody, visitation, and child support. Finally, it must be emphasized that the Charlottesville Mediation Project investigated only a single court and a single mediation program in a single state.

Each one of these characteristics of the sample potentially limits the generalizability of the study's findings. Partners who seek mediation on their own are likely to be more cooperative than those who petition for a custody hearing, and perhaps mediation is more successful with more cooperative partners. Spousal support and property division are crucial areas of dispute in divorce, and perhaps divorcing partners prefer to address these topics together with custody, visitation, and child support. Age or socioeconomic status may influence the outcome of mediation or litigation in any number of ways and thereby limit the study's findings. Finally, different approaches to the practice of mediation and different approaches to lawyering and litigation surely result in different outcomes for parents and for children. Similarly, the case laws and statutory laws that form the backdrop for both mediation and adversary settlement differ across states. Because of this, even identical interventions might produce different results in Virginia versus California, for example. In short, the external validity of the Charlottesville project can be questioned.

These limitations are noted for the sake of clarity, but such constraints are expected. No study can maintain a high degree of experimental control and simultaneously obtain a representative sample of the divorcing population. Researchers always must compromise between internal validity and external validity. The findings of the Charlottesville Mediation Project demonstrate causality, but it is readily acknowledged that their generalizability may be limited. In this chapter, questions about generalizability are addressed by contrasting the findings of these investigations with those obtained by other researchers studying other mediation programs in other states.

EFFICIENCY IN THE ADMINISTRATION OF JUSTICE

The first set of questions to ask about mediation is whether or not it improves efficiency in the administration of justice. Crowded court dockets and long delays in setting hearing dates are motivations for developing mediation programs, particularly among the members of the judiciary. If few agreements are reached in mediation, the alternative clearly does not achieve the goal of reducing the number of custody hearings. If so, mediation will delay, rather than hasten, dispute resolution by adding an inefficient layer of procedure to the judicial process. A closely related question is whether or not mediation results in lower or higher rates of relitigation, a frequent occurrence in divorce and custody cases. Finally, a more general question is whether or not the content of mediated agreements differs from settlements reached through adversary procedures. Similar agreements would be preferred by those who wish the reforms of mediation to be limited to procedure, but advocates for broader reform might hope that mediated and litigated settlements would differ widely in their substance.

Rates of Agreement and Diversion from Court

In the Charlottesville Mediation Project, it was clearly demonstrated that the implementation of a custody mediation program can cause a dramatic reduction in court hearings. Of the 35 families who attempted mediation in the study, 27 (77%) reached either a verbal or a written agreement. In addition, an out-of-court settlement was reached by another 4 of the 8 families who failed to reach an agreement in mediation. Thus, only 4 (11%) of the 35 families assigned at random to mediation at the beginning of the study proceeded to a custody hearing (see Figure 8.1).

These figures cannot be evaluated adequately, however, without considering the number of settlements reached after the petition was filed for the families in the litigation control group. Attorneys frequently schedule court hearings as a means of "upping the ante" in their negotiations. They still may hope or expect that a settlement will be reached out of court. In fact, 10 of the 36 families in the litigation group did settle prior to a court hearing, but 72% (26 of 36) proceeded on to court (see Figure 8.1). The different percentage of cases proceeding to a court hearing was statistically significant when comparing the two groups (Emery et al., 1991). More practically, the difference translates into a dramatic reduction in the number of court hearings as a result of implementing the custody mediation program.

Other researchers similarly have found that mediation produces a large number of agreements and leads to a substantial reduction in the number of court hearings. Rates of reaching agreement in mediation vary widely across studies from a low of approximately 20% to a

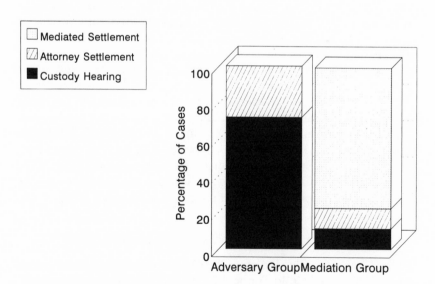

N=36 for adversary group and N=35 for mediation group

Figure 8.1. Cases proceeding to a custody hearing following random assignment to mediation or adversary settlement.

high of about 80% (Kressel & Pruitt, 1989). These figures apply to the mediation of all categories of disputes (including disputes between strangers), but considerable variation also has been found in evaluation research on custody mediation in different courts. Perhaps the best evaluation statistics come from studies of large numbers of families who were seen in highly regarded public mediation programs, where reports indicate agreement rates of 55% (McIsaac, 1982) and 64% (Salius & Maruzo, 1982). A statewide evaluation of California's mandatory custody mediation programs found a comparable rate of settlement (Depner, Cannata, & Simon, 1992).

These figures can be somewhat misleading, because court mediation programs deal with the most acrimonious separated and divorced parents. Court mediators settle between one-half and two-thirds of custody disputes in cases headed for a court hearing. It is likely that programs who deal with parents who seek mediation voluntarily will have considerably higher rates of reaching a settlement. In one such study of comprehensive mediation (which included all financial matters), 59% of the partners reached a complete divorce agreement and 15% reached a partial agreement (Kelly & Duryee, 1992).

As noted, some cases are settled out of court by lawyers after they file a petition for a custody hearing but before the hearing is held. It therefore is crucial to include a control group in order to determine whether or not mediated agreements actually reduce the number of custody hearings. In addition to the Charlottesville project, at least two studies that used random assignment to conditions also demonstrated that mediation directly caused a reduction in court hearings (Irving, Benjamin, Bohm, & MacDonald, 1981; Pearson & Thoennes, 1984.) Thus, the Charlottesville Mediation Project and several other studies have clearly established that mediation can cause a substantial, meaningful reduction in the number of custody hearings, and evaluation research indicates that the results can be generalized to other programs and populations. In fact, the dramatic reduction in court hearings has been enthusiastically noted by judges sitting in courts before and after the implementation of mediation programs (e.g., King, 1982).

Compliance with Mediated and Adversary Agreements

In the Charlottesville Mediation Project, court records and the records of the Office for Child Support Enforcement were monitored for a period of 2 years following parents' entry into the study. Relitigation rates were very high for the entire sample, as nearly two-thirds of families returned to court over some dispute during this 2-year period. Relitigation rates were slightly higher for parents who used adversary settlement rather than mediation, but the differences were not statistically significant. Differences between the two groups fell just short of statistical significance for compliance with child support, however. Fifty-one percent of parents in the mediation group had to be sent notices for overdue child support compared to 71% of the families who reached a settlement through the adversary system (Emery et al., 1994).

Other studies have obtained data that are more optimistic about compliance following mediation and adversary settlement. One early report noted that relitigation was six times higher following adversary settlement than after mediation (Margolin, 1973), but no other investigator has found a difference of this magnitude. In one study of the mediation of divorce issues, Pearson and Thoennes (1989) found that relitigation was three times higher following adversary settlement (35%) versus mediation (13%), but smaller differences were found in a second study and no differences were found in a third investigation. In her comparison of comprehensive divorce mediation and adversary settlement, Kelly (1990) found more compliance immediately after the final divorce among the parents who mediated, but differences were no longer statistically significant 2 years later. In this study, 84% of the former spouses across both groups were complying with the financial terms of their agreements. Rates of actual relitigation were too small to analyze.

Together the findings from the Charlottesville project and other studies suggest a prudent but positive conclusion. Mediation clearly does *not* lead to an frenzy of relitigation, as some have feared that it might. In fact, evidence suggests that custody mediation results in higher compliance and lower rates of relitigation. Differences in relitigation following mediation and adversary settlement are not large, however, especially when compared to the success of mediation in settling new cases prior to a court hearing. It would seem that there are some former partners who are bound to appear in court repeatedly irrespective of whether they initially attempt mediation or adversary settlement.

Content of Agreements

The content of the actual agreements that were reached in the Charlottesville Mediation Project were quite similar whether they were negotiated in mediation or through adversary procedures. The two sets of agreements did not differ significantly in terms of primary residence (physical custody), the number of days to be spent with the nonresidential parent, or the amount of child support to be paid.

There was a significant difference between groups in terms of legal custody. Joint *legal* custody was more common in the mediation group, although sole maternal legal and physical custody was the norm irrespective of the method of dispute resolution (Emery et al., 1991). This "traditional" outcome likely reflects a number of factors, including the preferences of the legal community and the mediators, the lower socioeconomic status of the sample, and the absence of any mention of the term "joint custody" in the statutory law of Virginia that was in effect during the time of the study.

The content of the mediated and adversary agreements in the Charlottesville study differed only in one respect other than legal custody. The residential arrangements were more detailed in the mediated agreements than in the adversary ones. Mediated agreements specified days and times for exchanging the children, and also included agreements about other aspects of parenting such as childrearing goals. Adversary settlements were much more general, including such imprecise residential arrangements as "physical custody to the mother, liberal rights of visitation to the father."

Similar findings have been reported by other investigators who have compared the content of agreements reached through mediation and adversary procedures. Joint legal custody was more common in mediated than in adversary settlements according to the results of two of the Denver studies (Pearson and Thoennes, 1989). Visitation was more frequent for nonresidential parents in the mediation group in only one of these investigations (Pearson & Thoennes, 1989).

In Kelly's (1990) studies of adversary settlement and comprehensive mediation, no significant differences were found for joint legal custody in mediated and adversary agreements. Joint legal custody was agreed upon by 100% of the mediation parents and by 90% of the adversary parents, a reflection of the differing norms across states. Other aspects of the content of the agreements were different between the two groups of parents in this study, however. Mediated agreements were more specific about the details of both residential arrangements and parental decision-making, and they also specified more balanced residential arrangements. Primary father residence and limited father visitation *both* were more common among parents who reached an adversarial settlement, while a more equal time-sharing arrangement was more common among parents who mediated. Kelly (1990) termed this last result an "either/or" outcome, a reflection of the win–lose orientation of one approach and the win–win goal of the alternative. Mediated agreements also included more provisions for the children's health insurance and for continuing child support beyond the age of 18 than did the adversary settlements that were reached in this study.

Consistent with the results of these studies, other researchers also have found that mediated agreements are more specific, contain more joint legal custody provisions, and include more details or innovations in providing financial support to the children when compared to adversary settlements (Koopman, Hunt, & Stafford, 1984). While these differences are consistent, the similarities in the agreements reached by the two methods are at least as noteworthy. Mediated and adversary agreements generally have not been found to differ in terms of joint physical custody, an important outcome because mediators have been accused of imposing this arrangement upon unwilling parents (Fineman, 1988; Grillo, 1991). In fact, there is a considerable overlap between mediated and adversary agreements. This indicates that many differences in party satisfaction following the two methods of dispute resolution are likely to be caused by the alternative procedures rather than by differences in the substance of the final agreements.

Conclusions

Overall, mediation compares very favorably to adversary settlement in terms of outcomes related to facilitating the administration of justice. Mediation typically ends in an agreement for between one-half and three-quarters of parents whose custody disputes seem sufficiently intractable to lead them to request a court hearing. Without mediation, some of these parents would settle out of court as a result of their own, informal discussions or through attorney negotiations. Nevertheless, it has been clearly demonstrated in experimental and evaluation research that mediation programs directly cause a substantial reduction in the number of custody hearings.

Other evidence indicates that disputes are resolved more quickly in mediation than in adversary settlement (Emery et al., 1991). Another extremely important finding is that parents who reach an agreement through mediation are somewhat more likely to comply with it than are parents who reach a settlement with their attorneys or in court. Finally, the content of the settlements reached in mediation or through adversary settlement does not differ dramatically. Evidence does indicate, however, that mediated agreements tend to include more joint legal custody, more specific details about parenting plans, more information about financial arrangements concerning the children, and perhaps slightly more balance in the time children spend with mothers and fathers.

Ironically, perhaps the major concern about custody mediation from the perspective of administration of justice is that it may be *too* successful. In their enthusiasm about diverting cases from court, judges and other court personnel sometimes overemphasize agreement rates as a measure of the success or failure of mediation. This can lead to subtle pressures on mediators to become increasingly coercive in order to obtain a goal that may be a dubious indicator of success. Mediators occasionally need to remind themselves and others about the intervention's more ambitious goals of empowerment, education, and protecting ongoing relationships against unnecessary conflict. Fortunately, research also indicates that mediation does achieve more than just "getting agreements," as is discussed in the following section.

SATISFACTION WITH MEDIATION AND ADVERSARY SETTLEMENT

In the Charlottesville Mediation Project, mothers and fathers who participated in mediation or adversary settlement were contacted approximately 1 month after reaching an agreement or having a decision rendered by a judge. All parents were interviewed in their own homes, where they completed a 19-item questionnaire rating their satisfaction with different aspects of the dispute resolution process. The identical instrument was administered to parents in each group. Parents were interviewed again about 1 year later, and they responded to the same questionnaire at that time. Some items addressed satisfaction with the psychological aspects of mediation (e.g., satisfaction with control over decisions, feeling understood, or the good/bad effect on family members). Other items addressed satisfaction with the traditional goals of legal settlement (e.g., satisfaction with the fairness of decisions, protection of rights, reaching a lasting agreement).

In comparing the groups statistically, parents were included in the mediation sample even when they failed to reach an agreement, and they were included in the litigation group even when they settled out of court. This procedure provided a conservative test of the hypothesized benefits of mediation, and it preserved the integrity of the random assignment. Another important approach to the analysis of the satisfaction findings was comparing mothers and fathers separately following mediation or litigation. The samples were combined across gender in some earlier research.

Parents' ratings of satisfaction following mediation and litigation have been a major focus of several reports from the Charlottesville project (Emery & Wyer, 1987a; Emery et al., 1991; Emery et al., 1994).

Therefore, these findings will not be reiterated in great detail here. Rather, the results of these studies can be summarized by noting four broad patterns in the findings. First, fathers were significantly and substantially more satisfied with mediation than with litigation in virtually every domain of assessment. This was true whether the items assessed satisfaction with the psychological or the legal aspects of the dispute resolution. Second, few differences were found between mothers in terms of the satisfaction with mediation or litigation that they reported. Some evidence favoring each method was obtained, but the strongest pattern in the findings was the similarity between the two groups of the mothers. Third, whether they mediated or litigated their custody dispute, mothers were more satisfied than fathers with the process, outcome, and impact of the dispute settlement. Fourth, these patterns of findings were consistent across the initial study, a replication study, and a 1-year longitudinal follow-up study.

A Closer Look at Differences between Mothers and Fathers

The findings of the Charlottesville studies are clear and consistent, but they have been misinterpreted nevertheless. The most common misinterpretation is that they mean that mediation is "bad" for mothers and "good" for fathers (e.g., Grillo, 1991). Disparities in intepreting the data certainly have been affected by political concerns, as some "mothers' rights" advocates have opposed mediation, while some "fathers' rights" advocates have embraced it. Part of the reason for misinterpretation, however, is likely due to the manner in which the data have been presented. The separate comparisons of men and women are advantageous statistically, because they maximize statistical power and accommodate missing data. However, the plan of analysis can cause one to overlook comparisons between men and women *within* mediation and litigation.

In order to facilitate such comparisons, findings for five representative items from the satisfaction questionnaire are summarized in Figure 8.2. These figures are based on data from the combined original and replication samples, and they were obtained about a month after settlement (see Emery et al., 1991). The figure includes findings for men and women who mediated or litigated, thus facilitating comparisons between the four subgroups. A quick glance at this figure indicates a consistent pattern of results. For most items, mothers who mediated, mothers who litigated, and fathers who mediated all reported a high average level of satisfaction. On these same items, however, fathers who litigated reported a notably lower level of satisfaction.

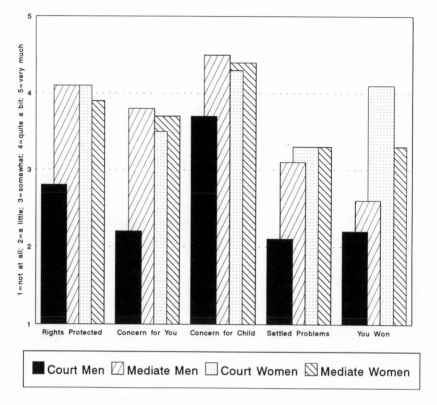

Figure 8.2. Satisfaction ratings of mothers and fathers following mediation or adversary settlement.

Fathers in Litigation

Consider the results specifically. For the item, "feel your rights were protected," the mean for mothers who mediated was 3.9; for mothers who litigated it was 4.1; for fathers who mediated it was 4.1. The members of each of these groups felt their rights had been protected "quite a bit" according to the rating scale that was used. For fathers who litigated, the mean was 2.8, or "somewhat" on the same scale. For the item, "concern was shown for you," the means were 3.7 for mediation mothers, 3.5 for litigation mothers, and 3.8 for mediation fathers. On average, these parents felt that "quite a bit" of concern was shown for them. For fathers who litigated, the mean was 2.2, which corresponds to "a little" concern. For the item, "concern was shown for the children," the means were 4.4, 4.3, and 4.5 for mediation mothers, litigation mothers, and mediation fathers, respectively. For fathers who litigated, the mean was 3.7. For the item "settled problems with spouse," the means were 3.3, 3.3, and 3.1 for mediation mothers, litigation mothers, and mediation fathers. On average, they reported that the problems had been settled "somewhat." For fathers who litigated, the mean was 2.1 or "a little" (see Figure 8.2). In fact, this pattern held for virtually every item on the satisfaction questionnaire (see Emery et al., 1991).

Winning and Losing

The one exception to this pattern occurred for the item "won what you wanted" (see Figure 8.2) and the parallel item "lost what you wanted" (not shown here). For the former item, the means for mothers and fathers who mediated were relatively close to one another, 3.3 and 2.6 respectively, whereas the means for mothers and fathers in the litigation group were far apart, 4.1 and 2.2. Mediation partners each thought that they won "somewhat" of what they wanted, while litigation mothers won "quite a bit" and litigation fathers won "a little."

In the reports of the study's findings, mothers who mediated were compared with women who litigated. This makes the women who mediated appear to be at a disadvantage, winning only "somewhat" rather than "quite a bit." This interpretation of the findings fails to consider two essential aspects of the data, however. First, it ignores the fact that, whether they mediated or litigated, mothers generally were satisfied on other measures of outcome. The majority of the study's findings point to the disadvantage of men in litigation, not to the disadvantage of women in mediation. Second, the conclusion ignores the possibility that the "somewhat" findings for the mediation mothers may be a *good* outcome. Perhaps the parents in mediation arrived at win–win outcomes, while the parents who litigated reached win–lose outcomes.

One way of testing this theoretical possibility is to examine the correlations between the scores of mothers and fathers within each of the two settlement groups. A positive correlation would indicate that the more one parent was satisfied, the *more* the other parent also was satisfied—a win–win outcome. A negative correlation would indicate that the more one parent was satisfied, the *less* the other parent was satisfied—a win–lose consequence. In fact, a positive correlation was found between mothers' and fathers' ratings within the mediation group, but a negative correlation was found for mothers' and fathers' ratings in the litigation group (Emery et al., 1991).

This extended discussion of the findings for mothers and fathers is intended to clarify the results of the Charlottesville Mediation Project, not to dismiss gender issues in custody dispute resolution. As I have discussed elsewhere (Emery & Wyer, 1987a; Emery et al., 1991; Emery et al., 1994), the findings do suggest that mediation holds more potential to benefit fathers than mothers. This is not because men are advantaged relative to women in mediation, however. If anything, the data from this study indicated the reverse. This study found that men who mediated were more satisfied than men who litigated, while few differences were apparent for mothers. However, this was because women who litigated held a strong advantage over men who litigated. In short, the research documented much stronger gender differences following *litigation* than following mediation.

At the same time, it is true that this research found that mediation gave fathers more voice in the custody dispute resolution than they would have had in litigation. Fathers' gains in mediation did not come at the expense of mothers' satisfaction—further evidence of the win–win possibilities of mediation. Nevertheless, the fact that men experience more of the added benefit indicates that advocates for mediation might also advocate for reforms that will be of more direct benefit to women. More equitable and stringently enforced child support payment is one such important goal (Emery, 1988).

Other Research on Party Satisfaction

Party satisfaction following mediation has been examined in several studies in addition to the Charlottesville project. As with this investigation, more satisfaction with the process and outcome of mediation has been reported in several studies in which it has been compared with adversary settlement (Irving et al., 1981; Kelly, 1990; Pearson & Thoennes, 1984). In addition, evaluation research typically has found a high degree of satisfaction with mediation, indicating that the positive results obtained in experimental or quasi-experimental research do generalize to other settings (e.g., Depner et al., 1992; Keilitz, Daley, & Hanson, 1992). With one exception (Pearson & Thoennes, 1984), however, gender differences either have not been examined carefully or have not been found in other investigations.

The most notable counterpoint to the Charlottesville findings with respect to gender differences is Joan Kelly's (1989, 1990; Kelly & Gigy, 1989; Kelly, Gigy, & Hausman, 1988) study of comprehensive mediation in California. Few differences in the experiences of men and women in mediation or litigation were reported in this study. Differences in favor of mediation over adversary settlement were found in terms of the clients' feelings of empowerment, the impact on spousal relationships, views about the professionals' effectiveness and sensitivity, and satisfaction with both the substantive and the emotional aspects of the settlements. In general, satisfaction ratings favored mediation over adversary settlement equally for both men and women (Kelly, 1989), a pattern that clearly differs from the Charlottesville project.

The differences between the Virginia and California studies could be due to any number of factors. The California sample was comprised of higher income families who voluntarily sought mediation, while the Virginia sample included lower income families who agreed to mediate only after petitioning for a custody hearing. The studies also differed in that mediation was limited to child-related issues in the Virginia study, but mediation included property and spousal support disputes in the California study.

The most powerful influence on the gender results obtained in the two studies, however, likely was the differing legal climate in the two states. California has embraced gender neutrality in divorce and custody law much more rapidly and completely than Virginia. In the results of the two sets of studies, the differing legal background was evident in the much higher rates of joint legal custody and more frequent parent–child contact in the California sample than among the Virginia subjects—differences found for both the mediation and the adversary settlement groups. If the contrasting gender results obtained in the two studies were due to the contrasting legal climates of California and Virginia, this again focuses attention back on the differing experiences of men and women in *litigation*, not in mediation.

The emphasis on gender differences in adversary settlement was underscored by a recent study by Kelly and Duryee (1992). These investigators compared the satisfaction of men and women in two mediation samples: a public custody mediation group and a private comprehensive mediation group. Few gender differences were found in either of these samples, and when they were found, more satisfaction was reported by women than men who mediated. These results may appear to contradict findings from the Charlottesville project, but they actually are perfectly consistent. The Charlottesville findings also indicated that, in comparison to men, women were consistently more satisfied with both litigation *and* mediation (Emery & Wyer, 1987a; Emery et al., 1991; Emery et al., 1994).

Conclusions

In summary, several independent research groups have found that, relative to adversary settlement, mediation increases parents' satisfaction with a number of aspects of dispute resolution, including the decisions that are reached, the process of reaching those decisions, and the impact of the process on oneself, the children, and ongoing family relationships. There is no evidence, moreover, that men hold advantages over women in mediation. In fact, data from at least two studies indicate that women are more satisfied with mediation than are men. All of these conclusions apply to averages, of course. Variability across individual cases must be expected.

Thus, the controversy about whether or not mediation is "bad" for women and "good" for men is not attributable to contradictory research findings. Rather, the debate can be attributed to broader political considerations that determine which aspects of the fairly consistent data are emphasized. Women are *advantaged* relative to men in custody mediation. However, women are *more advantaged* relative to men in custody litigation than in custody mediation. (Or, in states like California, women until recently were more advantaged relative to men in custody litigation.) Evidence for these conclusions is apparent in the data found in the Charlottesville Mediation Project (see Figure 8.2).

Perhaps the greatest benefit of mediation is that it creates excess satisfaction—a win–win outcome. This has helped to maintain mothers' satisfaction with custody dispute resolution at quite a high level at the same time that fathers have gained more equal footing through substantive and procedural reforms in custody law.

PSYCHOLOGICAL OUTCOMES

Research on party satisfaction with mediation supports the alternative method of dispute resolution despite the controversies about gender issues. This support is particularly strong when considered together with evidence that mediation facilitates the administration of justice. The final question about the impact of mediation relates to what may be its highest goal: improving postdivorce family relationships and thereby promoting mental health among parents and children.

The consequences of mediation for coparental and parent–child relationships, as well as for parents' and children's mental health, were a focus of considerable effort in the Charlottesville Mediation Project. Measures of parents' depression and acceptance of the end of their marriage were the major indices of their mental health. Assessments of children's mental health were attempted in numerous ways, but because of the young age of most of the children in the study, it was necessary to rely primarily on parents' reports on standard child behavior checklists. Both conflict and closeness in the coparental

relationship also was assessed, while warmth was the major consideration in assessing parent–child relationships (Emery et al., 1991; Emery
et al., 1994; Kitzmann & Emery, in press).

The findings from virtually all of these broader measures of
psychological well-being can be summarized simply: no differences
were observed between members of the mediation and litigation
groups in terms of their broader psychological outcomes. Mothers
who mediated were found to be more depressed than mothers who
litigated in an early report (Emery & Wyer, 1987a), but the opposite
pattern was obtained in a replication study, and the differences
vanished when the samples were combined (Emery et al., 1991). At
1-year follow-up, both groups of mothers showed a substantial decline
in depression, but there continued to be no differences between
mothers who mediated or litigated (Emery et al., 1994). In addition,
no differences between groups were found for mothers' or fathers'
acceptance of the end of the marriage or fathers' depression for either
sample at any point in time. The one positive finding for parents was
a tendency for fathers who mediated to report less coparenting
conflict a year after dispute settlement in comparison to fathers who
litigated (Emery et al., 1994).

Some evidence indicated that fathers who mediated remained
more involved with their children than did fathers who litigated
(Emery et al., 1994), and this may be considered to be a positive
outcome for children. Similar to the results for parents, however, no
differences between groups were found on measures of children's
mental health or warmth in parent–child relationships (Kitzmann &
Emery, in press). Evidence did support the goal of reducing coparenting conflict, and a decline in parental conflict over time was associated
with improved child mental health across both the mediation and
litigation groups (Kitzmann & Emery, in press).

Very little additional research has focused on the mental health
outcomes for families following mediation and litigation. The data
that have been collected have failed to demonstrate differences between groups. No differences in child outcome were found in a brief
assessment in the Denver studies (Pearson & Thoennes, 1984). A
detailed assessment of the former partners in the California studies
similarly found no differences between mediation and adversary
settlement groups in terms of the adults' psychological adjustment
immediately after dispute resolution or at follow-up (Kelly et al., 1988;
Kelly, 1990).

There are a number of alternative explanations for this failure to
demonstrate differences in terms of general psychological adjustment. One set of explanations is methodological. Only a small number

of studies have been conducted, limited domains of psychological functioning have been assessed, and the time between intervention and follow-up assessment has been relatively short. Mediation has not been demonstrated to improve family mental health, but more research clearly is needed and mental health benefits still may be detected.

Another reason for the limited demonstration of mental health benefits may be the modest increase in psychological disturbance associated with divorce (see Chapter 9). It will be difficult to demonstrate the effectiveness of any preventative intervention on traditional measures of mental health, because the psychological fallout of divorce is not great as indexed by these measures. Nevertheless, many parents and children report considerable psychological distress due to divorce in domains of functioning that are difficult to assess. This again suggests the need for more research, particularly for research that incorporates innovative measures of more subtle psychological processes.

Of course, the most parsimonious conclusion at this point in time is that mediation does not directly produce improved mental health. In fact, it may be too much to expect mediation to improve parents' depression or children's divorce adjustment. Mediation is a brief intervention that may last no longer than a few hours. Mediation explicitly focuses on negotiating agreements as opposed to attempting to improve ongoing relationships or individual mental health. It may be that the psychological health of the members of divorcing families can only be promoted by more direct and intensive intervention inside or outside of mediation. This possibility also deserves further research. The promise of mediation does not rest on mental health outcomes, however, as has been demonstrated by the encouraging research reviewed in this chapter.

SUMMARY

Several important conclusions can be reached based on existing research, despite the fact that custody mediation is a recent development in need of further study. One conclusion is that mediation clearly facilitates the administration of justice. A high percentage of cases seen in custody mediation end in an agreement, even when other forms of negotiation have broken down and a court hearing is imminent. This means that custody mediation programs produce a substantial reduction in the number of court hearings. Other evidence indicates that, in comparison to adversary settlements, mediated agreements are reached more quickly and compliance with their terms is somewhat higher. The content of mediated agreements is not radically different from those reached through the adversary system, although mediated agreements typically contain more progressive provisions with respect to legal custody, specific childrearing arrangements, and mechanisms for providing financial support to children.

The people who use mediation also are quite satisfied with the process, and party satisfaction is higher following mediation than adversary settlement. In the Charlottesville Mediation Project, fathers who mediated were more satisfied when compared to fathers who litigated, although the same comparison for mothers yielded few differences. This pattern of findings must be considered carefully in order to avoid misinterpretation, however. The gender difference was caused primarily by the unhappiness of fathers who litigated. Men's satisfaction improves when they mediate rather than litigate, but women's satisfaction remains high—higher than that of men who mediate. Thus, research suggests that gains in fathers' satisfaction following mediation are produced by a "win–win" outcome, not by a loss for mothers.

Finally, there is little evidence that mediation leads to improvements in the mental health of parents or children following separation and divorce. Although more research is needed on the effects of mediation on family relationships and psychological well-being, perhaps such broad benefits should not be expected of this brief intervention that does not focus directly on emotional concerns. The limited evidence with respect to mental health outcomes perhaps makes other positive findings in favor of mediation more believable. In any case, it should not cloud the promise of mediation for reducing acrimonious court hearings, increasing compliance with agreements, and improving party satisfaction in the process.

CHAPTER 9

Psychological Research on Children, Parents, and Divorce

Mediators must be familiar with empirical evidence on the experience of divorce for children for several reasons. One reason is to set realistic expectations for postdivorce parenting. Substantial modifications in custody have occurred in legal theory, but far fewer dramatic changes have taken place in the practice of raising children. The number of children living with their fathers or in joint physical custody after divorce is large in absolute terms, but still proportionately small. The overwhelming majority of children continue to reside primarily with their mothers after divorce. Other evidence indicates that children see their nonresidential parents infrequently on average. In short, demographic realities depart considerably from many perceptions of postdivorce coparenting.

Empirical evidence also is important to mediators in educating parents about children and divorce. The popular media frequently report sweeping, adverse effects of divorce on children's mental health, but research consistently points to children's *resilience*. Studies reveal only small differences in the psychological adjustment of children whose parents are married or divorced; children seem to cope with divorce despite substantial changes in their family life. This optimistic conclusion must be tempered with the caution that coping with distress can take a psychological toll. Psychological disturbance is not a common consequence of divorce for children, but psychological distress is. The various stressors caused by divorce range from troubled parent–child relationships to a decline in living standards. Most children successfully cope with these sources of distress, but it is obviously preferrable to insulate children from such difficulties.

Mediators also must heed psychological research, because it helps to shape the goals of mediation. In particular, researchers consistently have found that the quality of postdivorce family relationships is linked with better or worse adjustment among children. Authoritative parent–child relationships and cooperative parent–parent relationships are well-established predictors of superior adjustment among children both during marriage and following divorce. Such findings indicate that containing conflict should be an ongoing goal of mediation. Indeed, conflict containment is an essential goal for all interventions with divorced parents, including mediation, lawyering, therapy, and education.

For these reasons, an overview of research on children and divorce is presented in this chapter. The more limited evidence on parents' psychological adjustment to divorce also is considered briefly. This latter research reminds us that divorce is a time of upheaval for parents as well as for children. Establishing a businesslike coparenting arrangement is not a simple emotional or practical task for parents. Even as they work toward containing conflict, mediators must legitimize the adult's perspective on divorce. Former spouses are hurt, angry, sad, and lonely. Their task is not to eliminate their emotions, but to find a way of coping that minimizes harm to their children.

DEMOGRAPHICS OF DIVORCE

Divorce rates stabilized in the 1980s, but approximately two-thirds of today's marriages still are projected to end in divorce (Cherlin, 1992; Martin & Bumpass, 1989). Estimates indicate that at least one-third of the current generation of children will experience a parental divorce before the age of 18 (Bumpass, 1984; Furstenberg, Peterson, Nord, & Zill, 1983). The risk for divorce differs in meaningful ways for different groups of children, however. African-American children are four times as likely as whites to be born outside of marriage, and African-Americans also are more likely to divorce and to remain separated without a legal divorce (Select Committee on Children, Youth, and Families [SCCYF], 1989). In fact, one estimate indicated that 75% of all black children born to married parents would experience a divorce by the age of 18. Among white children, the comparable projection was 38% (Bumpass, 1984).

Children's age and the length of the marriage also are important predictors of the risk for divorce. About 60% of all divorces involve children, but divorce is about half as likely among couples with preschoolers than among childless couples who have been married for the same length of time. The likelihood of divorce is about equal among couples who have older children, however, in comparison with childless marriages of the same length (Cherlin, 1977; Waite, Haggstrom, & Kanouse, 1985). Many parents apparently *do* stay married for their children's sake, but most children who experience divorce do so at a young age nevertheless. Of all children who experience a divorce by age 12, for example, approximately two-thirds experience it before the age of 6 (Furstenberg et al., 1983). This is because divorce is far more likely to occur early in a marriage, whether or not a couple has children.

Children's Primary Residence

According to 1988 census data, of all children who lived with a parent following separation or divorce, 87% lived with their mothers, and 13% lived with their fathers. Although the absolute number of single fathers has been growing, so has the number of single mothers. Thus, the proportion of children living in their father's custody has remained relatively stable since 1960 (U.S. Census Bureau, 1989). Somewhat more boys (15.8%) than girls (11.5%) lived in the custody of their fathers, and older boys, but not older girls, were more likely to live with their fathers (see Table 9.1).

Age and Changes over Time

Census statistics mask developmental differences in children's residence that may be due to their age at divorce, current age, or changes that occur over time (Emery & Kitzmann, in press). There are no

Table 9.1. Boys and Girls Living with Separated or Divorced Mothers and Fathers

	Boys		Girls	
Child's Age	Mothers	Fathers	Mothers	Fathers
All ages	84.2	15.8	88.5	11.5
Under 3	84.0	16.0	88.0	12.0
3 to 5	86.8	13.2	87.6	12.4
6 to 9	84.1	15.9	90.9	9.1
10 to 14	85.0	15.0	87.7	12.3
15 to 17	80.7	19.3	87.7	12.3

Note: From U.S. Bureau of the Census (1989). Marital status and living arrangements: March 1988. *Current Population Reports*, Series P-20, No. 433. Washington, D.C.: U.S. Government Printing Office.

national data on such influences, but a longitudinal study on a large California sample indicates their importance (Maccoby & Mnookin, 1992). Children who were older at the time of divorce were more likely to live primarily with their fathers, but this increase resulted from a decline in joint physical custody, not in mother custody. Twice as many teenagers as toddlers lived primarily with their fathers, but only 3% of children 15 years of age or older lived in joint physical custody compared to 17% of children aged 3 and under (Maccoby & Mnookin, 1992).

The percentage of families maintaining each type of custody arrangement remained fairly stable over the 3 years of the longitudinal study. Like the census data, however, these cross-sectional figures hide important developmental changes. Over 80% of mother residence families maintained this arrangement 3 years later, as did 70% of father residence families. In contrast, only slightly more than half of all families maintained joint physical custody, and less than one-third of families with split custody kept the arrangement 3 years later (Maccoby & Mnookin, 1992).

The relative instability of the more complicated joint physical and split custody arrangements is important to note. However, perhaps the most striking aspect of the data is the most obvious: children's primary residence changes frequently over time. Whether decisions are reached in mediation, through attorney negotiations, or in court, custody arrangements are not final either theoretically in the law or empirically in parenting practices. In fact, it may be helpful to raise this likelihood of change when custody is first negotiated. As noted in Chapter 7, raising the possibility of change may not only anticipate the future, but it may also alleviate some of the pressure that parents feel to make a permanent childrearing decision. Parents may consider new options for sharing time with their children when they view residence as evolving over time.

Joint Custody

The census bureau does not track legal custody or joint physical custody, but other research provides information on developments in these areas. Nearly 80% of families in the California sample had joint legal custody, while less than 20% had joint physical custody (Maccoby & Mnookin, 1992). Similar statistics were found in a study of Washington state families, where 69% of parents had joint legal custody and 20% had joint physical custody (Ellis, 1990). A New Hampshire study found joint legal custody in 65% of cases and joint physical custody among 7% (Racusin, Albertin, Wishik, Schnurr & Mayberry, 1989). A study of a large sample of Wisconsin families found 20% with joint legal custody and 2% with joint physical custody (Seltzer, 1991). As noted in Chapter 8, increases in joint legal custody and much smaller increases in joint physical custody also are common following mediation.

These statistics across studies appear to indicate two important trends about joint custody. First, joint legal custody is far more common than joint physical custody across all jurisdictions. Second, although wide differences still are found across states, joint legal custody appears to be the developing norm for most parents. In contrast, joint physical custody is an arrangement elected by only a minority of families even in states where laws encourage this option.

Involvement of Nonresidential Parents

The high degree of involvement that characterizes joint physical custody may be the exception, not the rule, but it still is possible for nonresidential parents to remain closely involved in their children's lives even without joint physical custody. National evidence indicates that this is not typically the case, however. A recent national survey indicated that, according to mothers' reports, approximately one-third of divorced fathers had seen their children only once or not at all in the past year. About 4 out of 10 fathers saw their children a few times a year up to three times a month, while about a one-quarter saw them once a week or more (Seltzer, 1991; see Table 9.2).

Few fathers made up for the lack of contact with letters or telephone calls. For example, only 10% of fathers who had not seen their children in the past year wrote or phoned them. Not surprisingly, most mothers also made decisions about the children on their own. According to mothers' reports, only 17% of nonresidential fathers had "a great deal" of influence on decisions concerning their children's education, medical care, and religious training. Approximately half of the women reported that the fathers had no influence on these decisions at all (Seltzer, 1991).

The degree of father's involvement was strongly related to the length of time since separation. Among fathers separated for 2 years or less, for example, 13% had seen their children once a year or less, while 43% saw them once a week or more. In contrast, among fathers separated for 11 years or more, 50% saw their children once a year or less, while 12% saw them once a week or more. Other influences related to increased paternal involvement included higher socioeconomic status, being black rather than nonblack, a shorter distance between residences, and neither parent having remarried (Seltzer, 1991).

Table 9.2. Divorced Fathers' Contact with Their Children[a]

Frequency of contact	See in person[b]	Phone or write	Talk to mother[c]
Not at all	18.2%	21.2%	26.9%
Once a year	13.6%	7.5%	8.9%
Several times a year	22.1%	22.7%	27.1%
One to three times a month	21.2%	19.4%	17.4%
Once a week	12.4%	14.2%	11.1%
Several times a week	12.4%	15.1%	8.6%

[a]All percentages are based on the responses of 717 divorced mothers about their former husbands' contact with the children who lived with the mothers. Interviews took place in 1987–1988 as a part of the National Survey of Families and Households.
[b]Of the fathers who saw their children at all in the past year, 36.6% were reported to have had extended visits with them.
[c]These data refer to how often fathers were reported to have talked with mothers about their children.
Note: Adapted from J. A. Seltzer (1991). Relationships between fathers and children who live apart: The father's role after separation. *Journal of Marriage and the Family, 53*, p. 86. Copyright 1991 by National Council on Family Relations. Adapted by permission.

The findings of this survey are similar to those reported in two other national surveys with the exception of inconsistent findings for race (Furstenberg et al., 1983; Seltzer and Bianchi, 1988). These disheartening findings about nonresidential parents are tempered somewhat by two more optimistic patterns. First, nonresidential mothers consistently have been found to maintain more contact with their children than nonresidential fathers. Second, contact between nonresidential fathers and their children is somewhat higher in more recent cohorts, suggesting that there may be some, small increase in the childrearing involvement of divorced fathers in more recent years.

CHILDREN'S DIVORCE OUTCOMES

The adjustment of children from divorced families has been a topic of vigorous debate. Some authors indicate that the ill-effects of divorce on children are substantial and long-lasting, and may emerge after lying dormant for a number of years (e.g., Wallerstein & Blakeslee, 1989). Others have suggested that the damage that divorce causes for children has been overstated, and that this has created unnecessary fears among parents, children, and the public at large (e.g., Edwards, 1987). In a detailed review of the research literature on children and divorce, I concluded that both of these extreme views are erroneous (Emery, 1988). It is empirically inaccurate and socially unjust to conclude that divorce does substantial damage to children's mental health. It is equally inaccurate and personally insensitive to ignore the practical and emotional struggles that children face as a result of divorce.

A Focus on Resilience

A focus on children's *resilience* may help to explain some of the conflicting conclusions about the adjustment of children following divorce (Emery & Forehand, in press). Three observations about research on children and divorce make a focus on resilience particularly compelling. First, research indicates that divorce is accompanied by considerable emotional distress, psychological confusion, relationship strain, and life upheaval for parents and for children. Second, research clearly indicates that most children function competently following divorce despite the often dramatic changes in their family life. Third, children frequently express disappointment, longing, and resentment about divorce even years later, and their relationships with their parents are likely to be strained. In short, most children cope successfully with divorce, but even successful coping takes a psychological toll.

The Average Adjustment of Children from Divorced Families

Evidence on the average adjustment of children from divorced families is an important starting point for understanding research on children and divorce. Many qualitative literature reviews have concluded that the overall effects of divorce on children are statistically significant but small in magnitude, including several reviews of my own (Emery, 1982, 1988; Emery, Hetherington, & DiLalla, 1984; Emery & Forehand, in press; Emery & Kitzmann, in press). This conclusion is strongly supported by a recent meta-analysis of the divorce literature (Amato & Keith, 1991b). An average effect size of .14 SD units was found when all studies of children from married and divorced families were compared on all measures. Slightly larger effect sizes were found for some measures, but the differences remained modest nevertheless (see Table 9.3). A related meta-analysis on the adult adjustment of children from divorced families indicated slightly larger, but similarly modest differences (Amato & Keith, 1991a).

　　　　Overall, it can be concluded that the differences in the average adjustment of children from married and divorced families are small in

Table 9.3. Mean Effect Size for Adjustment Outcomes: Children Whose Parents Divorced or Remained Married

Measure of adjustment	Number of studies	Mean effect size[a]
School achievement	39	.16*
Conduct	56	.23*
Psychological adjustment	50	.08*
Self-concept	34	.09*
Social adjustment	39	.12*
Mother–child relations	22	.19*
Father–child relations	18	.26*

[a]All effect sizes are expressed in standard deviation units. For example, on an IQ test with an SD of 15, an effect size of .2 = 3 IQ points. All effects indicate more difficulties among those from divorced families.

*$p < .05$

Note: Adapted from P. R. Amato & B. Keith (1991b). Parental divorce and the well-being of children: A meta-analysis. *Psychological Bulletin, 110*, p. 30. Copyright 1991 by the American Psychological Association. Adapted by permission.

magnitude. This conclusion must be tempered by several qualifications, however. It is limited to demonstrated areas of measurement, the average adjustment of children, and relatively stable psychological outcomes. Greater differences might be found in areas of psychological health not measured in research conducted to date. Moreover, evidence on the average adjustment obscures the fact that some children suffer considerably as a result of divorce. Finally, the small differences found on measures of psychological disturbance do not mean that children feel no emotional distress about divorce. In fact, the resilience concept suggests that children are distressed by divorce, even as time passes and they cope successfully. Competence is not the same as invulnerability; disturbance may be absent but distress typically is present.

A Prospective View of Children's Adjustment to Divorce

This list of qualifications suggests caution about underestimating the distress that divorce causes for children, but some very important recent research raises the opposite concern. Research to date may overestimate the psychological disturbance produced by divorce, because studies have examined children's psychological functioning only *after* divorce. Psychological difficulties among children may develop *before* divorce, and if they do, they obviously cannot be consequences of divorce.

This possibility was first addressed in a small, but intensive longitudinal study of normal children and their families (Block, Block, & Gjerde, 1986). Children were followed throughout their childhood in this study of normal development, but because many parents divorced after the study began, the researchers could examine the adjustment of children both prior to and after divorce. Analysis of the longitudinal data indicated that, in comparison to boys whose parents were married, higher levels of aggression were found among boys after divorce. In fact, however, the increased aggression was present as many as 11 years prior to the marital separation (Block et al., 1986).

Another research group reported that difficulties found after divorce among adolescent girls actually were present before the marital separation. The same was not true for boys (Doherty & Needle, 1991). A third investigation of two large, nationally representative samples, one of 14,476 British children and the second of 2,279 American children, reached a similar conclusion about the timing of psychological problems, but a different one about gender. Predivorce problems accounted for many of the difficulties found among boys after divorce in comparison to boys whose parents were married. Few pre- or postdivorce difficulties were found for girls whose parents were divorced, however (Cherlin et al., 1991).

An independent analysis of the national sample of British children reached perhaps the most straightforward conclusion (Elliott & Richards, 1991). No effects attributable to a parental divorce occurring when children were 7 to 16 years old were found on measures of children's "unhappy and worried" behavior or their "disruptive" behavior. As is shown in Figure 9.1, mean differences between children from married and divorced families were present at age 16, but the same differences existed at age 7 when all of the children's parents were still married. Divorce was found to exacerbate preexisting differences on measures of children's math achievement, however (Elliott & Richards, 1991; see Figure 9.1).

Specific Outcomes of Concern

The global results of literature reviews and especially of prospective research are important, but evidence in some specific areas of psychological outcome deserves some further discussion. One such finding is contact with mental health professionals. Data from one nationally representative sample indicated that children from divorced homes were two to three times as likely to see a therapist as were children who lived with their married, biological parents (Zill, Morrison, & Coiro, 1993). Mental health utilization is an imperfect indicator of

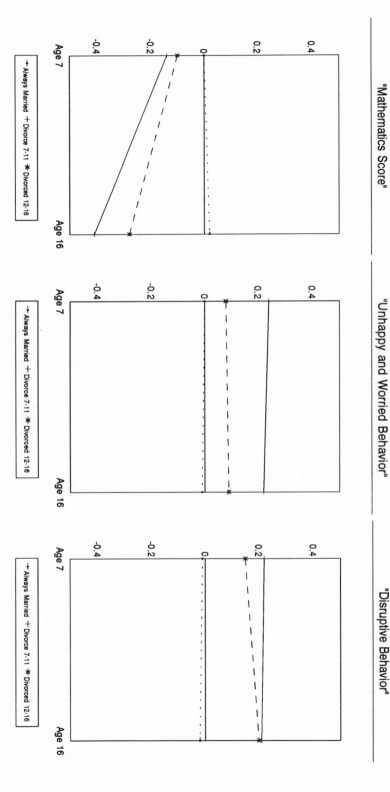

"Mathematics Score"

Age 7   Age 16

Always Married   + Divorce 7-11   ✳ Divorced 12-16

"Unhappy and Worried Behavior"

Age 7   Age 16

Always Married   + Divorce 7-11   ✳ Divorced 12-16

"Disruptive Behavior"

Age 7   Age 16

Always Married   + Divorce 7-11   ✳ Divorced 12-16

Figure 9.1. Children's psychological and academic functioning before and after divorce. All children with married parents at age 7, but some children experienced divorce before age 16. All scores were standardized.

children's psychological health, as it likely reflects parental overconcern in addition to children's emotional difficulties. Nevertheless, the finding does document parents' worries. For this reason alone, mediators should be prepared to answer questions about mental health services in their communities.

Another noteworthy finding is that externalizing problems such as disobedience, aggression, and conduct problems are more consistently linked to divorce than are internalizing difficulties such as fears, depression, and low self-esteem (Emery, 1988). Divorced parents' preoccupation with their own distress and difficulties in coordinating rules between households both can disrupt normal discipline. The less effective discipline, in turn, often is reflected in children's misbehavior. While most parents reestablish their roles as disciplinarians as time passes (Hetherington, 1991), evidence on externalizing problems indicates that maintaining consistency in discipline should be one of parents' foremost goals throughout the divorce transition.

A third outcome of special interest is evidence that experiencing a parental divorce increases the likelihood that one's own marriage will end in divorce. This intergenerational transmission of divorce has raised much concern, and some of these exaggerated worries border on suggestions of predestination: if your parents were divorced, you will get divorced too. Research demonstrates that a parental divorce is associated with an increase in divorce rates on the order of 5 to 10 percentage points (Martin & Emery, 1994). Such a moderate increase in risk is far from predestination, however, and other evidence suggests that it may be explained by factors such as earlier marriage and increased acceptance of divorce as a solution to an unhappy marriage (Martin & Emery, 1994). Still, the increased intergenerational risk is real, and marital stability often is a substantial concern among young adults from divorced families.

In summary, differences in the psychological adjustment of children from married and divorced families generally are modest in magnitude, and many of these differences antecede the parents' separation. These findings indicate that it is wrong to conclude that divorce places children at great risk for experiencing psychological disorder. Nevertheless, the emotional distress that divorce causes for resilient children must not be ignored, and concerns about certain areas of outcome seem well founded. In fact, the outcome of greatest concern has yet to be considered: a decline in the quality of ongoing family relationships. Evidence indicates that troubled family relationships form the most common negative outcome of divorce for children (Amato & Keith, 1991b; Zill et al., 1993). It is important to note that troubled family relationships are linked with children's psychological disturbance in both married and divorced families.

CHILDREN'S ADJUSTMENT AND THE PROCESS OF DIVORCE

Research indicates that most divorces involve an extremely difficult set of experiences that can last over an extended period of time. Divorce is a process of transition, not a discrete event. Pre- and postdivorce conflict between parents, uncertainty surrounding the marital separation, strained parent–child relationships, financial worries, and continuing changes such as remarriage are among the sources of potential distress. The extent and duration of these upheavals in family life are linked both with distress during the divorce transition and with an increased risk for psychological disturbances among children.

Parental Conflict

Conflict between parents is a consistent predictor of increased psychological difficulties among children from divorced—and married—families. Numerous experimental and field studies point to the detrimental role of parental conflict, particularly conflict that is extended, open, angry, unresolved, and involves the child (Cummings, 1987; Emery, 1982, 1988; Grych & Fincham, 1990). Parental conflict in divorce typically begins well before parents separate, and may continue long after the divorce is final. Conflict often is exacerbated by predictable events in the divorce process, such as marital separation, legal proceedings, relocation, and remarriage, which can adversely influence children in a number of ways.

Parental Anger as a Stressor

The stress caused by exposure to anger is perhaps the most notable consequences of parental conflict on children. Children as young as 18 months old become emotionally upset when they witness angry exchanges between adults, and by the age of 5 or 6, children's distress is evident in their attempts to intervene in the conflict (Cummings, Zahn-Waxler, & Radke-Yarrow, 1981, 1984). Children's emotional upset in reaction to anger between their parents or unfamiliar adults has even been demonstrated using psychophysiological measures (El-Sheikh, Cummings, & Goetsch, 1989; Gottman & Katz, 1989).

Moreover, laboratory studies have demonstrated that at least some of the effects of conflict on children are direct and do not result from other family problems such as troubled parent–child relationships (Cummings, 1987; Emery, Cummings, & Fincham, 1992).

Interventions and Alliances

The emotional distress that conflict creates for children can motivate them to intervene in parental disputes (Emery, 1989, 1992). Research indicates that children do become involved in these conflicts, and they form an alliance with one side against the other about half of the time that they intervene (Vuchinich, Emery, & Cassidy, 1988). Intervention strategies and alliances are meaningful not only for the immediate conflict, but also for ongoing family relationships (Emery, 1989, 1992). As discussed in Chapter 3, parents in the midst of a custody dispute can heighten children's dilemma by actively involving and competing for the children. Not surprisingly, children who feel caught in their parents' divorce disputes are more likely to have emotional difficulties. In one study, increased parental conflict was related to adolescents' adjustment problems only when the teens also felt caught in the middle of their parents' disputes (Buchanan et al., 1991).

Modeling and Discipline

Parental conflict also can directly and indirectly affect children through modeling and disruptions in discipline. Parents' angry and unresolved arguments serve as a model of inappropriate conflict resolution, and research has linked open marital conflict with increased aggression among children (Porter & O'Leary, 1980). Conflict also can disrupt children's socialization by altering discipline practices, particularly by making discipline inconsistent between the two parents. In one study, married parents' disagreements about childrearing not only predicted children's adjustment difficulties in school several years later, but it also predicted the parents' subsequent divorce (Block, Block, & Morrison, 1981). Such inconsistent discipline is a common correlate of emotional problems among children from both married and divorced families (Maccoby & Martin, 1983).

Other Triadic Processes

A number of other cognitive, emotional, and interpersonal processes may mediate the risk for children's psychological problems that accompanies parental conflict (Emery, 1982; Emery et al., 1992;

Emery, Joyce, & Fincham, 1987; Grych & Fincham, 1990). Children's perceptions of the conflict are likely to be particularly important, including the extent to which they see conflicts as being resolved, and the extent to which they believe it is their responsibility to help their parents to resolve them. Parents' perceptions are important too. Parents may project the hurt, sadness, or anger that they feel toward a former spouse onto their children, and thereby incorrectly conclude that their children feel the same way that they do (see Chapter 2). Alternatively, parents can displace their loving, lonely, or angry feelings toward a former spouse onto their children, and become overly invested or overly rejecting of their children as a result. Parents may be more likely to project hurt or sadness onto a child they view as being like themselves, while they may displace anger onto a child who resembles the former spouse.

Separation from Attachment Figures

Another major source of upset for children is the physical separation from one of their parents and the subsequent diminished and perhaps erratic contact with that parent. Attachment theory offers a valuable perspective on children's experiences of this separation distress (Bowlby, 1973). A period of protest or anger followed by despair is a predictable reaction to separation from an attachment figure. Protest and despair may be followed by detachment depending on the frequency, regularity, and quality of contact with the nonresidential parent. Children may eventually show little interest in the former attachment figure if contact is infrequent and emotionally distant. If contact with the nonresidential parent is fairly frequent but unpredictable, children may become preoccupied with the parent rather than detached. Such anxious attachments may continue over long periods of time, or they may eventually end in detachment.

Children's experience of separation distress also can be prolonged by each parent's ambivalence about divorce. Nearly half of all divorced couples separate and reconcile at least once before the final break (Kitson & Raschke, 1981). A quarter reconcile after filing a petition for a divorce (Kitson, Holmes, & Sussman, 1983). These episodes can cause children to experience repeated episodes of separation distress, and they also can make the final loss more uncertain and difficult for both children and parents to accept.

The limited cognitive capacity of young children means that they cannot grasp the concept of divorce; thus they can be expected to be particularly unprepared for the changes caused by the separation. Older children may anticipate the possibility of a separation, but its occurrence is likely to bring new fears and uncertainties. Whatever their age, children are likely to seek out and derive reassurance from whatever sources of security remain stable during the transition. Attachment researchers have found that separation distress can be alleviated by continuity in alternative sources of security (Bowlby, 1973). During a divorce, residential parents are the most important source of stability, but children's added needs for reassurance come at precisely the time when residential parents may be least able to meet them. In fact, the stability of virtually every source of security may be called into question by a divorce, including the family home, a familiar school, and friendships.

Ongoing Parent–Child Relationships

Many other changes in parent–child relationships are likely to occur beyond the immediate separation. The changes are not uniform across mothers and fathers, residential and nonresidential parents, different families, or for the same family over time, but researchers have documented some general patterns. Residential parents typically are overworked, overwrought, and overwhelmed by their children's needs, while nonresidential parents are more likely to feel unwanted, unimportant, and unappreciated. Evidence suggests that such parenting problems are particularly prominent in the first years following a separation, a time when emotional and practical demands on family members are at a peak (Hetherington, 1989; Hetherington, Cox, & Cox, 1982). Gender differences in parenting strain are found, as fathers report more difficulty monitoring their children's behavior, school work, and health, while mothers report more troubles with being firm and patient irrespective of residence (Maccoby & Mnookin, 1992). In general, however, the contrasting issues faced by residential and nonresidential parents apply to both women and men.

Residential Parents

It is helpful to consider changes in parent–child relationships in terms of the dimensions of warmth and discipline—love and power—and the categorizations derived from these dimensions; the authoritative, authoritarian, indulgent, and neglectful parenting styles (Maccoby & Martin, 1983; see Chapter 3). Several investigators have found divorced, residential mothers to be either less warm or less effective in their discipline. That is, divorced mothers tend to be more permissive or disengaged than their married counterparts (e.g., Capaldi & Patterson, 1991; Fauber, Forehand, Thomas, & Wierson, 1990; Forehand,

Thomas, Wierson, Brody, & Fauber, 1990; Hess & Camara, 1979; Wallerstein & Kelly, 1980). Recent research indicates that at least some of these parenting difficulties are present before the marital separation, however (Block, Block, & Gjerde, 1988; Shaw, Emery, & Tuer, 1993), and other findings point to the dynamics of change in parent–child relationships after divorce.

Hetherington's (1989, 1991; Hetherington, Cox, & Cox, 1982) longitudinal study of mother custody families provides a wealth of information on the evolution of residential mother–child relationships after divorce. In this study, parenting strain was found to be at a peak one year after divorce. Divorced mothers made fewer maturity demands, communicated less well, were less affectionate, more inconsistent, and less effective in controlling their children when compared to mothers who remained married. Particular difficulties were found in mother–son relationships. Two years after divorce, mothers were more nurturant, consistent, and in control of their children than they had been previously, but they remained less so than married mothers. By six years after divorce, residential mothers were as affectionate as nondivorced mothers, but they continued to be more negative and less effective in discipline, especially with sons. Divorced mothers also gave their children more responsibility at home and more independence in their own lives. In short, over time divorced mothers moved from being more neglectful to more indulgent than married mothers (Hetherington, 1989, 1991; Hetherington, Cox, & Cox, 1985).

Little research has been conducted on residential fathers. Investigators have noted that residential fathers share many common struggles with residential mothers, but each typically faces greater challenges in the role traditionally fulfilled by the opposite sex (Luepnitz, 1982). Residential fathers have more difficulties with parenting and household responsibilities, while mothers worry more about finances. In general, such gender differences are outweighed by the similar experiences of residential parents of either sex, however (Risman & Park, 1988). Furthermore, while some researchers have found that children fare best when living with a same-sex residential parent (Warshak, 1986), recent evidence has challenged this finding (Downey & Powell, 1993).

Divorce permanently changes residential parenting from a more to a less adaptive style for some families. Residential parents who are depressed, who are cut off from kin and friendship support networks, who have more severe economic concerns, or who have a number of young children are more likely to have lasting difficulties (Emery et al., 1984). In turn, children have more psychological disturbances when residential parent–child communication is poor, problem solving is ineffective, children's behavior is monitored less closely, and parent–child relationships lack warmth (Capaldi & Patterson, 1991; Fauber et al., 1990; Forehand et al., 1990). Simply put, children from divorced families have more psychological problems when their residential parents are disengaged rather than authoritative, a pattern that is consistent with the general literature on parenting styles (Maccoby & Martin, 1983).

Nonresidential Parents

As noted earlier, many children have little contact with their nonresidential fathers (see Table 9.2). Other evidence documents changes in the quality of these relationships as well. In general, nonresidential father–child relationships are less close and more indulgent in divorced than in married families (e.g., Hetherington, Cox, & Cox, 1976; Peterson & Zill, 1986). Much of the interaction between nonresidential fathers and their children is social in nature, and teenagers report feeling both less close to and less disciplined by nonresidential than married fathers (Furstenberg & Nord, 1985). Although teenagers report having a better relationship with nonresidential mothers, problems also develop with mothers by the time children become young adults (Zill et al., 1993).

Over time, nonresidential parent–child relationships tend to normalize, but divorced fathers continue to be less restrictive than married fathers (Hetherington et al., 1982). Thus, many nonresidential parent–child relationships fall into the category of indulgent parenting. For another substantial group of parents, a neglectful style clearly is suggested by the data on infrequent contact. It is essential to note, however, that children regard their nonresidential parents as vital figures in their lives nevertheless. In one national survey, for example, half of all adolescents listed their nonresidential fathers as members of their family despite low average levels of contact (Furstenberg & Nord, 1985).

Given the vehement debates about the topic, it is surprising how little research has focused on the link between nonresidential parenting and children's psychological well-being. In one of the best studies conducted to date, no consistent relations were found between the amount of contact and children's adjustment. Similarly, a measure of children's perceived closeness to their nonresidential fathers was unrelated to indices of their adjustment (Furstenberg, Morgan, & Allison, 1987). Other researchers have found either no or inconsistent relations between visitation frequency and children's mental health (Kline, Johnston, & Tschann, 1991; Kurdek, 1986; Kurdek, Blisk, & Siesky, 1981; Luepnitz, 1982).

Visitation duration, but not frequency, was related to better child adjustment in one study (Hess & Camara, 1979), and other investigators have found more frequent visitation to be associated with better adjustment among children under circumscribed conditions (Hetherington, Cox, & Cox, 1978; Wallerstein & Kelly, 1980). Two of the most important constraints identified in research are the presence of conflict and the quality of residential parent–child relationships. Frequent contact with nonresidential parents may create more problems for children when parental conflict is intense (Buchanan et al., 1991). Other research suggests that a good relationship with at least one parent may buffer the ill effects of a bad relationship with the other (Camara & Resnick, 1987; Peterson & Zill, 1986).

Given the small body of evidence and limited outcome measures, it would be premature to conclude that nonresidential parents are of little importance to children from divorced families. In one national survey, 76% of teenagers living with single mothers reported that their fathers loved and were interested in them, as did 93% of children living with remarried mothers, and 83% of children living in married families (Furstenberg & Nord, 1985). Such findings suggest that children have important, conflicted, and largely undocumented feelings about their nonresidential parents. These relationships appear to be at least of symbolic importance to adolescents, even if frequent contact has not been found to be related to improvements in teenagers' psychological adjustment. In short, great caution must be exercised about drawing conclusions about children's relationships with their nonresidential parents when so much has gone unmeasured in research to date.

Joint versus Sole Physical Custody

Another caution has been noted by advocates of joint physical custody. These proponents argue that it is not surprising that "visitation" is unrelated to children's adjustment, because parent–child relationships are marginalized by this arrangement. It can be noted, for example, that nonresidential fathers saw their children as little as 25 days per year (two days a month) in the *high* contact group in one of the major studies of visitation (Furstenberg et al., 1987). Others point out that many fathers are not "dropout dads," but they are interested fathers who are actively discouraged from investing in their children's lives after divorce (Braver et al., 1993).

Several researchers have compared children living under joint and sole custody arrangements. This evidence cannot be conclusive, because joint custody parents are older, wealthier, and better educated than sole custody parents (Luepnitz, 1982; Racusin et al., 1989), and they also may be especially cooperative coparents. Studies are of value nevertheless if only for providing evidence about what is possible in postdivorce parenting.

Researchers have found that children can function well even under complex joint physical custody arrangements, thus alleviating concerns that such arrangements are inappropriate (Clingempeel & Reppucci, 1982). However, evidence is not strong that joint custody improves children's mental health. In one of the better early studies no differences were found between children living in maternal, paternal, or joint custody, but the degree of parental conflict predicted children's adjustment in all three arrangements (Luepnitz, 1982). Other investigators have reported positive if small differences in favor of joint custody, although the influence of family processes again appears to outweigh the influence of custody structures (Folberg, 1991; Shiller, 1986; Wolchik, Braver, & Sandler, 1985).

Some investigators have indicated, moreover, that children suffer under joint physical custody when their parents are in conflict (Johnston, Kline, & Tschann, 1989). In fact, recent evidence suggests that joint physical custody may be either the best or the worst alternative for children. When parents are fighting, children suffer under joint physical custody. When fighting is contained, children do better with joint than with sole physical custody (Maccoby, Buchanan, Mnookin, & Dornbusch, 1993). However, one researcher found that even in the face of considerable conflict, joint custody can work if mutual parenting respect is maintained, personal feelings are distinguished from the needs of the children, and parental and spousal roles are separated (Steinman, Zemmelman, & Knoblauch, 1985).

Joint *legal* custody also has been found to be linked with some modest improvements in postdivorce family relationships. Contact between nonresidential parents and their children is somewhat greater (Bowman & Ahrons, 1985; Grief, 1979), and compliance with child support awards is better (Braver et al., 1993; Pearson & Thoennes, 1985). Thus, joint legal or physical custody is no solution for contentious couples, but it offers some benefits for children when parents can agree to work together as parents.

Remarriage, Economic Decline, and Other Family Changes

Changes in relationships between members of the former nuclear family are the primary concern of this chapter, but the relation between children's mental health and a few additional strains that accompany divorce must be elaborated at least briefly. Remarriage is one of the most important of these. Recent evidence suggests that gender differences in children's adjustment to remarriage may be the opposite of what is sometimes found following divorce. Girls have more difficulties following remarriage, while boys have an easier time with remarriage than with divorce (Needle, Su & Doherty, 1990; Vuchinich, Hetherington, Vuchinich, & Clingempeel, 1991). However, contradictory findings have been reported (Hetherington & Clingempeel, 1992), and the appropriate focus of remarriage research is on family processes not structures, as is the case with divorce research.

Children's relationships with the custodial parents may influence their adjustment to remarriage. The new stepparent may have a positive influence on children when single parenting has been troubled. When children have developed a close and involved relationship with their custodial parent, however, it may be more difficult for them to accept a stepparent (Furstenberg & Spanier, 1984; Hetherington & Clingempeel, 1992). This may explain why sex differences sometimes have been found in children's coping with remarriage. Girls may be more likely than boys to view the stepfather as an intruder, because they are closer to their mothers following divorce (Peterson & Zill, 1986; Vuchinich et al., 1991).

The quality of children's developing relationship with their new stepparent is another factor of obvious importance to their adjustment to remarriage. Of particular concern is that stepparents strike a balance in their new role. Problems have been reported both when stepfathers become involved in parenting too quickly and when they remain aloof and disengaged from their stepchildren (Hetherington, 1991; Hetherington & Clingempeel, 1992). Good relationships with stepparents seem to be achieved more readily with young children, while teenagers have more difficulty.

Remarriage can also rekindle old marital tensions and create new loyalty dilemmas for children (Wallerstein & Kelly, 1980). As noted earlier, visitation with the nonresidential parent decreases following remarriage. In addition, custody battles may be renewed, as the remarried parent may feel better equipped to care for the children, or the unremarried parent may feel threatened by the presence of a same-sex stepparent (Furstenberg & Spanier, 1984). Finally, the fact that remarriages often are followed by a second divorce means that many children experience multiple, difficult transitions (Cherlin, 1992).

Financial Difficulties

Divorce entails a variety of economic challenges, as well as social and psychological changes. The most notable is a lowered standard of living, particularly for divorced women and their custodial children. The economic problems are of sufficient magnitude to be a growing concern for public welfare agencies. In 1987, 46.1% of families with children that were headed by women had incomes below poverty level, and 60.5% of female-headed families with children under the age of 6 were living in poverty (SCCYF, 1989). Moreover, 35% of families receiving AFDC benefits in 1987 were divorced or separated (SCCYF, 1989).

The fact that marital dissolution rates are higher among low-income families explains part of these statistics, but longitudinal data indicate that separation and divorce directly affect the proportion of families living in poverty. Between 1966 and 1981, 9.9% of white women with minor children had family incomes below the poverty level when married, but that percentage increased to 28.7% following divorce. For nonwhite women, 33.4% were below the poverty line when married, 44.3% after divorce. In contrast, the percentage of men living at poverty levels actually *decreased* following divorce. For whites, 9.2% of the men had incomes below the poverty level when married, while 4.8% were impoverished following divorce. Among nonwhite men, 35.7% lived in poverty when married, 26.1% following divorce (Nichols-Casebolt, 1986).

A variety of factors contribute to the lower standard of living of divorced families, and declining living standards can set into motion a series of changes that tax children's coping resources. Important life events may include moving from the family home, changing schools, losing contact with old friends, spending more time in childcare settings while their mother is working, and dealing with their parents' preoccupation with and conflict over financial matters. In fact, it has been suggested that economics alone may account for the psychological difficulties experienced by children following divorce. In their influential review, Herzog and Sudia (1973) noted that socioeconomic controls attenuate or eliminate many of the differences in delinquency, academics, and sex-role behavior found in studies comparing children from father-absent and father-present households. More recent evidence indicates that differences between one- and two-parent families generally decrease, but do not disappear, when income controls are introduced (Amato & Keith, 1991; Emery, 1988).

Parental Mental Health

Studies of adult mental health invariably find a link between marital status and psychopathology, such that married or remarried adults have fewer mental health problems than single or divorced adults. In fact, marital status has been found to be a better predictor of adult mental health than age, race, socioeconomic status, or childhood experience (e.g., Gove, Hughes, & Styles, 1983). As with other issues, however, the question arises as to whether the adult mental health problems are consequences of divorce, and therefore constitute a new stressor for children, or whether the parental problems predate and perhaps precipitate the divorce.

In reviewing evidence on marriage and adult mental health, Gotlib and McCabe (1990) concluded that research suggests both that preexisting psychological problems increase the risk for divorce and that divorce increases the risk for psychological problems. They argue that evidence that psychopathology causes divorce is strongest for severe emotional disorders such as schizophrenia and alcoholism, while less severe problems such as depression and anxiety appear to be partially a consequence of divorce, especially among women. Although divorce may not be the cause of severe, prolonged mental health problems among adults, such a conclusion is consistent with the common clinical view that divorce precipitates a period of grief among adults (Kitson, 1992; Somary & Emery, 1991; Weiss, 1988; see Chapter 2).

Other evidence indicates that maternal depression explains significant variance in adolescents' psychological difficulties after divorce, even when the effects due to parenting are statistically controlled (Forehand et al., 1990). Although it is possible that preexisting parental psychological problems account both for divorce and for psychological difficulites among children (e.g., Lahey et al., 1988), research and clinical observation suggest that yet another challenge that children face in divorce is coping with parents who are dealing with their own emotional struggles. In part because the parents' emotional state is significant for children but more because it plays a crucial role in many custody disputes, this chapter concludes with a brief review of adults' coping with divorce.

PARENTS' ADJUSTMENT AND THE DIVORCE PROCESS

Divorce has been ranked as being second only to the death of a spouse in terms of the amount of stress it places on adults (Holmes & Rahe, 1967). A variety of adverse emotional reactions have been described including anger, sadness, and regret. In interviews conducted an average of 16 months after a divorce, Spanier and Thompson (1984) found a strong sense of anger, for example, but found feelings of guilt and remorse to be more common. Almost all of the individuals in the study also reported feeling lonely, with 30% having periods of severe loneliness.

Such feelings are directly linked with the marital breakup, and to varying degrees they dissipate with time (Kitson, 1992). Other research has tied divorce to more enduring problems that are not necessarily directly linked to feelings about the marriage. People from disrupted marriages have a higher rate of psychopathology, as indicated by a wide range of measures (Bloom, Asher, & White, 1978; Gotlib & McCabe, 1990). In particular, considerable depression has been found among divorced adults (Menaghan & Lieberman, 1986), particularly among those who remain more attached to their former spouse (Kitson, 1992).

The degree of predivorce marital conflict may be related to postdivorce adjustment. It is essential to note, however, that the association for adults may be the inverse of what is found for children. Adults whose marriage was extremely unhappy may have an *easier* time accepting its termination. In one study, increased bickering and irritation made for easier acceptance of the divorce, whereas both spouses found it difficult to end the marriage if their marital relationship had been calm (Spanier & Thompson, 1984).

Contact with the children also seems to influence adults' adjustment to divorce. Lack of contact with the children is a correlate of distress among men (Kitson, 1992), while more symptoms of depression are found among custodial mothers who have either three or more children, young children, or boys rather than girls (Price-Bonham & Balswick, 1980). Apparently, some contact with the children serves a supportive function for parents, while single parents can be overwhelming when child care demands are particularly high. Social isolation from family and friends also is related to adults' maladjustment (Kitson, 1992), and the association between remarriage and improved adjustment may be explained by the supportive functions that marriage offers (Weingarten, 1983). Together, this evidence clearly highlights the importance of positive relationships to parents' as well as children's mental health.

SUMMARY

Research on children and divorce is important to examine if for no other reason than that the evidence contradicts much conventional wisdom. Custody arrangements largely continue to be "traditional" (with mother residence as the norm, father residence as the exception), and joint physical custody is an important alternative chosen only by a minority of parents. Data indicate that joint legal custody has become a new norm in certain regions of the country, but demographics also highlight the large number of fathers who drop out of their children's lives following separation and divorce.

Another surprise in empirical research is that relatively small differences are found between children whose parents have divorced and children whose parents remain married. Evidence establishes children's resilience, their competence in coping with the multiple stressors introduced by divorce. Successful coping must be distinguished from the absence of distress, however, and it is clear that children do experience much distress before, during, and after divorce. Sensitivity is needed both in recognizing children's strengths and in supporting them in their struggles.

The quality of ongoing family relationships is a key predictor of more or less adequate adjustment to divorce among children. Parental conflict throughout the divorce transition is a consistent predictor of maladjustment among children, as is the less adequate parenting that characterizes most divorces, at least temporarily. Economic problems strain all members of the divorced family system, and while remarriage may solve many financial woes, it typically introduces rather than alleviates relationship concerns. Like divorce, remarriage is best construed as a developmental transition that unfolds and generally is managed more adequately with the passage of time.

Divorce poses many immediate and long-term challenges for adults as well as children. These difficulties must be recognized by mediators. Parents in mediation often are preoccupied with their own, conflicting emotions. Mediators must not attempt to squelch parents' understandable and strong emotions. Rather, the goal is to help them to express these feelings in more appropriate ways in mediation and hopefully in their everyday lives as well.

CHAPTER 10

His and Her Divorce Revisited

The discussion of psychological research on parents' and children's mental health brings the focus back to the major issues raised in the first chapter of this book. Based on both clinical practice and empirical research, it is clear that the tone of custody disputes and children's experience of the divorce transition depend greatly on the parents' emotions, which, in turn, depend heavily on their past, present, and future relationship with their former spouse.

Even as they decide to end their marriage, former partners who remain parents must renegotiate their relationship. The task is unavoidable. Some former partners will meet regularly to discuss their circumstances. Others will refuse to speak to one another once they have separated. Through these and other actions, the partners inevitably define new boundaries for relating to one another and to their children.

The lack of correspondence between parents' and children's emotional needs during this extremely difficult transition is a major dilemma in divorce—perhaps the central emotional dilemma. In particular, conflict helps former partners to achieve the needed distance in their relationship. The venting of anger also can temporarily ease grief. However, parental battles only exacerbate the difficulties for children who already are torn by divorce.

The negotiation of custody agreements reflects the partners' struggle to balance their own needs with their children's. The former partners' attempts to renegotiate their relationship can be expected to continue throughout mediation. At the same time, the substantive details of a custody agreement—and the process of negotiating it—are major steps toward redefining the relationships between the members of the postdivorce family. Mediation involves negotiating agreements and renegotiating relationships.

Having come full circle in discussing the psychological and legal rationales for mediation, methods for conducting the process, and empirical evidence on mediation and divorce, some of the major themes of this book can be recapitulated by briefly returning to the case studies presented in Chapter 1. Let us reconsider Sheila and John, the couple whose case history was used to illustrate "his" and "her" divorce.

THE CASE OF SHEILA AND JOHN REVISITED

Sheila and John had recently separated in the case history presented in Chapter 1. Sheila initiated the separation much to John's great dismay. The parents had an informal arrangement whereby their 5- and 7-year-old children resided with Sheila, but the children would spend every Saturday night and Sunday daytime with John. The case history ended with John's refusal to return the two children after a weekend visit. He had heard that "possession is nine-tenths of the law," and he told Sheila that he would not return the children until she agreed to joint physical custody. John's actions appeared to reflect his struggle to save the marriage at least as much as his concern for the children.

It is easy to envision a number of alternative scenarios for John and Sheila at this point in time. The possibilities range from John calling Sheila back to apologize and return the children, to Sheila calling her lawyer to schedule an emergency custody hearing on Monday morning. As discussed in Chapters 2 and 3, the key to achieving a more adaptive outcome rests with John's awareness of his own conflicting emotions, as well as his recognition of the children's needs. John may be incapable of achieving such insights during the emotional weeks, months, and even years following the end of his marriage. On the other hand, perhaps his hurt, longing, and loneliness might come rushing into his awareness once he slammed down the telephone on Sunday night. Although his immediate reactions are uncertain, it is clear that John will need considerable time to cope with his grief and eventually accept the end of his marriage.

It is also possible that John's actions in withholding the children were motivated by his continued attempts to manipulate Sheila rather than by his desperate love for her. While this possibility suggests a very different scenario to follow, in either case, it is obvious that John's refusal to return the children reflected his feelings for Sheila at least as much as his feelings for the children. At some level, John wanted to get Sheila's attention, and he succeeded.

It is easy to empathize with the terror that Sheila must have felt when John refused to return the children. If John really was cold, calculating, and manipulative, an emergency custody hearing might be Sheila's best option, perhaps her only one. In fact, it may be easier to empathize with Sheila in general. As with most partners' who initiate a separation, Sheila had a much longer time to cope with her grief. Her actions therefore are likely to be better planned, and she is much less likely to seem erratic or out of control.

However, it may be too easy for mediators to empathize with the more rational partner who leaves a marriage. If Sheila was caught up in the fantasies of an affair, John's actions still would be very wrong, but more readily understood. How can we expect John to be rational when his wife just left him for someone else, and he is confronted with losing his children as well? John and Sheila both need to be able to see the children's perspective on the separation, but perhaps Sheila also needs to try to understand John's perspective, which is very different from her own.

Perhaps an emergency custody hearing would be the best recourse for both John and Sheila. Both of them may need legal protection. Sheila may need to be protected from an action that borderd on child snatching. John may need a legal advocate to help him overturn an informal arrangement that he negotiated while he was emotionally distraught. In considering the option of going to court, clear guidance from the law would be extremely helpful. As discussed in Chapter 4, however, the law is indeterminate. The uncertain outcome of a custody hearing would be likely to exacerbate conflict between John and Sheila, as they each tried to convince a judge that one was right and the other was wrong.

Certainly, the judge who heard this case would wish for concrete guidance from the law. Perhaps an hour would be allotted to an emergency hearing. In this time, it would be impossible for the judge to uncover the truth about John and Sheila, if there was some ultimate truth. Certainly, the judge could not be expected to discern what would be in the children's best interests during this short period of time.

Consider what might happen if the court required Sheila and John first to attend a mediation session on Monday morning. The judge would enter the case only if one of the parents still wanted an emergency hearing after this meeting. The ground rules discussed in Chapter 6 would be much needed both by the mediator and the parents in order to structure the emotionally intense meeting. In fact, it might be wise for John and Sheila to meet with the mediator separately. Whether they met together or individually, the mediation session might be a waste of time. John might be unyielding. Sheila might be hysterical. It might be necessary for a judge to make a decision for them.

Of course, mediation could lead to a more positive outcome. John might be adamant and angry in Sheila's presence, but perhaps he would burst into tears during a caucus. A mediator's empathy—or confrontation—might help him to recognize his underlying feelings and the error in his actions. Sheila too might gain insight during this mediation session. She might realize that the separation was more complicated than she had hoped or planned. As a result of their increased awareness, perhaps John and Sheila would agree to return temporarily to their informal plan for the children. Additional meetings could be scheduled, and the parents could work toward developing a more permanent arrangement during these subsequent meetings.

As noted throughout the book, John and Sheila would hardly be expected to "be friends" after this first mediation session. Rather, one goal of mediation is simply to avoid a custody hearing, and it can be successful in meeting this goal (Chapter 8). Perhaps mediation might not have been effective for Sheila and John, but without mediation, it is easy to envision the beginning of a legal feud between them. Whoever lost the temporary custody hearing would not be likely to stop there. In the coming weeks and months, both John and Sheila might concentrate on building a case against the other. During this time, their individual past failings as spouses and parents—distorted by the pending trial and their strong emotions—could be garnered as potential evidence to be used in the ultimate court battle. Friends, family, and the children all would be likely to be interviewed by one side or the other. John and Sheila surely would become enemies, not friends, under this scenario.

This outcome would be particularly unfortunate if Sheila and John continued to paint overly harsh portraits of each other and to exaggerate their true bargaining positions, as suggested by research on adversarial negotiations (Chapter 5). Their negotiations and their emotions would doubtless become polarized by positional bargaining, but perhaps the truth of their marriage was not so extreme. Perhaps John was cold and indifferent, not in any extreme sense, but only according to what Sheila discovered that she wanted in a man and in a marriage. In this circumstance, mediation might give the couple a chance to negotiate an agreement in a relatively calm manner, while the process also would give Sheila and John time to cope with their conflicting feelings about each other and themselves.

Sheila might have to cope with her own guilt about the children and her lingering concern for John's well-being. These feelings might cause Sheila to do things that are well-intentioned but confusing both to John and to the children. She might plan occasional activities for the four of them, telephone John just to talk, or frequently ask him to take care of the children during her times with them. The structured parenting plans that the mediator encourages (see Chapters 3 and 7) could help the couple to develop clearer boundaries. Sheila might recognize that her actions send mixed messages to John, and that he may never be able to be friendly in the way she wants.

The relief from time pressures, the structure, and the support offered in mediation also could help John to begin to accept his circumstances over time. He might be unprepared to sign a final agreement any time soon, but he is likely to be willing to agree to a temporary plan, perhaps one that was modified to work better for both the parents and the children. The mediator might well give John the name of a therapist who would help John express and understand his conflicting emotions. If John and Sheila return to mediation 6 months later in order to review the temporary agreement, John should be more prepared emotionally to reach a more permanent agreement. Both he and Sheila certainly would know much more about how their arrangement was working; hence they also might want to renegotiate some details of the agreement.

This scenario would not lead to a "happy ending" for Sheila and John. At best, perhaps the ending only would be less harmful than the alternatives.

A COMMENT ON THE FUTURE OF CUSTODY MEDIATION

The times were ripe for the emergence of custody mediation in the 1980s. Divorce rates rose to an all-time high as divorce laws were being rewritten to reflect gender neutrality and increasing pluralism in American family life. Dissatisfaction with lawyering also was widespread during this time. Litigation increasingly was criticized as being expensive, time consuming, and divisive, and alternative dispute resolution was embraced across the spectrum of legal conflicts. Finally, concerns about the psychological functioning of children from divorced families were raised repeatedly during the 1980s. Although many issues remain unresolved, mental health professionals agreed that conflict between married and divorced parents was dysfunctional for children. Mediation promised to reduce litigation, encourage new ways of resolving disputes, and contain family conflict in the process. Clearly, the times were ripe for this social innovation.

Research indicates that custody mediation can fulfill the first two of these three promises, while at the same time possibly preventing the occurence of psychological difficulties among parents and children—even though there is a lack of positive evidence to support this to date. Despite its subtantial impact in a very short period of time, however, broad questions still can be raised about the future of custody mediation.

Was the convergence of events in the 1980s unusual? Will new societal changes soon make custody mediation outdated? Will gender neutrality become a less pressing value in American family life? Will divorce laws be rewritten to be more determinative about postdivorce parenting? Will divorce rates decline and make custody a less pressing issue? Will the entrenched adversary system undermine efforts at establishing alternative dispute resolution? Does custody mediation really offer a win–win–win alternative that is simultaneously more healthy and more fair to children, mothers, and fathers?

These broad questions will be investigated by researchers, policy makers, and the public in the 1990s and beyond. In whatever way these questions are answered, I am certain that the ultimate goal of custody mediation is the right one. If children's interests are to be taken seriously, new ways to divorce must be invented in order to protect children from becoming caught in the crossfire of their parents' conflicts.

References

Amato, P. R. (1991). The "child of divorce" as a person prototype: Bias in the recall of information about children in divorced families. *Journal of Marriage and the Family, 53,* 59–69.

Amato, P. R., & Keith, B. (1991a). Parental divorce and adult well-being: A meta-analysis. *Journal of Marriage and the Family, 53,* 43–58.

Amato, P. R., & Keith, B. (1991b). Parental divorce and the well-being of children: A meta-analysis. *Psychological Bulletin, 110,* 26–46.

American Bar Association. (1969). *Code of professional responsibility.* Washington, DC: Author.

Axelrod, R. (1984). *The evolution of cooperation.* New York: Basic Books.

Bainham, A. (1990). The privatisation of the public interest in children. *Modern Law Review, 53,* 206–221.

Bandura, A. (1977). Self-efficacy: Toward a unifying theory of behavioral change. *Psychological Review, 84,* 191–195.

Baumrind, D. (1971). Current patterns of parental authority. *Developmental Psychology Monograph, 4* (1, Pt 2).

Benjamin, L. S. (1974). Structural analysis of social behavior. *Psychological Review, 81,* 392–425.

Bernard, J. (1972). *The future of marriage.* New York: World.

Bienenfeld, F. (1983). *Child custody mediation: Techniques for counselors, attorneys and parents.* Science and Behavior Books.

Bishop, T. A. (1988). Standards of practice for divorce mediators. In J. Folberg & A. Milne (Eds.), *Divorce mediation: Theory and practice* (pp. 403–428). New York: Guilford Press.

Block, J. H., Block, J., & Gjerde, P. F. (1986). The personality of children prior to divorce: A prospective study. *Child Development, 57,* 827–840.

Block, J. H., Block, J., & Gjerde, P. F. (1988). Parental functioning and the home environment in families of divorce: Prospective and concurrent analyses. *Journal of the American Academy of Child and Adolescent Psychiatry, 27,* 207–213.

Block, J. H., Block, J., & Morrison, A. (1981). Parental agreement–disagreement on child-rearing orientations and gender-related personality correlates in children. *Child Development, 52,* 965–974.

Bloom, B. L., Asher, S. J., & White, S. W. (1978). Marital disruption as a stressor: A review and analysis. *Psychological Bulletin, 85,* 867–894.

Bohannon, P. (1970). The six stations of divorce. In P. Bohannon (Ed.), *Divorce and after: An analysis of the emotional and social problems of divorce* (pp. 29–55). New York: Doubleday.

Bowlby, J. (1969). *Attachment and loss: Attachment* (Vol. 1). London: Hogarth Press.

Bowlby, J. (1973). *Attachment and loss: Separation* (Vol. 2). London: Hogarth Press.

Bowlby, J. (1979). *The making and breaking of affectional bonds.* London: Tavistock.

Bowlby, J. (1980). *Attachment and loss: Loss* (Vol. 3). London: Hogarth Press.

Bowman, M. E., & Ahrons, C. R. (1985). Impact of legal custody status on fathers' parenting postdivorce. *Journal of Marriage and the Family, 47,* 481–488.

Bowman, S. C. (1990). Idaho's decision on divorce mediation. *Idaho Law Review, 26,* 547–573.

Braver, S. L., Wolchik, S. A., Sandler, I. N., Sheets, V. L., Fogas, B., & Bay, R. C. (1993). A longitudinal study of noncustodial parents: Parents without children. *Journal of Family Psychology, 7,* 9–23.

Buchanan, C. M., Maccoby, E. E., & Dornbusch, S. M. (1991). Caught between parents: Adolescents' experience in divorced homes. *Child Development, 62,* 1008–1029.

Bumpass, L. (1984). Children and marital disruption:A replication and update. *Demography, 21,* 71–82.

Camara, K. A., & Resnick, G. (1987). Marital and parental subsystems in mother-custody, father-custody and two-parent households: Effects on children's social development. In J. Vincent (Ed.), *Advances in family assessment, intervention and research* (Vol. 4, pp. 165–196). Greenwich, CT: JAI.

Cameron, N., & Rychlak, J. F. (1985). *Personality development and psychopathology: A dynamic approach.* Boston: Houghton Mifflin.

Capaldi, D. M., & Patterson, G. R. (1991). Relation of parental transitions to boys' adjustment problems: I. A linear hypothesis. II. Mothers at risk for transitions and unskilled parenting. *Developmental Psychology, 3,* 489–504.

Catania, F. J. (1992). Accounting to ourselves for ourselves: An analysis of adjudication in the resolution of child custody disputes. *Nebraska Law Review, 71,* 1228–1271.

Cherlin, A. J. (1977). The effect of children on marital dissolution. *Demography, 14,* 265–272.

Cherlin, A. J. (1992). *Marriage, divorce, remarriage* (2nd ed.). Cambridge, MA: Harvard University Press.

Cherlin, A. J., Furstenberg, F. F., Chase-Lansdale, P. L., Kiernan, K. E., Robins, P. K., Morrison, D. R., & Teitler, J. O. (1991). Longitudinal studies of effects of divorce on children in Great Britain and the United States. *Science, 252,* 1386–1389.

Clingempeel, W. G., & Reppucci, N. D. (1982). Joint custody after divorce: Major issues and goals for research. *Psychological Bulletin, 91,* 102–127.

Cochran, R. F. (1987). Mediation of marital disputes before it is too late: A proposal for premarital contract provisions for mediation of disputes within the intact family and at separation. *Pepperdine Law Review, 15,* 51–64.

Coogler, O. J. (1978). *Structured mediation in divorce settlement.* Lexington, MA: Heath.

Cummings, E. M. (1987). Coping with background anger in early childhood. *Child Development, 58,* 976–984.

Cummings, E. M., Zahn-Waxler, C., & Radke-Yarrow, M. (1981). Young children's responses to expressions of anger and affection by others in the family. *Child Development, 52,* 1274–1282.

Cummings, E. M., Zahn-Waxler, C., & Radke-Yarrow, M., (1984). Developmental changes in children's reactions to anger in the home. *Journal of Child Psychology and Psychiatry, 25,* 63–74.

Depner, C. E., Cannata, K. V., & Simon, M. B. (1992). Building a uniform statistical reporting system: A snapshot of California Family Court services. *Family and Conciliation Courts Review, 30,* 185–206.

Derdeyn, A. P. (1976). Child custody contests in historical perspective. *American Journal of Psychiatry, 133,* 1369–1376.

Doherty, W. J., & Needle, R. H. (1991). Psychological adjustment and substance use among adolescents before and after a parental divorce. *Child Development, 62,* 328–337.

Downey, D. B., & Powell, B. (1993). Do children in single-parent households fare better living with same-sex parents? *Journal of Marriage and the Family, 55,* 55–71.

Duncan, G. J., & Hoffman, S. D. (1985). Economic consequences of marital instability. In M. David & T. Smeeding (Eds.), *Horizontal equity, uncertainty and well-being* (pp. 427–469). Chicago: University of Chicago Press.

D'Zurrilla, T., & Goldfried, M. (1971). Problem solving and behavior modificatin. *Journal of Abnormal Psychology, 78,* 107–126.

Edwards, J. N. (1987). Changing family structure and youthful well-being: Assessing the future. *Journal of Family Issues, 8,* 355–372.

Eekelaar, J. (1991). *Regulating divorce.* New York: Oxford University Press.

Elliott, B. J., & Richards, M. P. M. (1991). Children and divorce: Educational performance and behaviour before and after parental separation. *International Journal of Law and the Family, 5,* 258–276.

Ellis, J. W. (1990). Plans, protections, and professional intervention: Innovations in divorce custody reform and the role of legal professionals. *University of Michigan Journal of Law Reform, 24,* 65–188.

El-Sheikh, M., Cummings, E. M., & Goetsch, V. (1989). Coping with adults' angry behavior: Behavioral, physiological, and verbal responses in preschoolers. *Developmental Psychology, 25,* 490–498.

Elster, J. (1987). Solomonic judgments: Against the best interests of the child. *University of Chicago Law Review, 54,* 1–43.

Emery, R. E. (1982). Interparental conflict and the children of discord and divorce. *Psychological Bulletin, 92,* 310–330.

Emery, R. E. (1988). *Marriage, divorce, and children's adjustment.* Beverly Hills, CA: Sage.

Emery, R. E. (1989). Family violence. *American Psychologist, 44,* 321–328.

Emery, R. E. (1992). Family conflict and its developmental implications: A conceptual analysis of deep meanings and systemic processes. In C. U. Shantz & W. W. Hartup (Eds.), *Conflict in child and adolescent development* (pp. 270–298). London: Cambridge University Press.

Emery, R. E., Fincham, F. D., & Cummings, E. M. (1992). Parenting in context: Systemic thinking about parental conflict and its influence on children. *Journal of Consulting and Clinical Psychology, 60,* 909–912.

Emery, R. E., & Forehand, R. (in press). Parental divorce and children's well-being: A focus on resilience. In R. J. Haggerty, N. Garmezy, M. Rutter, & L. Sherrod (Eds.), *Risk and resilience in children.* London: Cambridge University Press.

Emery, R. E., Hetherington, E. M., & DiLalla, L. F. (1984). Divorce, children, and social policy. In H. W. Stevenson & A. E. Siegel (Eds.) *Child development research and social policy* (pp. 189–266). Chicago: University of Chicago Press.

Emery, R. E., Joyce, S. A., & Fincham, F. D. (1987). The assessment of marital and child problems. In K. D. O'Leary (Ed.), *Assessment of marital discord* (pp. 223–262). Hillsdale, NJ: Erlbaum.

Emery, R. E., & Kitzmann, K. M. (in press). The child in the family: Disruptions in family functions. In D. Cicchetti & D. J. Cohen (Eds.), *Manual of developmental psychopathology.* New York: Wiley.

Emery, R. E., Matthews, S., & Kitzmann, K. M. (1994). Child custody mediation and litigation: Parents' satisfaction and functioning a year after settlement. *Journal of Consulting and Clinical Psychology, 62,* 124–129.

Emery, R. E., Matthews, S., & Wyer, M. M. (1991). Child custody mediation and litigation: Further evidence on the differing views of mothers and fathers. *Journal of Consulting and Clinical Psychology, 59,* 410–418.

Emery, R. E., & Rogers, K. C. (1990). The role of behavior therapists in child custody cases. In M. Hersen & R. M. Eisler (Eds.), *Progress in behavior modification* (pp. 60–89). Beverly Hills, CA: Sage.

Emery, R. E., Shaw, D. S., & Jackson, J. A. (1987). A clinical description of a model of child custody mediation. In J. P. Vincent (Ed.), *Advances in family intervention, assessment, and theory* (Vol. 4, pp. 309–333). Greenwich, CT: JAI.

Emery, R. E., & Tuer, M. (1993). Parenting and the marital relationship. In T. Luster & L. Okagaki (Eds.), *Parenting: An ecological perspective* (pp. 121–148). Hillsdale, NJ: Erlbaum.

Emery, R. E., & Wyer, M. M. (1987a). Child custody mediation and litigation: An experimental evaluation of the experience of parents. *Journal of Consulting and Clinical Psychology, 55,* 179–186.

Emery, R. E., & Wyer, M. M. (1987b). Divorce mediation. *American Psychologist, 42,* 472–480.

Erikson, E. H. (1959, 1980). *Identity and the life cycle.* New York: Norton.

Espenshade, T. J. (1979). The economic consequences of divorce. *Journal of Marriage and the Family, 41,* 615–625.

Fauber, R., Forehand, R., Thomas, A. M., & Wierson, M. (1990). A mediational model of the impact of marital conflict on adolescent adjustment in intact and divorced families: The role of disruptive parenting. *Child Development, 61,* 1112–1123.

Fine, M. A., McKenry, P. C., Donnelly, B. W., & Voydanoff, P. (1982). Perceived adjustment of parents and children: Variations by family structure, race, and gender. *Journal of Marriage and the Family, 54,* 118–127.

Fineman, M. (1988). Dominant discourse, professional language, and legal change in child custody decisionmaking. *Harvard Law Review, 101,* 727–774.

Fisher, R., & Ury, W. (1981). *Getting to yes.* New York: Houghton Mifflin.

Folberg, J. (1984). *Joint custody and shared parenting.* Washington, DC: BNA.

Folberg, J. (1988). Confidentiality and privilege in divorce mediation. In J. Folberg & A. Milne (Eds.), *Divorce mediation: Theory and practice* (pp. 319–340). New York: Guilford Press.

Folberg, J. (1991). *Joint custody and shared parenting.* New York: Guilford Press.

Folberg, J., & Taylor, A. (1984). *Mediation: A comprehensive guide to resolving conflicts without litigation.* San Francisco: Jossey-Bass.

Forehand, R., Thomas, A. M., Wierson, M., Brody, G., & Fauber, R. (1990). Role of maternal functioning and parenting skills in adolescent functioning following parental divorce. *Journal of Abnormal Psychology, 99,* 278–283.

Foster, H. H., & Freed, D. J. (1973–74). Divorce reform: Breaks on breakdown. *Journal of Family Law, 74,* 443–493.

Freed, D. J., & Walker, T. B. (1986). Family law in the fifty states: An overview. *Family Law Quarterly, 19,* 331–411.

Freed, D. J., & Walker, T. B. (1991). Family law in the fifty states: An overview. *Family Law Quarterly, 24,* 309–405.

Furstenberg, F. F., Morgan, S., & Allison, P. (1987). Paternal participation and children's well-being after marital dissolution. *American Sociological Review, 52,* 695–701.

Furstenberg, F. F., & Nord, C. W. (1985). Parenting apart: Patterns of childrearing after marital disruption. *Journal of Marriage and the Family, 47,* 893–904.

Furstenberg, F. F., Peterson, J. L., Nord, C. W., & Zill, N. (1983). The life course of children of divorce:Marital disruption and parental contact.*American Sociological Review, 48,* 656–668.

Furstenberg, F. F., & Spanier, G. B. (1984). *Recycling the family: Remarriage after divorce.* Beverly Hills, CA: Sage.

Greif, J. B. (1979). Fathers, children, and joint custody. *American Journal of Orthopsychiatry, 49,* 311–319.

Gold, L. (1988). Lawyer and therapist team mediation. In J. Folberg & A. Milne (Eds.), *Divorce mediation: Theory and practice* (pp. 209–224). New York: Guilford Press.

Gold, L. (1992). *Between love and hate: A guide to civilized divorce.* New York: Plenum Press.

Goldberg, S. B., Green, E. D., & Sander, F. E. A. (1985). *Dispute resolution.* Boston: Little, Brown.

Gotlib, I. H., & McCabe, S. B. (1990). Marriage and psychopathology. In F. D. Fincham & T. N. Bradbury (Eds.), *The psychology of marriage* (pp. 226–257). New York: Guilford Press.

Gottman, J. M., & Katz, L. F. (1989). Effects of marital discord on young children's peer interaction and health. *Developmental Psychology, 25,* 373–381.

Gove, W. R., Hughes, M., & Styles, C. B. (1983). Does marriage have positive effects on the psychological well-being of the individual? *Journal of Health and Social Behavior, 24,* 122–132.

Grillo, T. (1991). The mediation alternative: Process dangers for women. *Yale Law Journal, 100,* 1545–1610.

Grossberg, M. (1985). *Governing the hearth.* Chapel Hill, NC: University of North Carolina Press.

Grych, J. H., & Fincham, F. D. (1990). Marital conflict and children's adjustment: A cognitive-contextual framework. *Psychological Bulletin, 108,* 267–290.

Halem, L. C. (1981). *Divorce reform.* New York:Free Press.

Haynes, J. M. (1981). *Divorce mediation: A practical guide for therapists and counselors.* New York: Springer.

Herzog, E., & Sudia, C. E. (1973). Children in fatherless families. In B. Caldwell & H. Ricciuti (Eds.), *Review of child development research* (Vol. 3, pp. 141–232). Chicago: University of Chicago Press.

Hess, R. D., & Camara, K. A. (1979). Post-divorce relationships as mediating factors in the consequences of divorce for children. *Journal of Social Issues, 35,* 79–96.

Hetherington, E. M. (1989). Coping with family transitions: Winners, losers, and survivors. *Child Development, 60,* 1–14.

Hetherington, E. M. (1991). Presidential address: Families, lies, and videotapes. *Journal of Research on Adolescence, 1,* 323–348.

Hetherington, E. M., & Clingempeel, W. G. (1992). Coping with marital transtions. *Monographs of the Society for Research in Child Development, 57,* 1–229.

Hetherington, E. M., Cox, M., & Cox, R. (1976). Divorced fathers. *Family Coordinator, 25,* 417–428.

Hetherington, E. M., Cox, M., & Cox, R. (1978). The aftermath of divorce. In J. H. Stevens & M. Matthews (Eds.), *Mother–child, father–child relations* (pp. 110–155). Washington, DC: National Association for the Education of Young Children.

Hetherington, E. M., Cox, M., & Cox, R., (1982). Effects of divorce on parents and children. In M. Lamb (Ed.), *Nontraditional families* (pp. 233–288).Hillsdale, N. J.:Erlbaum.

Hetherington, E. M., Cox, M., & Cox, R. (1985). Long-term effects of divorce and remarriage on the adjustment of children. *Journal of the American Academy of Child Psychiatry, 24,* 518–530.

Holmes, T. H., & Rahe, R. H. (1967). The social readjustment rating scale. *Journal of Psychosomatic Research, 11,* 213–218.

Horney, K. (1939). *New ways in psychoanalysis.* New York: International Universities Press.

Irving, H. H. (1980). *Divorce mediation:A rational alternative to the adversary system.* New York:Universe Books.

Irving, H. H., Benjamin, M., Bohm, P., & MacDonald, G. (1981). *Final research report.* Toronto, Canada: Provinicial Court (Family Division).

Johnston, J. R., & Campbell, L. E. G. (1988). *Impasses of divorce: The dynamics of and resolution of family conflict.* New York: Free Press.

Johnston, J. R., Kline, M., & Tschann, J. M. (1989). Ongoing post-divorce conflict in families contesting custody: Effects on children of joint custody and frequent access. *American Journal of Orthopsychiatry, 59,* 576–592.

Keilitz, S. L., Daley, H. W. K., & Hanson, R. A. (1992). *Multi-state assessment of divorce mediation and traditional court processing.* Project report, State Justice Institute, Williamsburg, VA.

Kelly, J. B. (1983). Mediation and psychotherapy:Distinguishing the differences. *Mediation Quarterly, 1,* 33–44.

Kelly, J. B. (1989). Mediated and adversarial divorce: Respondents' perceptions of their processes and outcomes. *Mediation Quarterly, 24,* 71–88.

Kelly, J. B. (1990). Final report. Mediated and adversarial divorce resolution processes: An analysis of post-divorce outcomes. Available from the author, Northern California Mediation Center, 100 Tamal Plaza, Suite 175, Corte Madera, CA 94925.

Kelly, J. B., & Duryee, M. A. (1992). Women's and men's views of mediation in voluntary and mandatory mediation settings. *Family and Conciliation Courts Review, 30,* 34–49.

Kelly, J. B., & Gigy, L. (1989). Divorce mediation: Characteristics of clients and outcomes. In K. Kressel & D. G. Pruitt (Eds.), *Mediation research* (pp. 263–283). San Francisco: Jossey-Bass.

Kelly, J. B., Gigy, L., & Hausman, S. (1988). Mediated and adversarial divorce: Initial findings from a longitudinal study. In J. Folberg & A. Milne (Eds.), *Divorce mediation: Theory and practice* (pp. 453–474). New York: Guilford Press.

King, D. K. (1982). *Custody and visitation disputes under the new mandatory mediation law.* 3 California Law 41.

Kitson, G. C. (1992). *Portrait of divorce.* New York: Guilford Press.

Kitson, G. C., & Holmes, W. (1982). Attachment to the spouse in divorce:A scale and its application. *Journal of Marriage and the Family, 44,* 379–391.

Kitson, G. C., Holmes, W., & Sussman, M. (1983). Withdrawing divorce petitions: A predictive test of the exchange model of divorce. *Journal of Divorce, 7,* 51–66.

Kitson, G. C., & Langlie, J. D. (1984). Couples who file for divorce but change their minds. *American Journal of Orthopsychiatry, 54,* 469–489.

Kitson, G. C., & Raschke, H. (1981). Divorce research: What we know and what we need to know. *Journal of Divorce, 4*, 1–37.

Kitzmann, K. M., & Emery, R. E. (1993). Procedural justice and parents' satisfaction in a field study of child custody dispute resolution. *Law and Human Behavior, 17*, 553–567.

Kitzmann, K. M., & Emery, R. E. (in press). Child and family coping 1 year after mediated and litigated child custody disputes. *Journal of Family Psychology.*

Kline, M., Johnston, J. R., & Tschann, J. M. (1991). The long shadow of marital conflict: A model of children's postdivorce adjustment. *Journal of Marriage and the Family, 53*, 297–309.

Koopman, E. J., Hunt, E. J., & Stafford, V. (1984). Child-related agreements in mediated and non-mediated divorce settlements:A preliminary examination and discussion of implications. *Conciliation Courts Review, 22*, 19–25.

Kressel, K. (1985). *The process of divorce: How professionals and couples negotiate settlements.* New York: Basic Books.

Kressel, K., & Pruitt, D. G. (1989). Conclusion: A research perspective on the mediation of social conflict. In K. Kressel & D. G. Pruitt (Eds.), *Mediation research* (pp. 394–435). San Francisco: Jossey-Bass.

Kubler-Ross, E. (1969). *On death and dying.* New York: Macmillan.

Kurdek, L. A. (1986). Children's reasoning about parental divorce. In R. D. Ashmore & D. M. Brodzinsky (Eds.), *Thinking about the family: Views of parents and children* (pp. 233–276). Hillsdale, NJ: Erlbaum.

Kurdek, L. A., & Berg, B. (1987). Children's beliefs about parental divorce scale: Psychometric characteristics and concurrent validity. *Journal of Consulting and Clincal Psychology, 55*, 712–718.

Kurdek, L. A., Blisk, D., & Siesky, A. E. (1981). Correlates of children's long-term adjustment to their parents' divorce. *Developmental Psychology, 19*, 565–579.

Lahey, B. B., Hartdagen, S. E., Frick, P. J., McBurnett, K., Connor, R., & Hynd, G. W. (1988). Conduct disorder: Parsing the confounded relation to parental divorce and antisocial personality. *Journal of Abnormal Psychology, 97*, 334–337.

Lamborn, S., Mounts, N., & Steinberg, L. (1991). Patterns of competence and adjustment among adolescents from authoritative, authoritarian, indulgent, and neglectful families. *Child Development, 62*, 1049–1065.

Landsman, K. J., & Minow, M. L. (1978). Lawyering for the child: Principles of representation in custody and visitation disputes arising from divorce. *Yale Law Journal, 87*, 1126–1190.

Landstreet, E., & Takas, M. (1991). *Developing effective procedures for pro se modification of child support awards.* Washington, DC: Department of Health and Human Services.

Leary, T. (1957). *Interpersonal diagnosis of personality.* New York: Ronald Press.

Lemmon, J. A. (1985). *Family mediation practice.* New York: Free Press.

Lind, E., & Tyler, T. (1988). *The social psychology of procedural justice.* New York: Plenum Press.

Luepnitz, D. A. (1982). *Child custody: A study of families after divorce.* Lexington, MA: Lexington Books.

Maccoby, E. E., Buchanan, C. M., Mnookin, R. H., & Dornbusch, S. M. (1993). Postdivorce roles of mothers and fathers in the lives of their children. *Journal of Family Psychology, 7,* 24–38.

Maccoby, E. E., & Martin, J. A. (1983). Socialization in the context of the family: Parent–child interaction. In E. M. Hetherington (Ed.), *Handbook of Child Psychology* (4th ed., Vol. 4, pp. 1–101). New York: Wiley.

Maccoby, E. E., & Mnookin, R. H. (1992). *Dividing the child: Social and legal dilemmas of custody.* Cambridge, MA: Harvard University Press.

Margolin, F. M. (1973). An approach to the resolution of visitation disputes post-divorce:Short-term counseling. Unpublished doctoral dissertation, United States International University, San Diego: CA.

Martin, T. C., & Bumpass, L. L. (1989). Recent trends in marital disruption. *Demography, 26,* 37–52.

Martin, M. T., & Emery, R. E. (1994). *The intergeneratioal transmission of marital dissolution: A review of the explanatory hypotheses.* Unpublished manuscript, University of Virginia.

McIsaac, H. (1982). Court-connected mediation. *Conciliation Courts Review, 21,* 49–56.

McIsaac, H. (1985). Confidentiality: An exploration of the issues. *Mediation Quarterly, 8,* 57–66.

McKnight, M. (1991). Issues and trends in the law of joint custody. In J. Folberg (Ed.), *Joint custody and shared parenting* (2nd ed., pp. 209–217). New York: Guilford Press.

Melton, G. B., & Lind, E. A. (1982). Procedural justice in family court: Does the adversary model make sense? *Child and Youth Services, 5,* 63–81.

Menaghan, E. G., & Leiberman, M. A. (1986). Changes in depression following divorce: A panel study. *Journal of Marriage and the Family, 48,* 319–328.

Menkel-Meadow, C. (1984). Toward another view of legal negotiation: The structure of problem solving. *UCLA Law Review, 31,* 754–842.

Milne, A., & Folberg, J. (1988). The theory and practice of divorce mediation: An overview. In J. Folberg & A. Milne (Eds.), *Divorce mediation: Theory and practice* (pp. 2–26). New York: Guilford Press.

Minuchin, P. (1985). Families and individual development: Provocations from the field of family therapy. *Child Development, 56,* 289–302.

Minuchin, S. (1974). *Families and family therapy.* Cambridge, MA: Harvard University Press.

Mlyniec, W. J. (1977–1978). The child advocate in private custody disputes: A role in search of a standard. *Journal of Family Law, 16,* 1–17.

Mnookin, R. H. (1975). Child-custody adjudication:Judicial functions in the face of indeterminacy. *Law and Contemporary Problems, 39,* 226–292.

Mnookin, R. H., & Kornhauser, L. (1979). Bargaining in the shadow of the law: The case of divorce. *Yale Law Journal, 88,* 950–997.

Monahan, J. (Ed.). (1980). *Who is the client? The ethics of psychological intervention in the criminal justice system.* Washington, DC: American Psychological Association.

Moore, C. W. (1986). *The mediation process: Practical strategies for resolving conflicts*. San Francisco: Jossey-Bass.

Mumma, E. (1984). Mediating disputes. *Public Welfare, 10*, 22–30.

Myers, S., Gallas, G., Hanson, R., & Keilitz, S. (1988). Divorce mediation in the states: Institutionalization, use, and assessment. *State Court Journal*, 17–25.

National Institiue for Child Support Enforcement (NICSE). (1986). *History and fundamentals of child support enforcement*. (2nd ed.). Washington, DC: U. S. Government Printing Office.

Needle, R. H., Su, S. S., & Doherty, W. J. (1990). Divorce, remarriage, and adolescent substance use: A prospective longitudinal study. *Journal of Marriage and the Family, 52*, 157–169.

Nichols-Casebolt, A. (1986). The economic impact of child support reform on the poverty status of custodial and noncustodial families. *Journal of Marriage and the Family, 48*, 875–880.

Patterson, G. R. (1982). *Coercive family processes*. Eugene, OR: Castilia.

Pearson, J., & Thoennes, N. (1984). Final report of the divorce mediation research project. Unpublished manuscript. Available from authors, 1720 Emerson St., Denver, CO.

Pearson, J., & Thoennes, N. (1985). Child custody, child support arrangements and child support payment patterns. *Juvenile and Family Court Journal, 14*, 49–56.

Pearson, J., & Thoennes, N. (1989). Divorce mediation: Reflections on a decade of research. In K. Kressel & D. Pruitt (Eds.), *Mediation research* (pp. 9–30). San Francisco: Jossey-Bass.

Peterson, C.& Seligman, M. E. P. (1984). Causal explanations as a risk factor for depression:Theory and evidence. *Psychological Review, 91*, 347–374.

Peterson, J. L., & Nord, C. W. (1990). The regular receipt of child support: A multistep process. *Journal of Marriage and the Family, 52*, 539–551.

Peterson, J. L., & Zill, N. (1986). Marital disruption, parent–child relationships, and behavior problems in children. *Journal of Marriage and the Family, 48*, 295–307.

Plateris, A. (1974). 100 years of marriage and divorce statistics, 1867–1967. *Vital and Health Statistics* (Series 21, No. 24). (DHEW Publication No.(HRA) 74–1902. Health Resources Administration.) Washington, DC: U. S. Government Printing Office.

Porter, B., & O'Leary, K. D. (1980). Marital discord and child behavior problems. *Journal of Abnormal Child Psychology, 80*, 287–295.

Price-Bonham, S., & Balswick, J. O. (1980). The non-institutions: Divorce, desertion, and remarriage. *Journal of Marriage and the Family, 42*, 959–972.

Protecting confidentiality in mediation. (1984). *Harvard Law Review, 98*, 441–459.

Raiffa, H. (1982). *The art and science of negotiation*. Cambridge, MA: Harvard University Press.

Racusin, R. J., Albertini, R., Wishik, H. R., Schnurr, P., & Mayberry, J. (1989).

Factors associated with joint custody awards. *Journal of the American Academy of Child and Adolescent Psychiatry, 28,* 164–170.

Ricci, I. (1982). *Mom's house, Dad's house.* New York: Macmillan.

Risman, B. J., & Park, K. (1988). Just the two of us: Parent–child relationships in single-parent homes. *Journal of Marriage and the Family, 50,* 1049–1062.

Roman, M., & Haddad, W. (1978). *The disposable parent: The case for joint custody.* New York: Holt, Rinehart, & Winston.

Ross, L. H. (1980). *Settled out of court: The social process of insurance claims adjustment* (2nd ed.). Chicago: Aldine.

Rubin, J. (1980). Experimental research on third-party intervention in conflict: Toward some generalizations. *Psychological Bulletin, 87,* 379–391.

Salius, A. J., & Maruzo, S. D. (1982). *The use of mediation in contested child custody and visitation disputes.* Unpublished program report, Family Division, Superior Court of Connecticut, Hartford, CT.

Saposnek, D. T. (1983). *Mediating child custody disputes.* San Francisco: Jossey-Bass.

Schneider, C. E. (1985). Moral discourse and the transformation of American family law. *Michigan Law Review, 83,* 1803–1880.

Scott, E. S. (1992). Pluralism, parental preference, and child custody. *California Law Review, 80,* 615–172.

Scott, E. S., & Derdeyn, A. P. (1984). Rethinking joint custody. *Ohio State Law Journal, 45,* 455–474.

Scott, E. S., & Emery, R. E. (1987). Child custody dispute resolution: The adversarial system and divorce mediation. In L. A. Weithorn (Ed.), *Psychology and child custody determinations* (pp. 23–56). Lincoln, NE: University of Nebraska Press.

Select Committee on Children, Youth, and Families (SCCYF). (1989). *U. S. children and their families: Current conditions and recent trends, 1989.* Washington, DC: U. S. Government Printing Office.

Seltzer, J. A. (1991). Relationships between fathers and children who live apart: The father's role after separation. *Journal of Marriage and the Family, 53,* 79–101.

Seltzer, J. A., & Bianchi, S. M. (1988). Children's contact with absent parents. *Journal of Marriage and the Family, 50,* 663–677.

Shaw, D. S., Emery, R. E., & Tuer, M. (1993). Parental functioning and children's adjustment in families of divorce: A prospective look. *Journal of Abnormal Child Psychology, 29,* 119–134.

Shiller, V. M. (1986). Joint versus maternal custody for families with latency age boys: Parent characteristics and child adjustment. *American Journal of Orthopsychiatry, 56,* 486–489.

Sloman, L., Gardner, R., & Price, J. (1989). Biology of family systems and mood disorders. *Family Process, 28,* 387–398.

Somary, K., & Emery, R. E. (1991). Emotional anger and grief in divorce mediation. *Mediation Quarterly, 8,* 185–198.

Spanier, G. B., & Thompson, L. (1984). *Parting: The aftermath of separation and divorce.* Beverly Hills, CA: Sage.

Standards of practice for family mediators. (1984). *Family Law Quarterly, 17,* 455–460.

Steinman, S. B., Zemmelman, S. E., & Knoblauch, T. M. (1985). A study of parents who sought joint custody following divorce: Who reaches agreement and sustains joint custody and who returns to court. *Journal of the American Academy of Child Psychiatry, 24,* 554–562.

Sullivan, H. S. (1953). *The interpersonal theory of psychiatry.* New York: Norton.

Thibault, J., & Walker, L. A. (1978). A theory of procedure. *California Law Review, 66,* 541–566.

U. S. Census Bureau. (1989). Marital status and living arrangements: March 1988. *Current Population Reports* (Series P-20, No. 433). Washington, DC: U. S. Government Printing Office.

Vuchinich, S., Emery, R. E., & Cassidy, J. (1988). Family members as third parties in dyadic family conflict: Strategies, alliances, and outcomes. *Child Development, 59,* 1293–1302.

Vuchinich, S., Hetherington, E. M., Vuchinich, R. A., & Clingempeel, W. B. (1991). Parent–child interaction and gender differences in early adolescents' adaptation to stepfamilies. *Developmental Psychology, 27,* 618–626.

Waite, L. J., Haggstrom, G. W., & Kanouse, D. E. (1985). The consequences of parenthood for the marital stability of young adults. *American Sociological Review, 50,* 850–857.

Waldman, E. (1993). The role of legal norms in divorce mediation: An argument for inclusion. *Virginia Journal of Social Policy and the Law, 1,* 87–152.

Wallerstein, J. S. (1983). Children of divorce: The psychological tasks of the child. *American Journal of Orthopsychiatry, 53,* 230–243.

Wallerstein, J. S., & Blakeslee, S. (1989). *Second chances: Men, women, and children a decade after divorce.* New York: Ticknor & Fields.

Wallerstein, J., & Kelly, J. B. (1980). *Surviving the breakup: How children actually cope with divorce.* New York: Basic Books.

Warshak, R. A. (1986). Father-custody and child development: A review and analysis of psychological research. *Behavioral Sciences and the Law, 4,* 2–17.

Weingarten, H. R. (1983). Marital status and well-being: A national study comparing first-married, currently divorced, and remarried adults. *Journal of Marriage and the Family, 45,* 653–662.

Weiss, R. S. (1979a). Growing up a little faster: The experience of growing up in a single-parent household. *Journal of Social Issues, 35,* 97–111.

Weiss, R. S. (1979b). Issues in the adjudication of custody when parents separate. In G. Levinger & O. C. Moles (Eds.), *Divorce and separation* (pp. 324–336). New York: Basic Books.

Weiss, R. S. (1988). Loss and recovery. *Journal of Social Issues, 44,* 37–52.

Weithorn, L. A. (1987). Psychological considerations in divorce custody litigation: Ethical considerations. In L. A. Weithorn (Ed.), *Psychology and child custody determinations* (pp. 182–209). Lincoln, NE: University of Nebraska Press.

Weitzman, L. J. (1985). *The divorce revolution.* New York: Free Press.

Weitzman, L. J., & Dixon, R. B. (1979). Child custody awards: Legal standards and empirical patterns for child custody, support, and visitation after divorce. *University of California, Davis Law Review, 12,* 471–521.

Wiggins, J. S. (1982). Circumplex models of interpersonal behavior in clinical psychology. In P. C. Kendall & J. N. Butcher (Eds.), *Handbook of research methods in clinical psychology* (pp. 183–221). New York: Wiley.

Williams, G. R. (1983). *Legal negotiation and settlement.* St. Paul, MN: West.

Wilson, M. (1989). Child development in the context of the Black extended family. *American Psychologist, 44,* 380–385.

Wolchik, S. A., Braver, S. L., & Sandler, I. N. (1985). Maternal versus joint custody: Children's post-separation experiences and adjustment. *Journal of Clinical Child Psychology, 14,* 118–141.

Wortman, C. B., & Silver, R. C. (1989). The myths of coping with loss. *Journal of Consulting and Clinical Psychology, 57,* 349–357.

Yuzawa, Y. (1990). Recent trends of divorce and custody in Japan. *Journal of Divorce, 13,* 129–141.

Zill, N., Morrison, D. R., & Coiro, M. J. (1993). Long-term effects of parental divorce on parent–child relationships, adjustment, and achievement in young adulthood. *Journal of Family Psychology, 7,* 91–103.

Index